MATLAB Differential and Integral Calculus

César Pérez López

Apress®

MATLAB Differential and Integral Calculus

ISBN-13 (pbk): 978-1-4842-0305-7

ISBN-13 (electronic): 978-1-4842-0304-0

Publisher: Heinz Weinheimer
Lead Editor: Dominic Shakeshaft
Editorial Board: Steve Anglin, Mark Beckner, Ewan Buckingham, Gary Cornell, Louise Corrigan, Jim DeWolf, Jonathan Gennick, Robert Hutchinson, Michelle Lowman, James Markham, Matthew Moodie, Jeff Olson, Jeffrey Pepper, Douglas Pundick, Ben Renow-Clarke, Dominic Shakeshaft, Gwenan Spearing, Matt Wade, Steve Weiss
Coordinating Editor: Jill Balzano
Copy Editor: Barnaby Sheppard
Compositor: SPi Global
Indexer: SPi Global
Artist: SPi Global
Cover Designer: Anna Ishchenko

Distributed to the book trade worldwide by Springer Science+Business Media New York, 233 Spring Street, 6th Floor, New York, NY 10013. Phone 1-800-SPRINGER, fax (201) 348-4505, e-mail orders-ny@springer-sbm.com, or visit www.springeronline.com. Apress Media, LLC is a California LLC and the sole member (owner) is Springer Science + Business Media Finance Inc (SSBM Finance Inc). SSBM Finance Inc is a Delaware corporation.

For information on translations, please e-mail rights@apress.com, or visit www.apress.com.

Apress and friends of ED books may be purchased in bulk for academic, corporate, or promotional use. eBook versions and licenses are also available for most titles. For more information, reference our Special Bulk Sales–eBook Licensing web page at www.apress.com/bulk-sales.

Any source code or other supplementary material referenced by the author in this text is available to readers at www.apress.com. For detailed information about how to locate your book's source code, go to www.apress.com/source-code/.

Contents at a Glance

Contents

About the Author

César Pérez López is a Professor at the Department of Statistics and Operations Research at the University of Madrid. César is also a Mathematician and Economist at the National Statistics Institute (INE) in Madrid, a body which belongs to the Superior Systems and Information Technology Department of the Spanish Government. César also currently works at the Institute for Fiscal Studies in Madrid.

Coming Soon

- *MATLAB Programming for Numerical Analysis,* 978-1-4842-0296-8
- *MATLAB Differential Equations,* 978-1-4842-0311-8
- *MATLAB Control Systems Engineering,* 978-1-4842-0290-6
- *MATLAB Linear Algebra,* 978-1-4842-0323-1
- *MATLAB Matrix Algebra,* 978-1-4842-0308-8

CHAPTER 1

■ ■ ■

Introduction and the MATLAB Environment

1.1 Numerical Computation with MATLAB

You can use MATLAB as a powerful numerical computer. While most calculators handle numbers only to a preset degree of precision, MATLAB performs exact calculations to any desired degree of precision. In addition, unlike calculators, we can perform operations not only with individual numbers, but also with objects such as arrays.

Most of the topics of classical numerical analysis are treated by this software. It supports matrix calculus, statistics, interpolation, least squares fitting, numerical integration, minimization of functions, linear programming, numerical and algebraic solutions of differential equations and a long list of further methods that we'll meet as this book progresses.

Here are some examples of numerical calculations with MATLAB. (To obtain the results simply press *Enter* once the desired command has been entered after the prompt ">>".)

1. We calculate 4 + 3 to obtain the result 7. To do this, just type 4 + 3, and then *Enter*.

    ```
    >> 4 + 3

    ans =

    7
    ```

2. We find the value of 3 to the power of 100, without having previously set the precision. To do this we simply enter 3 ^ 100.

    ```
    >> 3 ^ 100

    ans =

    5. 1538e + 047
    ```

3. We can use the command "format long e" to obtain results to 15 digits (floating-point).

    ```
    >> format long e

    >> 3^100

    ans =

    5.153775207320115e + 047
    ```

4. We can also work with complex numbers. We find the result of the operation raising
    $(2 + 3i)$ to the power 10 by typing the expression $(2 + 3i) \wedge 10$.

    ```
    >> (2 + 3i) ^ 10
    ```

    ans =

    -1 415249999999998e + 005 - 1. 456680000000000e + 005i

5. The previous result is also available in short format, using the "format short" command.

    ```
    >> format short
    >> (2 + 3i)^10
    ```

    ans =

    -1.4152e + 005- 1.4567e + 005i

6. We can calculate the value of the Bessel function J_0 at 11.5. To do this we type
    besselj(0,11.5).

    ```
    >> besselj(0,11.5)
    ```

    ans =

    -0.0677

7. We can also perform numerical integration. To calculate the integral of $\sin(\sin(x))$ between
    0 and π we type int('sin((sin(x));' 0, pi).

    ```
    >> int ('sin(sin(x))', 0, pi)
    ```

    ans =

    1235191162052677/2251799813685248 * pi

These ideas will be treated more thoroughly later in the book.

1.2 Symbolic Computation with MATLAB

MATLAB perfectly handles symbolic mathematical computations, manipulating and performing operations on formulae and algebraic expressions with ease. You can expand, factor and simplify polynomials and rational and trigonometric expressions, find algebraic solutions of polynomial equations and systems of equations, evaluate derivatives and integrals symbolically, find solutions of differential equations, manipulate powers, and investigate limits and many other features of algebraic series.

To perform these tasks, MATLAB first requires all the variables (or algebraic expressions) to be written between single quotes. When MATLAB receives a variable or expression in quotes, it is interpreted as symbolic.

Here are some examples of symbolic computations with MATLAB.

1. We can expand the following algebraic expression: $((x+1)(x+2) - (x+2)^2)^3$. This is done by typing: expand('$((x+1)(x+2) - (x+2)^2)^3$'). The result will be another algebraic expression:

```
>> syms x; expand(((x + 1) *(x + 2)-(x + 2) ^ 2) ^ 3)
```

ans =

*-x ^ 3-6 * x ^ 2-12 * x-8*

2. We can factor the result of the calculation in the above example by typing: factor('$((x+1)*(x+2) - (x+2)^2)^3$')

```
>> syms x; factor(((x + 1)*(x + 2)-(x + 2)^2)^3)
```

ans =

-(x+2)^3

3. We can find the indefinite integral of the function $(x^2)\sin(x)^2$ by typing: int('$x^2 * \sin(x)^2$', 'x')

```
>> int('x^2*sin(x)^2', 'x')
```

ans =

*x ^ 2 *(-1/2 * cos(x) * sin(x) + 1/2 * x)-1/2 * x * cos(x) ^ 2 + 1/4 * cos(x) * sin(x) + 1/4 * 1/x-3 * x ^ 3*

4. We can simplify the previous result:

```
>> syms x; simplify(int(x^2*sin(x)^2, x))
```

ans =

*sin(2*x)/8 -(x*cos(2*x))/4 -(x^2*sin(2*x))/4 + x^3/6*

5. We can present the previous result using a more elegant mathematical notation:

```
>> syms x; pretty(simplify(int(x^2*sin(x)^2, x)))
```

ans =

$$\frac{\sin(2\,x)}{8} - \frac{x\,\cos(2\,x)}{4} - \frac{x^2\,\sin(2\,x)}{4} + \frac{x^3}{6}$$

6. We can find the series expansion up to order 12 of the function $x \wedge 2 * \sin(x) \wedge 2$, presenting the result in elegant form:

    ```
    >> pretty(taylor('x^2*sin(x)^2',12))
    ```

    ```
        4        6        8          10         12
    x  -  1/3  x  +  2/45  x  -  1/315  x  +  o  (x)
    ```

7. We can solve the equation $3ax - 7 x \wedge 2 + x \wedge 3 = 0$ (where a is a parameter):

    ```
    >> solve('3*a*x-7*x^2 + x^3 = 0', 'x')
    ```

    ans =

    ```
    [                          0]
    [7/2 + 1/2 *(49-12*a) ^(1/2)]
    [7/2-1/2 *(49-12*a) ^(1/2)]
    ```

8. We can find the five solutions of the equation $x \wedge 5 + 2 x + 1 = 0$:

    ```
    >> solve('x^5+2*x+1','x')
    ```

    ans =

    RootOf(_Z^5+2*_Z+1)

As the result does not explicitly give five solutions, we apply the "allvalues" command:

```
>> allvalues(solve('x^5+2*x+1','x'))
```

ans =

```
[-.7018735688558619-. 8796971979298240 * i]
[-. 7018735688558619 +. 8796971979298240 * i]
[-. 4863890359345430]
[.9450680868231334-. 8545175144390459 * i]
[. 9450680868231334 +. 8545175144390459 * i]
```

On the other hand, MATLAB can use the Maple program libraries to work with symbolic math, and can thus extend its field of action. In this way, MATLAB can be used to work on such topics as differential forms, Euclidean geometry, projective geometry, statistics, etc.

At the same time, Maple can also benefit from MATLAB's powers of numerical calculation, which might be used, for example, in combination with the Maple libraries (combinatorics, optimization, number theory, etc.)

1.3 MATLAB and Maple

Provided the "Extended Symbolic Math Toolbox" is installed then MATLAB can extend its symbolic calculation abilities by making use of the Maple libraries. To use a Maple command from MATLAB, use the command 'maple' followed by the corresponding Maple syntax.

To use a Maple command from Matlab, the syntax is as follows:

```
maple ('Maple_command_syntax')
```

or alternatively:

```
maple 'Maple_command_syntax'
```

To use a Maple command with N arguments from Matlab, the syntax is as follows:

```
maple('Maple_command_syntax', argument1,
       argument2,..., argumentN)
```

Here are some examples.

1. We can calculate the limit of the function (x ^ 3-1) / (x-1) as x tends to 1:

    ```
    >> maple('limit((x^3-1)/(x-1),x=1)')
    ```

    ans =

    3

    We could also have used the following syntax:

    ```
    >> maple limit('(x^3-1)/(x-1),x=1)';
    ```

    ans =

    3

2. We can calculate the greatest common divisor of 10,000 and 5,000:

    ```
    >> maple('gcd', 10000, 5000)
    ```

    ans =

    5000

1.4 Graphics with MATLAB

MATLAB can generate two- and three-dimensional graphs, as well as contour and density plots. You can graphically represent data lists, controlling colors, shading and other graphics features. Animated graphics are also supported. Graphics produced by MATLAB are portable to other programs.

Some examples of MATLAB graphics are given below.

1. We can represent the function $x\sin(1/x)$ for x ranging between $-\pi/4$ and $\pi/4$, taking 300 equidistant points in the interval. See Figure 1-1.

    ```
    >> x = linspace(-pi/4,pi/4,300);
    >> y=x.*sin(1./x);
    >> plot(x,y)
    ```

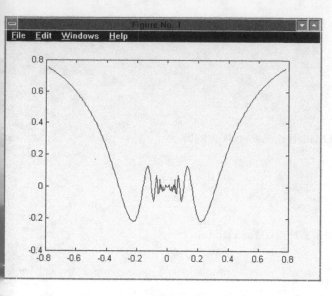

Figure 1-1.

2.   We can give the above graph a title and label the axes, and we can add a grid. See Figure 1-2.

```
>> x = linspace(-pi/4,pi/4,300);
>> y=x.*sin(1./x);
>> plot(x,y);
>> grid;
>> xlabel('Independent variable X');
>> ylabel('Dependent variable Y');
>> title('The function y=xsin(1/x)')
```

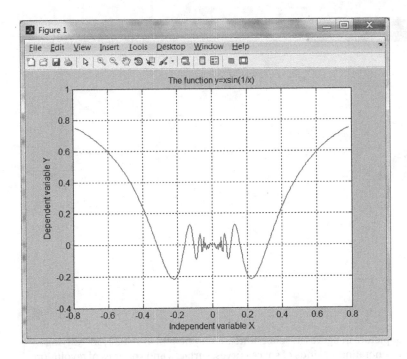

Figure 1-2.

3. We can generate a graph of the surface defined by the function $z = \sin(\text{sqrt}(x\^2+y\^2))$ / sqrt($x\^2+y\^2$), where x and y vary over the interval (–7.5, 7.5), taking equally spaced points 0.5 apart. See Figure 1-3.

```
>> x =-7.5:. 5:7.5;
>> y = x;
>> [X, Y] = meshgrid(x,y);
>> Z=sin(sqrt(X.^2+Y.^2))./sqrt(X.^2+Y.^2);
>> surf(X, Y, Z)
```

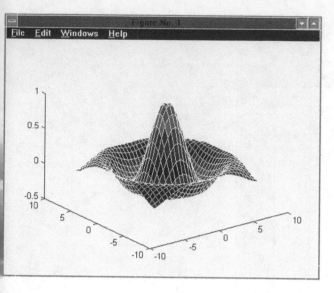

Figure 1-3.

These 3D graphics allow you to get a clear picture of figures in space, and are very helpful in visually identifying intersections between different bodies, and in generating all kinds of space curves, surfaces and volumes of revolution.

4. We can generate the three dimensional graph corresponding to the helix with parametric coordinates: $x = \sin(t)$, $y = \cos(t)$, $z = t$. See Figure 1-4.

```
>> t=0:pi/50:10*pi;
>> plot3(sin(t),cos(t),t)
```

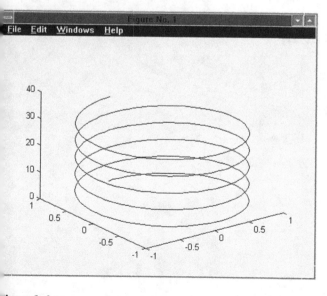

igure 1-4.

5. We can represent a planar curve given by its polar coordinates $r = \cos(2t) * \sin(2t)$ for t varying in the range between 0 and π by equally spaced points 0.01 apart. See Figure 1-5.

```
>> t = 0:. 1:2 * pi;
>> r = sin(2*t). * cos(2*t);
>> polar(t,r)
```

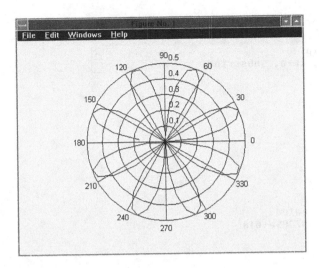

Figure 1-5.

6. We can make a graph of a symbolic function using the command "ezplot". See Figure 1-6.

```
>> y ='x ^ 3 /(x^2-1)';
>> ezplot(y,[-5,5])
```

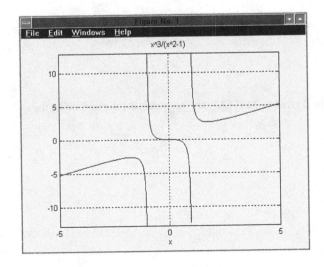

Figure 1-6.

We will see more on these concepts later.

1.5 Environment and General Notation

As for any program, the best way to learn MATLAB is to use it. By practicing on examples you become familiar with the syntax and notation peculiar to MATLAB. Each example we give consists of the header with the user input prompt ">>" followed by the MATLAB response on the next line. See Figure 1-7.

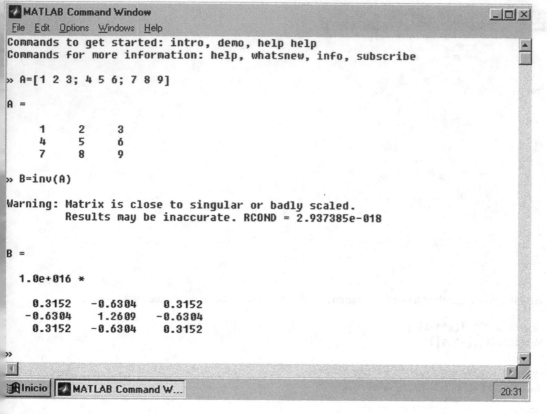

Figure 1-7.

At other times, depending on the type of entry (user input) given to MATLAB, the response is returned using the expression "ans =". See Figure 1-8.

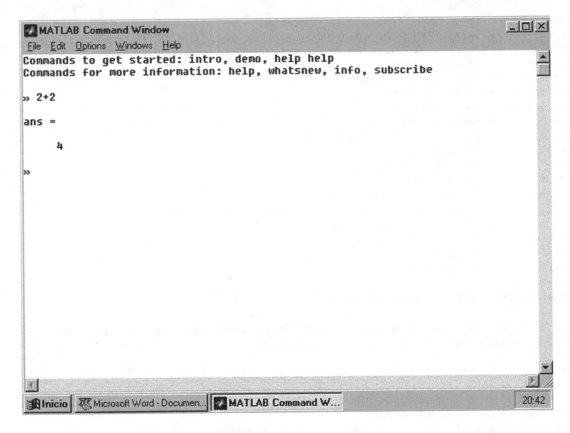

Figure 1-8.

It is important to pay attention to the use of uppercase versus lowercase letters, parentheses versus square brackets, spaces and punctuation (particularly commas and semicolons).

1.6 Help with Commands

You can get help using MATLAB's drop down menus, but, in addition, support can also be obtained via commands (instructions or functions), implemented as MATLAB objects.

You can use the help command to get immediate access to diverse information.

```
>> help
```

HELP topics:

matlab\general	- *General purpose commands.*
matlab\ops	- *Operators and special characters.*
matlab\lang	- *Programming language constructs.*
matlab\elmat	- *Elementary matrices and matrix manipulation.*
matlab\elfun	- *Elementary math functions.*
matlab\specfun	- *Specialized math functions.*
matlab\matfun	- *Matrix functions - numerical linear algebra.*

```
matlab\datafun        -  Data analysis and Fourier transforms.
matlab\polyfun        -  Interpolation and polynomials.
matlab\funfun         -  Function functions and ODE solvers.
matlab\sparfun        -  Sparse matrices.
matlab\graph2d        -  Two dimensional graphs.
matlab\graph3d        -  Three dimensional graphs.
matlab\specgraph      -  Specialized graphs.
matlab\graphics       -  Handle Graphics.
matlab\uitools        -  Graphical user interface tools.
matlab\strfun         -  Character strings.
matlab\iofun          -  File input/output.
matlab\timefun        -  Time and dates.
matlab\datatypes      -  Data types and structures.
matlab\winfun         -  Windows Operating System Interface Files(DDE/ActiveX)
matlab\demos          -  Examples and demonstrations.
toolbox\symbolic      -  Symbolic Math Toolbox.
toolbox\tour          -  MATLAB Tour
toolbox\local         -  Preferences.

For more help on directory/topic, type "help topic".
```

As we can see, the help command displays a list of program directories and their contents. Help on any given topic *topic* can be displayed using the command *help topic*. For example:

```
>> help inv

INV Matrix inverse.
INV(X) is the inverse of the square matrix X.
A warning message is printed if X is badly scaled or nearly singular.

See also SLASH, PINV, COND, CONDEST, NNLS, LSCOV.

Overloaded methods
help sym/inv.m

> help matlab\elfun

Elementary math functions.

Trigonometric.

sin           - Sine.
sinh          - Hyperbolic sine.
asin          - Inverse sine.
asinh         - Inverse hyperbolic sine.
cos           - Cosine.
cosh          - Hyperbolic cosine.
acos          - Inverse cosine.
acosh         - Inverse hyperbolic cosine.
tan           - Tangent.
tanh          - Hyperbolic tangent.
```

```
atan      - Inverse tangent.
atan2     - Four quadrant inverse tangent.
atanh     - Inverse hyperbolic tangent.
sec       - Secant.
sech      - Hyperbolic secant.
asec      - Inverse secant.
asech     - Inverse hyperbolic secant.
csc       - Cosecant.
csch      - Hyperbolic cosecant.
acsc      - Inverse cosecant.
acsch     - Inverse hyperbolic cosecant.
cot       - Cotangent.
coth      - Hyperbolic cotangent.
acot      - Inverse cotangent.
acoth     - Inverse hyperbolic cotangent.


Exponential.

exp       - Exponential.
log       - Natural logarithm.
log10     - Common(base 10) logarithm.
log2      - Base 2 logarithm and dissect floating point number.
pow2      - Base 2 power and scale floating point number.
sqrt      - Square root.
nextpow2  - Next higher power of 2.


Complex.

abs       - Absolute value.
angle     - Phase angle.
conj      - Complex conjugate.
imag      - Complex imaginary part.
real      - Complex real part.
unwrap    - Unwrap phase angle.
isreal    - True for real array.
cplxpair  - Sort numbers into complex conjugate pairs.


Rounding and remainder.

fix       - Round towards zero.
floor     - Round towards minus infinity.
ceil      - Round towards plus infinity.
round     - Round towards nearest integer.
mod       - Modulus(signed remainder after division).
rem       - Remainder after division.
sign      - Signum.
```

There is a command for help on a certain sequence of characters (*lookfor string*) which allows you to find all those functions or commands that contain or refer to the given string *string*. This command is very useful when there is no direct support for the specified string, or if you want to view the help for all commands related to the given sequence. For example, if we seek help for all commands that contain the sequence *complex*, we can use the *lookfor complex* command to see which commands MATLAB provides.

```
>> lookfor complex
```

```
ctranspose.m: %'   Complex conjugate transpose.
CONJ   Complex conjugate.
CPLXPAIR Sort numbers into complex conjugate pairs.
IMAG   Complex imaginary part.
REAL   Complex real part.
CDF2RDF Complex diagonal form to real block diagonal form.
RSF2CSF Real block diagonal form to complex diagonal form.
B5ODE  Stiff problem, linear with complex eigenvalues(B5 of EHL).
CPLXDEMO Maps of functions of a complex variable.
CPLXGRID Polar coordinate complex grid.
CPLXMAP Plot a function of a complex variable.
GRAFCPLX Demonstrates complex function plots in MATLAB.
ctranspose.m: %TRANSPOSE Symbolic matrix complex conjugate transpose.
SMOKE  Complex matrix with a "smoke ring" pseudospectrum.
```

1.7 Commands to Exit and Escape to the MS-DOS Environment

There are three ways you can escape from the MATLAB Command Window to the MS-DOS operating system environment in order to run temporary assignments. Entering the command ! *dos_command* in the Command Window allows you to run the specified DOS command in the MATLAB environment. For example:

```
! dir
```

```
The volume of drive D has no label
The volume serial number £ is 145 c-12F2
Directory of D:\MATLAB52\bin


               <DIR>       13/03/98   0:16 .
.              <DIR>       13/03/98   0:16 ..
BCCOPTS  BAT       1.872   19/01/98  14:14 bccopts.bat
CLBS110  DLL     219.136   21/08/97  22:24 clbs110.dll
CMEX     BAT       2.274   13/03/98   0:28 cmex.bat
COMPTOOL BAT      34.992   19/01/98  14:14 comptool.bat
DF5OOPTS BAT       1.973   19/01/98  14:14 df5oopts.bat
FENG     DLL      25.088   18/12/97  16:34 feng.dll
FMAT     DLL      16.896   18/12/97  16:34 fmat.dll
FMEX     BAT       2.274   13/03/98   0:28 fmex.bat
LICENSE  DAT         470   13/03/98   0:27 license.dat
W32SSI   DLL      66.560   02/05/97   8:34 w32ssi.dll
10 file(s)       11.348.865 bytes
    directory(s) 159.383.552 bytes free
```

The command ! *dos_command* & is used to execute the specified DOS command in background mode. The command is executed by opening a DOS environment window on the MATLAB Command Window, as shown in Figure 1-9. To return to the MATLAB environment simply right-click anywhere in the Command Window (the DOS environment window will close automatically). You can return to the DOS window at any time to run any operating system command by clicking the icon labeled *MS-DOS symbol* at the bottom of the screen.

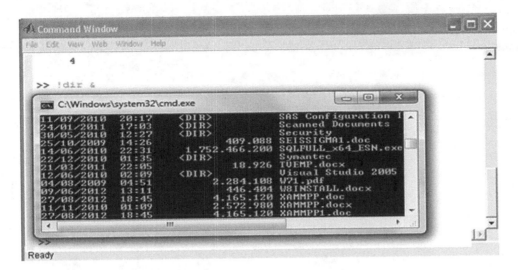

Figure 1-9.

The command >>*dos_command* is used to execute the DOS command in the MATLAB screen. Using the three previous commands, not only DOS commands, but also all kinds of executable files or batch tasks can be executed.

The command >>*dos dos_command* is also used to execute the specified DOS command in automatic mode in the MATLAB Command Window.

To exit MATLAB, simply type *quit* in the Command Window, and then press *Enter*.

1.8 MATLAB and Programming

By properly combining all the objects defined in MATLAB, according to the rules of syntax of the program, you can build useful mathematical programming code. Programs usually consist of a series of instructions in which values are calculated, are assigned names and are reused in further calculations.

As in programming languages like C or FORTRAN, in MATLAB you can write programs with loops, control flow and conditionals. MATLAB can write procedural programs, i.e., it can define a sequence of standard steps to run. As in C or Pascal, a Do, For, or While loop can be used for repetitive calculations. The language of MATLAB also includes conditional constructs such as If-Then–Else. MATLAB also supports different logical operators, such as AND, OR, NOT and XOR.

MATLAB supports procedural programming (with iterative processes, recursive functions, loops, etc.), functional programming and object-oriented programming. Here are two simple examples of programs. The first generates the Hilbert matrix of order *n*, and the second calculates all the Fibonacci numbers less than 1000.

```
% Generates the Hilbert matrix of order n
t = '1/(i+j-1)';
for i = 1:n
for j = 1:n
a(i,j) = eval(t);
end
end

% Calculates the Fibonacci numbers
f = [1 1]; i = 1;
while f(i) + f(i-1) < 1000
f(i+2) = f(i) + f(i+1);
i = i+1
end
```

CHAPTER 2

■ ■ ■

Limits and Continuity. One and Several Variables

MATLAB provides commands that allow you to calculate virtually all types of limits. The same functions are used to calculate limits of sequences and limits of functions. The commands for the analysis of one and several variables are similar. In this chapter we will present numerous exercises which illustrate MATLAB's capabilities in this field. The syntax of the commands concerning limits are presented below:

maple ('limit(sequence, n=infinity)') or **limit(sequence, n, inf)** or **limit(sequence, inf)** calculates the limit as *n* tends to infinity of the sequence defined by its general term.

maple ('limit(function, x=a)') or **limit(function, x, a)** or **limit(function, a)** calculates the limit of the function of the variable *x*, indicated by its analytical expression, as the variable *x* tends towards the value *a*.

maple ('limit(function, x=a, right)') or **limit(function, x, a, 'right')** calculates the limit of the function of the variable *x*, indicated by its analytical expression, as *the variable x tends to the value a from the right*.

maple ('limit(function, x=a, left)') or **limit(function, x, a, 'left')** calculates the limit of the function of the variable *x*, indicated by its analytical expression, as *the variable x tends to the value a from the left*.

maple ('limit(expr, var=a, complex)') is the complex limit of expr as the variable *var* tends to the value *a*.

maple ('limit(expr, {v1=a1, ..., vn=an})') is the n-dimensional limit of *expr* as *v1 tends to a1, v2 tends to a2,..., vn tends to an*.

maple ('Limit(expr, var=a)') or **maple ('Limit(expr, {v1=a1, ..., vn=an})')** is the inert limit of the expression *expr* for the specified values of the variable or variables.

2.1 Limits of Sequences

We present some exercises on the calculation of limits of sequences.

EXERCISE 2-1

Calculate the following limits:

$$\lim_{n\to\infty}\left(\frac{-3+2n}{-7+3n}\right)^4 \;,\; \lim_{n\to\infty}\frac{1+7n^2+3n^3}{5-8n+4n^3} \;,\; \lim_{n\to\infty}\left[\left(\frac{1+n}{2}\right)^4\frac{1+n}{n^5}\right] \;,\; \lim_{n\to\infty}\sqrt[n]{\frac{1+n}{n^2}}$$

In the first two limits we face the typical uncertainty given by the quotient ∞/∞:

```
>> syms n
>> limit(((2*n-3)/(3*n-7))^4, inf)
```

ans =

16/81

```
>> limit((3*n^3+7*n^2+1)/(4*n^3-8*n+5),n,inf)
```

ans =

3/4

The last two limits present an uncertainty of the form $\infty \cdot 0$ and ∞^0:

```
>> limit(((n+1)/2)*((n^4+1)/n^5), inf)
```

ans =

1/2

```
>> limit(((n+1)/n^2)^(1/n), inf)
```

ans =

1

EXERCISE 2-2

Calculate the following limits:

$$\lim_{n\to\infty}\left(\frac{3+n}{-1+n}\right)^n,\ \lim_{n\to\infty}\left(1-\frac{2}{3+n}\right)^n,\ \lim_{n\to\infty}\sqrt[n]{\frac{1}{n}},\ \lim_{n\to\infty}\frac{-\sqrt[3]{n}+\sqrt[3]{1+n}}{-\sqrt{n}+\sqrt{1+n}},\ \lim_{n\to\infty}\frac{n!}{n^n}$$

The first two examples are indeterminate of the form 1^∞:

```
>> limit(((n+3)/(n-1))^n, inf)
```

ans =

exp(4)

```
>> limit((1-2/(n+3))^n, inf)
```

ans =

exp (- 2)

The next two limits are of the form ∞^0 and $(\infty-\infty)\big/\infty$:

```
>> limit((1/n)^(1/n), inf)
```

ans =

1

```
>> maple('limit(((n+1)^(1/3)-n^(1/3))/((n+1)^(1/2)-n^(1/2)),n=infinity)')
```

ans =

0

The last limit is of the form $\infty\big/\infty$:

```
>> maple('limit(n!/n^n, n=infinity)')
```

ans =

0

2.2 Limits of Functions. Lateral Limits

To calculate the limits of functions one uses the same MATLAB commands as for limits of sequences. For functions, MATLAB allows you to calculate the limit at a point, and left and right limits (if these limits exist). If a function has a limit at a point then it necessarily has left and right limits at that point, and they coincide. If the left and right limits do not coincide then the function does not have a limit at the given point. Below are several exercises which illustrate how to calculate function limits. Some exercises are accompanied by graphics. The use of graphics is advisable if there are any doubts concerning the results.

EXERCISE 2-3

Calculate the following limits:

$$\lim_{x \to 1}\frac{-1-x}{-1+\sqrt{x}}, \; \lim_{x \to 2}\frac{x-\sqrt{2+x}}{-3+\sqrt{1+4x}}, \; \lim_{x \to 0}\sqrt[x]{1+x}, \; \lim_{x \to 0}\frac{\sin\left[(ax)^2\right]}{x^2}, \; \lim_{x \to 0}\frac{e^x-1}{\log(1+x)}.$$

Initially, we have two indeterminates of type 0/0 and one of the form 1^∞:

```
>> syms x
>> limit((x-1)/(x^(1/2)-1),x,1)
2
```

```
>> limit((x-(x+2)^(1/2))/((4*x+1)^(1/2)-3),2)

9/8
```

```
>> limit((1+x)^(1/x))
exp (1)
```

The last two are indeterminates of the form 0/0:

```
>> syms x a, limit(sin(a*x)^2/x^2,x,0)

a^2
```

```
>> numeric(limit((exp(1)^x-1)/log(1+x)))

1
```

EXERCISE 2-4

Calculate the following function limits:

$$\lim_{x \to 1} \frac{|x|}{\sin(x)}, \ \lim_{x \to 3}\left|x^2 - x - 7\right|, \ \lim_{x \to 1}\frac{x-1}{x^n - 1}, \ \lim_{x \to 0}\sqrt[x]{e}.$$

The first limit is calculated as follows:

```
>> limit(abs(x)/sin(x),x,0)
```

ans =

NaN

```
>> limit(abs(x)/sin(x),x,0,'left')
```

ans =

-1

```
>> limit(abs(x)/sin(x),x,0,'right')
```

ans =

1

As the lateral boundaries are not equal, the function has no limit at $x = 0$.

If we plot the function (see Figure 2-1), the limits become clear:

```
>> ezplot (abs (x) /sin (x), [- 1, 1])
```

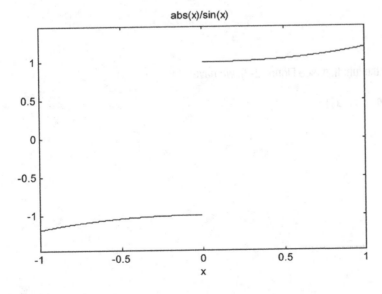

Figure 2-1.

By simple observation, we see that the limit from the right is 1 and the limit from the left is - 1.

For the next two limits we have:

```
>> limit(abs(x^2-x-7),x,3)
```

ans =

1

```
>> limit((x-1)/(x^n-1),x,1)
```

ans =

1/n

For the last limit we have the following:

```
>> limit(exp(1)^(1/x),x,0)
```

ans =

NaN

```
>> limit(exp(1)^(1/x),x,0,'left')
```

ans =

0

```
>> limit(exp(1)^(1/x),x,0,'right')
```

ans =

INF

Then, there is no limit at $x=0$. If we plot the function (see Figure 2-2), we have:

```
>> ezplot (exp(1)^(1/x), [- 10, 10 - 3, 3])
```

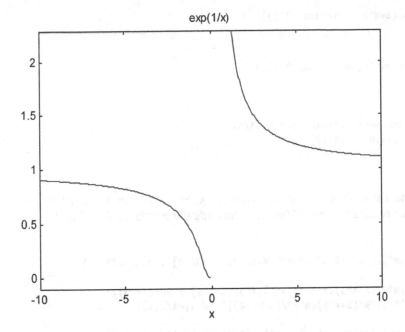

Figure 2-2.

We see that the function becomes (positive) infinite at 0 when approaching from the right, and it tends to 0 when approaching from the left. Thus we conclude that the function has no limit at $x = 0$.

2.3 Sequences of Functions

MATLAB enables you to analyze the convergence of sequences of functions. MATLAB's graphics capabilities can greatly help in understanding the concept of the limit of a sequence of functions and can also aid in the calculation of these limits.

EXERCISE 2-5

Calculate the limit function of the following sequences of functions:

$f_n(x) = x^n/n$, $g_n(x) = x^n/(1 + x^n)$, $h_n(x) = x^n/(n + x^n)$, $k_n(x) = sin^2(\pi x)$ if $1 / (n + 1) \le x \le 1/n$ and $k_n(x) = 0$ if $(x < 1/(n + 1)$ and $x > 1/n)$. In all cases x varies in $[0,1]$.

First of all, we impose the condition $x \in [0,1]$ using the syntax:

```
>> maple('assume(x, RealRange(0,1))');
```

We then calculate the limits of the function sequences as follows:

```
>> pretty(sym(maple('limit(x^n/n,n=infinity)')))
```

0

```
>> pretty(sym(maple('limit(x^n/(1+x^n),n=infinity)')))
```

0

```
>> pretty(sym(maple('limit(x^n/(n+x^n),n=infinity) ')))
```

0

```
>> pretty(sym(maple('limit(piecewise(x>=1/(n+1) and x<=1/n,
sin(Pi/x)^2,x<1/(n+1) and x<1/n,0),n=infinity) ')))
```

0

Now we support these results with the graphical representations shown in Figures 2-3, 2-4 and 2-5, which in each case illustrates the ***convergence of the sequence of functions towards the constant 0 function***. The syntax for the plots is as follows:

```
>> fplot('[x,x^2/2,x^3/3,x^4/4,x^5/5,x^6/6,x^7/7,x^8/8,x^9/9,x^10/10]',[0,1,-1/2,1])
```

```
>> fplot('[x/(1+x),x^2/(1+x^2),x^3/(1+x^3),x^4/(1+x^4),x^5/(1+x^5),x^6/(1+x^6),
         x^7/(1+x^7),x^8/(1+x^8),x^9/(1+x^9),x^10/(1+x^10)]',[0,1,-1/2,1])
```

```
>> fplot('[x/(1+x),x^2/(2+x^2),x^3/(3+x^3),x^4/(4+x^4),x^5/(5+x^5),x^6/(6+x^6),
         x^7/(7+x^7),x^8/(8+x^8),x^9/(9+x^9),x^10/(10+x^10)]',[0,1,-1/2,1])
```

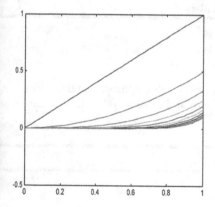

Figure 2-3.

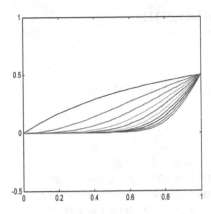

Figure 2-4.

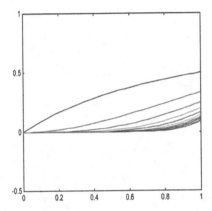

Figure 2-5.

EXERCISE 2-6

Calculate the limit of the following sequences of functions:

$$f_n(x) = (x^2 + nx)/n, \; x \in R$$

$$g_n(x) = 1 \text{ if } -n \le x \le n \text{ and } g_n(x) = 0 \text{ otherwise, } x \in R$$

$$h_n(x) = 2n^2x \text{ if } 0 \le x \le 1/2n, \; h_n(x) = 2n-2n^2x \text{ if } 1/2n \le x \le n, \; h_n(x) = 0 \text{ if } n \le x \le 1, \; x \in [0,1]$$

The limits of these sequences of functions are calculated as follows:

```
>> pretty(sym(maple('limit((x^2+n*x)/n,n=infinity)')))
```

x

```
>> pretty(sym(maple('limit(piecewise(x>=-n and x<=n,1,0),n=infinity)')))
```

1

```
>> maple('assume(x, RealRange(0,1))');
>> pretty(sym(maple('limit(piecewise(x>=0 and x<=1/(2*n), 2*n^2*x, x>=1/(2*n) and
1/n>=x, 2*n-2*x*n^2, 1/n<=x and x>=1, 0),n=infinity)')))
```

0

Now we support these results with the graphical representations shown in Figures 2-6, 2-7 and 2-8, which illustrate the ***convergence of the first sequence of functions towards the function f(x) = x, the second sequence to the function f(x) = 1 and the third sequence to the function f(x) = 0***. The syntax entered into the *Matlab/Editor debugger* to define the functions via the *M-File* sub-option of the *File* menu in the MATLAB command window is the following:

```
function f=seq1(x,n)
f=(x^2+n*x)/n;

function g=seq2(x,n)
   if x>=-n & x<n
   g=1;
   else g=0;
end

function h=seq3(x,n)
if x>=0 & x<=1/(2*n)
h=2*n^2*x;
elseif x>1/(2*n) & x<=1/n
h=2*n-2*n^2*x;
elseif x>1/n & x<=1
h = 0;
end
```

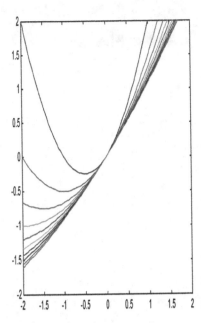

Figure 2-6.

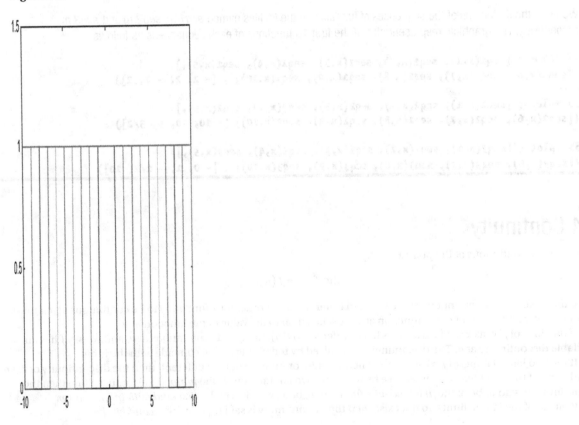

Figure 2-7.

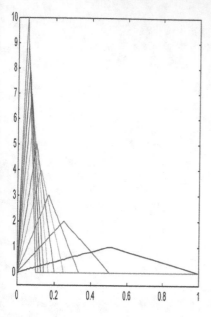

Figure 2-8.

We keep the definitions of the sequences of functions in the M-files named *seq1.m, seq2.m* and *seq3.m* respectively. The graphical resprestation of the first 10 functions of each sequence is as follows:

```
>> fplot ('[seq1(x,1), seq1(x,2), seq1(x,3), seq1(x,4), seq1(x,5),])
([seq1(x,6), seq1(x,7), seq1(x,8), seq1(x,9), seq1(x,10)]', [- 2, 2, - 2, 2])

>> fplot ('[seq2(x,1), seq2(x,2), seq2(x,3), seq2(x,4), seq2(x,5),])
([seq2(x,6), seq2(x,7), seq2(x,8), seq2(x,9), seq2(x,10)]'[- 10, 10, 0, 3/2])

>> fplot ('[seq3(x,1), seq3(x,2), seq3(x,3), seq3(x,4), seq3(x,5),])
([seq3(x,6), seq3(x,7), seq3(x,8), seq3(x,9), seq3(x,10)]', [- 0, 1, - 1/2, 10])
```

2.4 Continuity

A function *f* is continuous at the point $x = a$ if:

$$\lim_{x \to a} f(x) = f(a).$$

Otherwise, it is discontinuous at the point. In other words, in order for a function *f* to be continuous at *a* it must be defined at *a* and the limit of the function at *a* must be equal to the value of the function at *a*.

If the limit of $f(x)$ as *x* tends to *a* exists but is different to $f(a)$, then *f* is discontinuous at *a*, and we say *f* has an avoidable discontinuity at *a*. The discontinuity is resolved by redefining $f(a)$ to coincide with the limit.

If the two lateral limits of $f(x)$ at *a* exist (whether finite or infinite) but are different, then the discontinuity of *f* at *a* is said to be of the *first kind*. The difference between the two lateral limits is the *jump*. If the jump is finite then the discontinuity is said to be of the *first kind with finite jump*, otherwise it is of the *first kind with infinite jump*.

If either of the lateral limits do not exist, then the discontinuity is said to be of the *second kind*.

MATLAB provides the following commands relating to continuity:

maple ('readlib (discont): discont (function, variable)'): Determines the points of discontinuity of the real valued function given in the specified variable.

maple ('readlib (iscont): iscont(function,var=a..b)'): Determines when the given function is continuous on the interval [a, b]. The functional expression can contain piecewise-defined functions.

maple ('readlib (iscont): iscont(function,var=a..b, open)'): Determines when the given given function is continuous on the open interval (a, b).

We illustrate these concepts with several exercises:

EXERCISE 2-7

Study the continuity of the following functions of a real variable:

$$f(x) = \frac{\sin(x)}{x}, \ g(x) = \sin\left(\frac{1}{x}\right).$$

```
>> syms x a
>> limit(sin(x)/x,x,a)
```

ans =

sin(a)/a

The function f is continuous at any non-zero point a, so for any such point we have that $\lim_{x \to a} f(x) = f(a)$.

The problem arises at the point $x = 0$, at which the function f is not defined. Therefore, the function is discontinuous at $x = 0$, This discontinuity can be avoided by redefining the function at $x = 0$ with a value equal to $\lim_{x \to 0} f(x)$.

```
>> limit(sin(x)/x,x,0)
```

ans =

1

Thus we conclude that the function $f(x) = \sin(x) / x$ presents an avoidable discontinuity at $x = 0$ that is avoided by defining $f(0) = 1$. The function is continuous at all non-zero points.

The function g is continuous at any non-zero point a, so $\lim_{x \to a} g(x) = g(a)$.

```
>> limit (sin (1/x), x, a)
```

ans =

sin(1/a)

The problem arises at the point $x = 0$, where the function g is not defined. Therefore, the function is discontinuous at $x = 0$. To try to avoid the discontinuity, we calculate $\lim\limits_{x \to 0} g(x)$.

```
>> limit(sin(1/x),x,0)
```

ans =

-1 .. 1

```
>> limit(sin(1/x),x,0,'left')
```

ans =

-1 .. 1

```
>> limit(sin(1/x),x,0,'right')
```

ans =
-1 .. 1

We see that the limit does not exist at $x = 0$ (the limit has to be unique and here the result given is all points in the interval [– 1,1]), and neither of the lateral limits exist. Thus the function has a discontinuity of the second kind at $x=0$.

MATLAB responded to the calculation of the above limits with the expression *"– 1.. 1".* This is because the graph of $g\,(x)$ presents infinitely many oscillations between – 1 and 1. This is illustrated in Figure 2-9:

```
>> fplot ('sin (1/x)', [- 1, 1])
```

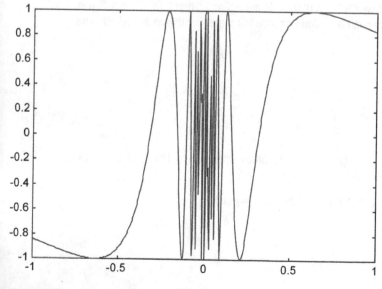

Figure 2-9.

EXERCISE 2-8

Study the continuity of the following function of a real variable:

$$f(x) = \frac{1}{1 + \sqrt[x]{e}} \text{ if } x \neq 0 \text{ and } f(x) = 1 \text{ if } x = 0.$$

The only problematic point is $x = 0$. Now, the function does exist at $x = 0$ (it has the value 1). We will try to find the lateral limits as x tends to 0:

```
>> syms x
>> limit(1/(1+exp(1/x)),x,0,'right')
```

ans =

0

```
>> limit(1/(1+exp(1/x)),x,0,'left')
```

ans =

1

As the lateral boundaries are different, the limit of the function at 0 does not exist. However, the lateral boundaries are both finite, so the discontinuity at 0 is of the first kind with a finite jump. We illustrate this result in Figure 2-10.

```
>> fplot('1/(1+exp(1/x))',[-5,5])
```

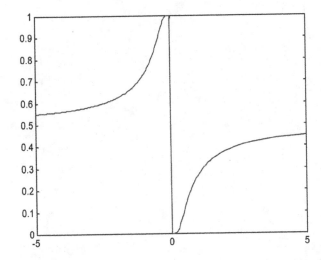

Figure 2-10.

EXERCISE 2-9

Study the continuity of the following function of a real variable:

$$f(x) = \sqrt[x]{e} \text{ if } x \neq 0 \text{ and } f(x) = 1 \text{ if } x = 0.$$

The only problematic point is $x = 0$. The function is defined at $x = 0$ (it has the value 1). We will try to find the lateral limits at 0:

```
>> limit ((exp (x)), x, 0, 'right')
```

ans =

inf

```
>> limit((exp(1/x)),x,0, 'left')
```

ans =

0

As the lateral boundaries are different, the limit of the function as x tends to 0 does not exist. As the right lateral limit is infinite, the discontinuity of the first kind at $x = 0$ is an infinite jump. We illustrate this result in Figure 2-11 above.

```
>> fplot ('exp (x)', [- 150, 150])
```

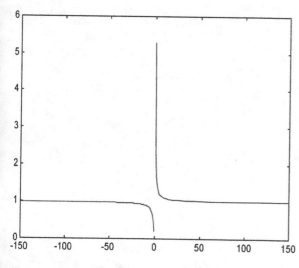

Figure 2-11.

2.5 Several Variables: Limits and Continuity. Characterization Theorems

The sequence $\{(a_{1n}, a_{2n}, ..., a_{mn})\}$ of points in m-dimensional space, where n runs through the natural numbers, has as limit the point $(a_1, a_2, ..., a_m)$ if, and only if:

$$\lim_{n \to \infty}(a_{1n}) = a_1, \lim_{n \to \infty}(a_{2n}) = a_2, ..., \lim_{n \to \infty}(a_{mn}) = a_m.$$

This characterization theorem allows us to calculate limits of sequences of points in m-dimensional space.

There is another theorem, similar to the above, which characterizes the limits of functions between spaces of more than one dimension. This theorem enables us to calculate the limits of multivariable functions.

If $f : R^n \to R^m$ is a function whose m components are $(f_1, ..., f_m)$. Then it follows that:

$$\lim_{x_1 \to a_1, x_2 \to a_2, ..., x_n \to a_n} \left(f_1(x_1, x_2, ..., x_n), f_2(x_1, x_2, ..., x_n), ..., f_m(x_1, x_2, ..., x_n) \right)$$

$$= (l_1, l_2, ..., l_m)$$

if and only if

$$\lim_{x_1 \to a_1, x_2 \to a_2, ..., x_n \to a_n} \left(f_1(x_1, x_2, ..., x_n) \right) = l_1,$$

$$\lim_{x_1 \to a_1, x_2 \to a_2, ..., x_n \to a_n} \left(f_2(x_1, x_2, ..., x_n) \right) = l_2,$$

$$...,$$

$$\lim_{x_1 \to a_1, x_2 \to a_2, ..., x_n \to a_n} \left(f_m(x_1, x_2, ..., x_n) \right) = l_m.$$

EXERCISE 2-10

Calculate the limit of the following three-dimensional sequence:

$$\lim_{n \to \infty} \left[\frac{1+n}{n}, \left(1 + \frac{1}{n} \right)^{2n}, \frac{n}{2n-1} \right]$$

```
>> pretty(sym(maple('vector([limit((n+1)/n,n=infinity),limit((1+1/n)^(2*n),
n=infinity),limit(n/(2*n-1),n=infinity)])')))
```

[1-exp (2) 1/2]

EXERCISE 2-11

Calculate the limit as $n \rightarrow \infty$ of the following four-dimensional sequence:

$$\lim_{n\to\infty}\left[\sqrt[n]{\frac{n}{1+n^2}},\ \sqrt[n]{\frac{1}{n}},\ \sqrt[n]{5n},\ \frac{1+n^2}{n^2}\right]$$

```
>> pretty(sym(maple('vector([limit((n/(n^2+1))^(1/n),n=infinity),limit((1/n)^(1/n),
n=infinity),limit((5*n)^(1/n) ,n=infinity),limit((n^2+1)/n^2,n=infinity)])')))
```

[1, 1, 1, 1]

EXERCISE 2-12

For the function $f : R \rightarrow R^2$ defined below, find $\lim_{x\to 0} f(x)$:

$$f(x) = \left(\frac{\sin(x)}{x},\ \sqrt[x]{1+x}\right).$$

```
>> pretty(sym(maple('vector([limit(sin(x)/x,x=0),limit((1+x)^(1/x),x=0)])')))
```

[1, exp (1)]

EXERCISE 2-13

For the function $f : R^2 \rightarrow R^2$ defined below, find $\lim_{(x,y)\to(0,0)} f(x,y)$:

$$f(x,y) = \left[\frac{2(1-\cos(y))}{y^2} + \frac{\sin(x)}{x},\ \sqrt[x]{1+x} - \frac{\tan(y)}{y}\right].$$

```
>> maple ('f:=(x,y) - > sin (x) / x+2 (1-cos (y)) / y ^ 2');
```

```
>> maple ('g:=(x,y) - >(1+x) ^ (1/x) - tan (y) / y ');
```

```
>> pretty(sym(maple('vector([limit(limit(f(x,y),x=0),y=0),limit(limit(g(x,y),
(((([(x=0), y = 0)])')))
```

[inf, exp (1) - 1]

2.6 Iterated and Directional Limits

Given a function $f: R^n \to R$ an *iterated limit* of f at the point $(a_1, a_2, ..., a_n)$ is the value of the limit (if it exists):

$$\lim_{x_1 \to a_1} \left(\lim_{x_2 \to a_2} \left(... \lim_{x_n \to a_n} f(x_1, x_2, ..., x_n) \right) \right)$$

or any of the other limits obtained by permuting the order of the component limits.

The *directional limit of f at the point* $(a_1, ..., a_n)$ depends on the direction of the curve $h(t) = (h_1(t), h_2(t), ..., h_n(t))$, where $h(t_0) = (a_1, a_2, ..., a_n)$, and is defined to be the value:

$$\lim_{t \to t_0}(f(h(t)) = \lim_{(x_1, x_2, ..., x_n) \to (a_1, a_2, ..., a_n)} f(x_1, x_2, ..., x_n)$$

A necessary condition for a function of several variables to have a limit at a point is that all the iterated limits have the same value (which will be equal to the value of the limit of the function, if it exists).

It can also happen that the directional limit of a function will vary according to the curve used, so that a different limit exists for different curves, or the limit exists for some curves and not others.

Another necessary condition for a function of several variables to have a limit at a point is that all directional limits, i.e. the limit for all curves, have the same value.

Therefore, to prove that a function has no limit at a point it is enough to show that either an iterated limit does not exist or that two iterated limits have a different value, or we can show that a directional limit does not exist or that two directional limits have different values.

A practical procedure for calculating the limit of a function of several variables is to change from cartesian to polar coordinates.

EXERCISE 2-14

Find $\lim_{(x,y) \to (0,0)} f(x,y)$ for the function $f: R^2 \to R$ defined by:

$$f(x,y) = \frac{xy}{x^2 + y^2}$$

```
>> syms x y
>> limit (limit ((x*y) /(x^2+y^2), x, 0), y, 0)

ans =

0

>> limit (limit ((x*y) /(x^2+y^2), y, 0), x, 0)

ans =

0
```

Thus the two iterated limits are the same. Next we calculate the directional limits corresponding to the family of straight lines $y = mx$:

```
>> syms m
>> limit((m*x^2)/(x^2+(m^2)*(x^2)),x,0)
```

ans =

m /(1+m^2)

The directional limits depend on the parameter m, which will be different for different values of m (corresponding to different straight lines). Thus, we conclude that the function has no limit at (0,0).

EXERCISE 2-15

Find $\lim\limits_{(x,y)\to(0,0)} f(x,y)$ for the function $f:R^2 \to R$ defined by:

$$f(x,y) = \frac{(y^2 - x^2)^2}{x^2 + y^4}$$

```
>> syms x y
>> limit (limit ((y^2-x^2) ^ 2 /(y^4+x^2), x, 0), y, 0)
```

ans =

1

```
>> limit (limit ((y^2-x^2) ^ 2 /(y^4+x^2), y, 0), x, 0)
```

ans =

0

As the two iterated limits are different, we conclude that the function has no limit at the point (0,0).

EXERCISE 2-16

Find $\lim\limits_{(x,y)\to(0,0)} f(x,y)$ for the function $f:R^2 \to R$ defined by:

$$f(x,y) = \frac{(y^2 - x)^2}{x^2 + y^4}$$

```
>> syms x y m, limit (limit ((y^2-x) ^ 2 /(y^4+x^2), y, 0), x, 0)
```

ans =

1

```
>> limit (limit ((y^2-x) ^ 2 /(y^4+x^2), x, 0), y, 0)
```

ans =

1

Thus the two iterated limits are the same. Next we calculate the directional limits corresponding to the family of straight lines $y = mx$:

```
>> limit(((m*x)^2-x)^2/((m*x)^4+x^2),x,0)
```

ans =

1

The directional limits corresponding to the family of straight lines $y = mx$ do not depend on m and coincide with the iterated limits. Next we find the directional limits corresponding to the family of parabolas $y \wedge 2 = mx$:

```
>> limit(((m*x)-x)^2/((m*x)^2+x^2),x,0)
```

ans =

(m-1) ^ 2-/(m^2+1)

Thus the directional limits corresponding to this family of parabolas depend on the parameter m, so they are different. This leads us to conclude that the function has no limit at (0,0).

EXERCISE 2-17

Find $\lim\limits_{(x,y)\to(0,0)} f(x,y)$ for the function $f: R^2 \to R$ defined by:

$$f(x,y) = \frac{x^2 y}{x^2 + y^2}$$

```
>> syms x y, limit (limit ((x^2*y) /(x^2+y^2), x, 0), y, 0)
```

ans =

0

```
>> limit (limit ((x^2*y) /(x^2+y^2), x, 0), y, 0)
```

ans =

0

```
>> limit(((x^2)*(m*x))/(x^2+(m*x)^2),x,0)
```

ans =

0

```
>> limit (((m*y) ^ 2) * y / ((m*y) ^ 2 + y ^ 2), y, 0)
```

ans =

0

We see that the iterated limits and directional limits corresponding to the given family of lines and parabolas coincide and are all zero. This leads us to suspect that the limit of the function may be zero. To confirm this, we transform to polar coordinates and find the limit:

```
>> syms a r, limit (limit (((r^2) * (cos (a) ^ 2) * (r) * (sin (a))) / ((r^2) *
(cos (a) ^ 2)+(r^2) * (sin (a) ^ 2)), r, 0), a, 0)
```

ans =

0

Therefore we conclude that the limit of the function is zero at the point (0,0).

This is an example where, as a last resort, we had to transform to polar coordinates. In the above examples we used families of lines and parabolas, but other curves can be used. The change to polar coordinates can be crucial in determining limits of functions of several variables. As we have seen, there are sufficient criteria to show that a function has no limit at a point. However, we do not have necessary and sufficient conditions to ensure the existence of the limit.

EXERCISE 2-18

Find $\lim\limits_{(x,y)\to(0,0)} f(x,y)$ for the function $f: R^2 \to R$ defined by:

$$f(x,y) = \frac{(x-1)^2 y^2}{(x-1)^2 + y^2}$$

```
>> syms x y m a r
>> limit (limit (y ^ 2 *(x-1) ^ 2 / (y ^ 2 +(x-1) ^ 2), x, 0), y, 0)
```

ans =

0

```
>> limit (limit (y ^ 2 *(x-1) ^ 2 / (y ^ 2 +(x-1) ^ 2), y, 0), x, 0)
```

ans =

0

```
>> limit((m*x)^2*(x-1)^2/((m*x)^2+(x-1)^2),x,0)
```

ans =

0

```
>> limit((m*x)*(x-1)^2/((m*x)+(x-1)^2),x,0)
```

ans =

0

We see that the iterated and directional limits coincide. We calculate the limit by converting to polar coordinates:

```
>> limit (limit ((r ^ 2 * sin (a) ^ 2) * (r * cos (a) - 1) ^ 2 / ((r ^ 2 * sin (a) ^ 2) +
(r * cos (a) - 1) ^ 2), r, 1), a, 0)
```

ans =

0

The limit is zero at the point (1,0). The surface is depicted in Figure 2-12 where we see the function tends to 0 in a neighborhood of (1,0):

```
>> [x, y] = meshgrid(0:0.05:2,-2:0.05:2);
>> z=y.^2.*(x-1).^2./(y.^2+(x-1).^2);
>> mesh(x,y,z), view ([- 23, 30])
```

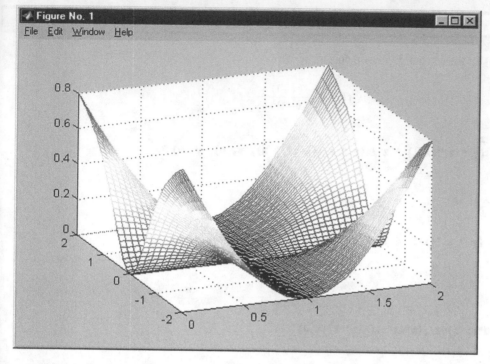

Figure 2-12.

2.7 Continuity in Several Variables

A function $f: R^n \rightarrow R^m$ is said to be continuous at the point $(a_1, a_2, ..., a_n)$ if:

$$\lim_{x_1 \rightarrow a_1, x_2 \rightarrow a_2, ..., x_n \rightarrow a_n} f(a_1, a_2, ..., a_n).$$

EXERCISE 2-19

Let the function $f: R^2 \rightarrow R$ be defined by:

$$f(x,y) = \frac{x^3 + y^3}{x^2 + y^2}.$$

Find $\lim_{(x,y) \rightarrow (1,0)} f(x,y)$ and study the continuity of f.

The only problematic point is the origin. We will analyze the continuity of the function at the origin by calculating its limit there.

```
>> syms x y m a r
>> limit (limit ((x^3+y^3) /(x^2+y^2), x, 0), y, 0)
```

ans =

0

```
>> limit (limit ((x^3+y^3) /(x^2+y^2), y, 0), x, 0)
```

ans =

0

```
>> limit((x^3+(m*x)^3)/(x^2+(m*x)^2),x,0)
```

ans =

0

We see that the iterated and the linear directional limits coincide. We try to calculate the limit by converting to polar coordinates:

```
>> maple ('limit (limit (((r * cos (a)) ^ 3 + (r * sin (a)) ^ 3) / ((r * cos (a)) ^ 2 +
(r * sin (a)) ^ 2), r = 0), a = 0)')
```

ans =

0

We see that the limit at (0,0) coincides with f(0,0), so the function is continuous at (0,0). The graph in Figure 2-13 confirms the continuity.

```
>> [x, y] = meshgrid(-1:0.007:1,-1:0.007:1);
>> z=(x.^3+y.^3)./(x.^2+y.^2);
>> mesh (x, y, z)
>> view ([50, - 20])
```

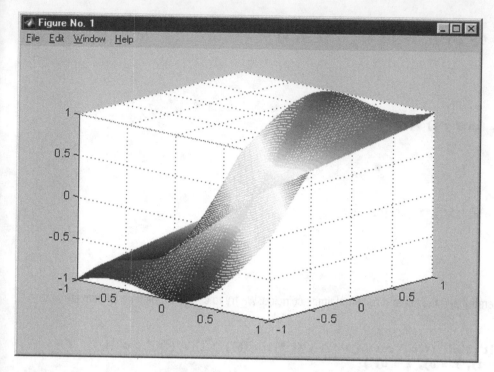

Figure 2-13.

EXERCISE 2-20

Define the function $f: R^2 \to R$ by

$$f(x,y) = x^2 + 2y \ \ if \ (x,y) \neq (1,2) \ \ and \ f(1,2) = 0$$

and study its continuity at the point (1,2).

```
>> limit (limit ((x^2+2*y), x, 1), y, 2).
```

ans =

5

```
>> limit (limit ((x^2+2*y), y, 2), x, 1)
```

ans =

5

We see that if the limit at (1,2) exists, then it should be 5. But the function has the value 0 at the point (1,2). Thus, the function is not continuous at the point (1,2).

EXERCISE 2-21

Consider the function $f: R^2 \to R$ defined by:

$$f(x,y) = \frac{[1-\cos(x)]\sin(y)}{x^3 + y^3} \text{ if } (x,y) \neq (0,0) \text{ and } f(0,0) = 0.$$

Study the continuity of f at the point (0,0).

```
>> maple ('limit (limit ((1-cos (x)) * sin (y) /(x^3+y^3), x = 0), y = 0)')
```

ans =

0

```
>> maple ('limit (limit ((1-cos (x)) * sin (y) /(x^3+y^3), x = 0), y = 0)')
```

ans =

0

```
>> maple ('limit ((1-cos (x)) * sin(m*x) / (x ^ 3, +(m*x) ^ 3), x = 0)')
```

ans =

1/2 * m /(1 + m^3)

We see that the limit at (0,0) does not exist, as there are different directional limits for different directions. Thus, the function is not continuous at (0,0). At the rest of the points in the plane, the function is continuous. The plot of the function in a neighborhood of the origin of radius 0.01 shown in Figure 2-14 shows that around (0,0) there are branches of the surface that soar to infinity, which causes the non-existence of the limit at the origin.

```
>> [x,y]=meshgrid(-1/100:0.0009:1/100,-1/100:0.0009:1/100);
>> z=(1-cos(x)).*sin(y)./(x.^3+y.^3);
>> surf (x, y, z)
>> view ([50, - 15])
```

4

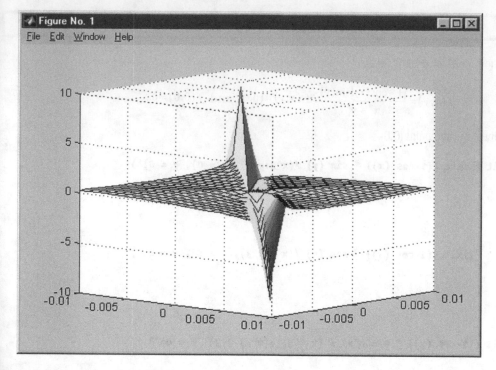

Figure 2-14.

CHAPTER 3

■ ■ ■

Numerical Series and Power Series

This chapter demonstrates the wide range of features that MATLAB offers which can be used to treat numerical series. These include the determination of the radius of convergence of a power series, summation of convergent series, alternating series and so on.

3.1 Series. Convergence Criteria

We distinguish between numerical series which have non-negative terms and series which have alternating terms. Some examples of the more classical criteria to determine whether a series of non-negative terms converges or diverges will be presented first, then we will go on to analyze alternating series.

3.2 Numerical Series with Non-Negative Terms

Among the most common of the convergence criteria is the *ratio test* or *d'Alembert criterion*, which reads as follows:

$$\sum_{n=1}^{\infty} a(n) \text{ is convergent if } \lim_{n\to\infty} \frac{a(n+1)}{a(n)} < 1$$

$$\sum_{n=1}^{\infty} a(n) \text{ is divergent if } \lim_{n\to\infty} \frac{a(n+1)}{a(n)} > 1$$

If the limit is 1, we don't know whether the series converges or diverges.
Another widely used criterion is the *Cauchy criterion* or *root test*, which reads as follows:

$$\sum_{n=1}^{\infty} a(n) \text{ is convergent if } \lim_{n\to\infty} \sqrt[n]{a(n)} < 1$$

$$\sum_{n=1}^{\infty} a(n) \text{ is divergent if } \lim_{n\to\infty} \sqrt[n]{a(n)} > 1$$

Again, if the limit is 1, we cannot say whether the series diverges or converges.
If a limit of 1 is obtained in both the ratio and root test, we can often use the *criterion of Raabe or Duhamel*, which reads as follows:

$$\sum_{n=1}^{\infty} a(n) \text{ is convergent if } \lim_{n\to\infty} \left[n\left(1 - \frac{a(n+1)}{a(n)} \right) \right] > 1$$

4

$$\sum_{n=1}^{\infty} a(n) \text{ is divergent if } \lim_{n\to\infty}\left[n\left(1-\frac{a(n+1)}{a(n)}\right)\right] < 1$$

However, if the limit is 1, we still cannot conclude anything about the convergence or divergence of the series. Another useful criterion is the following:

$$\sum_{n=1}^{\infty} a(n) \text{ and } \sum_{n=1}^{\infty} 2^n a(2^n) \text{ either both diverge or both converge.}$$

Other criteria such as Gauss majorization, comparison tests and so on can also be implemented via Maple. We will see some examples below:

EXERCISE 3-1

Study the convergence and, if possible, find the sum of the following series:

$$\sum_{n=1}^{\infty} \frac{1+n}{n(2+n)(3+n)}$$

We will apply the ratio test:

```
>> maple('a:=n -> (n+1)/(n*(n+2)*(n+3)):limit(a(n+1)/a(n), n=infinity);')
```

ans =

1

We see that the limit is 1, so we can't yet say anything about the convergence or divergence of the series. We will apply Raabe's criterion:

```
>> maple('a:=n-> (n+1) / (n * (n + 2) * (n)): limit (n * (1-a (n + 1) /a (n)),
n = infinity);')
```

ans =

2

As the limit is greater than 1, the series converges and will be summable:

```
>> maple('sum(a(n),n=1..+infinity)')
```

ans =

17/36

The MATLAB command *symsum* can be used to sum series, but it is not as strong as the command *maple('sum')*. The syntax of both is:

```
syms v, a, b
symsum(S,v,a,b) sums the series with general term S where the variable v ranges between a and b
```

`symsum(S,v)` sums the series with general term **S** in the variable **v**

`maple('sum(S,v=a..b)')` sums the series with general term **S** where the variable **v** ranges between **a** and **b**

The sum of the series can also be found as follows:

```
>> syms n
>> symsum((n+1)/(n*(n+2)*(n+3)),1,Inf)
```

ans =

17/36

EXERCISE 3-2

Study the convergence and, if possible, find the sum of the following series:

$$\sum_{n=1}^{\infty}\frac{n}{2^n}, \quad \sum_{n=1}^{\infty}\frac{n^n}{n!}, \quad \sum_{n=1}^{\infty}\frac{n^n}{3^n\,n!}$$

We apply the ratio test to the first series:

```
>> maple('a:=n -> n/2^n: limit(a(n+1)/a(n), n=infinity)')
```

ans =

1/2

The limit is less than 1, so the series converges. We find its sum:

```
>> maple('sum(a(n),n=1..+infinity)')
```

ans =

2

We apply the ratio test to the second series:

```
>> maple('a:=n -> n^n/n!: limit(a(n+1)/a(n), n=infinity)')
```

ans =

exp (1)

As the limit is greater than 1, the series diverges.

We apply the ratio test to the third series:

```
>> maple('a:=n -> n^n/((n!)*(3^n)): limit(a(n+1)/a(n), n=infinity)')
```

ans =

1/3 * exp (1)

The limit is less than 1, so the series is convergent. Trying to find the exact sum, we see that MATLAB does not solve the problem:

```
>> maple('sum(a(n),n=1..+infinity)')
```

ans =

sum(n^n/n!/(3^n),n = 1 .. inf)

EXERCISE 3-3

Study the convergence and, if possible, find the sum of the following series:

$$\sum_{n=1}^{\infty} \frac{3+2n}{7^n n(1+n)}, \quad \sum_{n=1}^{\infty} \frac{n}{p^n}, \quad \sum_{n=1}^{\infty} \frac{(n+p)!}{p^n n! p!}, \quad p = parameter$$

We apply the ratio test to the first series:

```
>> maple('a:=n -> (2*n+3)/(n*(n+1)*(7^n)): limit(a(n+1)/a(n), n=infinity)')
```

ans =

1/7

As the limit is less than 1, the series is convergent. We will calculate its sum. The result that is returned will sometimes be complicated, depending on certain functions that are implemented in MATLAB (in this case *hypergeom*):

```
>> maple('sum(a(n),n=1..+infinity)')
```

ans =

16/3+30*log(6/7)-13/49*hypergeom([2, 2],[3],1/7)

```
>> maple('evalf(")')
```

ans =

.3833972806909634

Now we apply the ratio test to the second series:

```
>> maple('a:=n -> n/p^n');
>> maple('limit(a(n+1)/a(n), n=infinity)')
```

ans =

1/p

Thus, if $p > 1$, the series converges, and if $p < 1$, the series diverges. If $p = 1$, we get the series with general term n, which diverges. For p greater than 1, we find the sum of the series:

```
>> maple('sum(a(n),n=1..+infinity)')
```

ans =

p /(-1+p) ^ 2

We apply the ratio test to the third series:

```
>> maple('a:=n ->(n+p)!/((p!)*(n!)*(p^n))');
>> maple('limit(a(n+1)/a(n), n=infinity)')
```

ans =

*limit((n+1+p)!/(n+1)!/(p^(n+1))/(n+p)!*n!*p^n,n = inf)*

Here MATLAB has not been able to find the limit, so we will try the Raabe criterion instead:

```
>> maple('limit(n*(1-a(n+1)/a(n)),n=infinity)')
```

ans =

limit(n(1-(n+1+p)!/(n+1)!/(p^(n+1))/(n+p)!*n!*p^n),n = inf)*

Again, the limit could not be found. We try to simplify the expression before finding the limit:

```
>> maple('limit(simplify(a(n+1)/a(n)), n=infinity)')
```

ans =

1/p

Thus, if $p > 1$, the series converges, if $p < 1$, the series diverges and if $p = 1$, we get the series wit$n + 1$, which diverges.

EXERCISE 3-5

Study the convergence and, if possible, find the sum of the following series:

$$\sum_{n=1}^{\infty} \frac{5}{2^n}, \quad \sum_{n=1}^{\infty} (\sqrt[n]{n}-1)^n, \quad \sum_{n=1}^{\infty} \left(\frac{n^2+2n+1}{n^2+n-1} \right)^{n^2}$$

For the first series, we apply the root test:

```
>> maple('a:=n ->5/(2^n)');
>> maple('limit((a(n))^(1/n), n=infinity)')
```

ans =

1/2

As the limit is less than 1, the series is convergent:

```
>> maple('sum(a(n),n=1..+infinity)')
```

ans =

5

Now we apply the root test to the second series:

```
>> maple('a:=n ->(n^(1/n)-1)^n');
>> maple('limit(simplify((a(n))^(1/n)), n=infinity)')
```

ans =

0

As the limit is less than 1, the series is convergent, but neither the exact nor an accurate approximate sum are calculable.

Now we apply the root test to the third series:

```
>> maple('a:=n->((n^2+2*n+1)/(n^2+n-1))^(n^2)');
>> maple('simplify(limit(simplify((a(n))^(1/n)), n=infinity))')
```

ans =

exp (1)

As the limit is greater than 1, the series diverges.

EXERCISE 3-6

Study the convergence and, if possible, find the sum of the following series:

$$\sum_{n=1}^{\infty} \tan^n\left(p+\frac{q}{n}\right).$$

We apply the root test:

```
>> maple ('a: = n - > (tan(p+q/n)) ^ n');
>> simple(maple('limit(simplify((a(n))^(1/n)), n=infinity)'))
```

ans =

$sin(p)/cos(p)$

Then, for values of *p* such that *tan(p)* < 1 the series converges. These values are 0 < *p* < *Pi*/4. And for values of *p* such that *tan(p)* > 1 the series diverges. These values are *Pi*/4 < *p* < *Pi*/2. MATLAB does not offer the exact or an accurate approximate sum of this series.

EXERCISE 3-7

Study the convergence and, if possible, find the sum of the following series:

$$\sum_{n=1}^{\infty} \frac{1}{n \, Log(n)}, \quad \sum_{n=1}^{\infty} \frac{1}{n\left[Log(n)\right]^p}, \quad p = parameter > 0$$

We apply the criterion that the series $\sum_{n=1}^{\infty} a(n)$ and $\sum_{n=1}^{\infty} 2^n a(2^n)$ either both diverge or both converge.

```
>> maple ('a: = n - > 1 / (n * log (n))');
>> maple('b:=(2^n)*a(2^n)');
>> pretty(maple('simplify(b)'))
```

```
      1
   ---------
   n log (2)
```

As the general term is a constant multiple of the general term of the divergent harmonic series, this series diverges, and we conclude that the original series diverges.

Let us now apply the same criteria to the second series:

```
>> maple('a:=n->1/(n*(log(n))^p)');
>> maple('b:=(2^n)*a(2^n)');
>> pretty(maple('simplify(b)'))
```

$$\begin{array}{cc} (-\,p) & (-\,p) \\ n & log(2) \end{array}$$

When $p < 1$, this series dominates the series with general term $n^{-p} = 1/n^p$. Thus the initial series also diverges.

When $p < 1$, this series is dominated by the convergent series with general term $n^{-p} = 1/n^p$. Thus the initial series also converges.

When $p = 1$, the series reduces to the series studied above, i.e. it diverges.

MATLAB does not offer the sum of either of the two series of this problem.

EXERCISE 3-8

Study the convergence and, if possible, find the sum of the following series:

$$\sum_{n=1}^{\infty} \frac{(n+1)(n+2)}{n^5}, \quad \sum_{n=1}^{\infty} \frac{1}{\left(1+\sqrt{n}\right)^2}$$

We will begin by studying the second series. We try to apply the ratio, Raabe and root tests:

```
>> maple('a:=n->1/(1+n^(1/2))^2');
>> maple('limit(a(n+1)/a(n), n=infinity)')
```

ans =

1

```
>> maple('limit(n*(1-a(n+1)/a(n)),n=infinity)')
```

ans =

1

```
>> maple('limit(simplify((a(n))^(1/n)), n=infinity)')
```

ans =

1

Thus all the limits are 1. Therefore, at the moment, we cannot conclude anything about the convergence of the series.

We now compare our series with the divergent harmonic series by finding the limit of the quotient of the respective general terms:

```
maple('limit(a(n)/(1/n),n=infinity)')
```

=

As the limit is greater than zero, the initial series is also divergent.

We will now analyze the first series of the problem directly, comparing it with the convergent series with general term $1/n^3$ by examining the limit of the quotient of the general terms:

```
>> maple('a:=n->(n+1)*(n+2)/n^5');
>> maple('limit(a(n)/(1/(n^3)),n=infinity)')
```

ans =

1

As the limit is greater than 0, the initial series is also convergent:

```
>> maple('sum(a(n),n=1..+infinity)')
```

ans =

*2 * zeta (5) + 1/30 * pi ^ 4 + zeta (3)*

Now, we try to approximate the result:

```
>> maple('evalf(sum(a(n),n=1..+infinity))')
```

ans =

6.522882114579747

We could have tried to determine whether the first series converges or diverges by using the ratio, root and Raabe criteria:

```
>> maple('limit(a(n+1)/a(n), n=infinity)')
```

ans =

1

```
>> maple('limit(simplify((a(n))^(1/n)), n=infinity)')
```

ans =

1

```
>> maple('limit(n*(1-a(n+1)/a(n)),n=infinity)')
```

ans =

3

The root and ratio tests tells us nothing, but since the limit is greater than 1, the Raabe criterion tells us that the series converges.

3.3 Alternating Numerical Series

We now consider numerical series that have alternating positive and negative terms.

A series $\sum a(n)$ is *absolutely convergent* if the series $\sum |a(n)|$ is convergent. As the series of moduli is a series of positive terms, we already know how to analyze it.

Every absolutely convergent series is convergent.

Apart from the criteria described earlier, there are, among others, two classical criteria that allow us to analyze the nature of alternating series, which will allow us to resolve most convergence problems concerning alternating series.

The *Dirichlet test* says that if the sequence of partial sums of $\sum a(n)$ is bounded and $\{b(n)\}$ is a decreasing sequence that has limit 0, then the series $\sum a(n)b(n)$ is convergent.

Abel's test says that if $\sum a(n)$ is convergent and $\{b(n)\}$ is a monotone convergent sequence, then the series $\sum a(n)b(n)$ is convergent.

EXERCISE 3-9

Study the convergence of the following series:

$$\sum_{n=1}^{\infty} \frac{(-1)^{1+n}}{1+2n^2}$$

This is an alternating series. Let us consider the series of moduli and analyze its character:

```
>> maple ('a: = n - > 1 /(2*n^2+1)');
```

We apply to this series of positive terms the criteria of comparison of the second kind, comparing with the convergent series with general term $1/n^2$:

```
>> maple('limit(a(n)/(1/(n^2)),n=infinity)')
```

ans =

½

As the limit is greater than zero, the given series of positive terms is convergent, so the initial series is absolutely convergent and, therefore, convergent.

EXERCISE 3-10

Study the convergence of the following series:

$$\sum_{n=1}^{\infty} \frac{(-1)^{1+n}\, n}{(1+n)^2}, \quad \sum_{n=1}^{\infty} \frac{(-1)^{1+n}}{n}$$

Defining $a(n) = (-1)^{1+n}$ and $b(n) = \dfrac{n}{(1+n)^2}$, we have that $\sum a(n)$ has bounded partial sums and $\{b(n)\}$ is monotone decreasing with limit 0.

Using the Dirichlet test we conclude that the series is convergent.

For the second series we similarly proceed as follows.

Defining $a(n)=(-1)^{1+n}$ and $b(n)=\dfrac{1}{n}$, we have that $\sum a(n)$ has bounded partial sums and $\{b(n)\}$ is monotone decreasing with limit 0.

Using the Dirichlet test we conclude that the series is convergent.

3.4 Power Series

Given the power series $\sum a(n)x^n$, the most pressing issue is to calculate the range of convergence, i.e., the range of values of x for which the series is convergent.

The most common convergence criteria that we use are the root and ratio tests applied to the series of moduli (absolute values). If we can show the series is convergent then the original series is absolutely convergent and hence convergent.

EXERCISE 3-11

Study the range of convergence of the following power series:

$$\sum_{n=0}^{\infty}\frac{4^{2n}}{n+2}(x-3)^n$$

We apply the ratio test:

```
>> maple('a:=n->(4^(2*n))*((x-3)^n)/(n+2)');
>> maple('limit(simplify(a(n+1)/a(n)), n=infinity)')
```

ans =

16 * x-48

The series will be convergent when | 16 (- 3 + x) | < 1 :

```
[solve('16*x-48=1'), solve('16*x-48=-1')]
```

ans =

49/16 47/16

Thus, the condition $|16(-3+x)|<1$ is equivalent to the following:

$\dfrac{47}{16}<x<\dfrac{49}{16}$.

We already know that for values of x in the previous interval the series is convergent. Now we need to analyze the behavior of the series at the end points of the interval. We first consider $x = 49/16$:

```
>> maple ('a: = x - > (4 ^(2*n)) * ((x-3) ^ n) / (n + 2)');
>> maple('simplify(a(49/16))')
```

ans =

1/(n+2)

We first apply convergence tests for non-negative series to see if any of them determine the convergence or divergence of the series.

The ratio, Raabe and root tests do not solve the problem. Next we apply the criterion of comparison of the second kind, comparing the series of the problem with the divergent harmonic series with general term *1/n*:

```
>> maple('a:=n->1/(n+2)');
>> maple('limit(simplify((a(n))^(1/n)), n=infinity)')
```

ans =

1

As the limit is greater than zero, the series is divergent.

We now analyze the behavior of the series at the other end point $x = 47/16$:

```
>> maple ('a: = x - > (4 ^(2*n)) * ((x-3) ^ n) / (n + 2)');
>> maple ('simplify (a(47/16))')
```

ans =

(- 1) ^ n / (n + 2)

We have to analyze the alternating series $\sum\limits_{n=1}^{\infty} \dfrac{(-1)^n}{n+2}$.

The series with general term $(-1)^n$ has bounded partial sums, and the sequence with general term $1 / (n + 2)$ is decreasing toward 0. Then, by the Dirichlet test, the alternating series converges. Therefore the interval of convergence of the power series is the half-closed interval $[47/16, 49/16)$.

EXERCISE 3-12

Study the range of convergence of the following power series:

$$\sum_{n=0}^{\infty} \frac{1}{(-5)^n} x^{2n+1}$$

We apply the root test:

```
>> maple('a:=n->x^(2*n+1)/(-5)^n');
>> maple('limit(simplify(a(n+1)/a(n)), n=infinity)')
```

ans =

*-1/5 * x ^ 2*

The series is absolutely convergent when $|-x\wedge 2/5| < 1$.

The condition $|-x \wedge 2/5| < 1$ is equivalent to $-Sqrt\,(5) < x < Sqrt\,(5)$. Thus, we have determined a possible interval of convergence of the power series. We will now analyze the end points:

```
>> maple ('a: = x - > x ^(2*n+1) /(-5) ^ n');
>> [maple('simplify(a(sqrt(5)))'),maple('simplify(a(-sqrt(5)))')]
```

ans =

```
(- 1) ^(-n) * 5 ^(1/2)            -(-1) ^ n * 5 ^(1/2)
```

Both series are obviously divergent alternating series. Therefore, the interval of convergence of the power series is the open interval $\left(-\sqrt{5}, \sqrt{5}\right)$.

3.5 Formal Power Series

MATLAB implements the package *powseries*, which can be loaded into memory using the command *with(powseries)*. This package provides commands which allow you to create, manipulate and perform symbolic calculations with formal power series. The command **maple** must first be used. Among these commands are the following:

> powcreate(eqn,eqn1,eqn2,..,eqnn): Creates a formal power series, where *eqn* is an equation of the form $f(n) = expression\,(n)$, and where the equations *eqni*, which are of the form $f(ni) = value$, define the initial conditions that will give the values of the coefficients of the power series

> powpoly (polynomial, variable): Creates a formal power series equivalent to the polynomial given in the specified variable

> powadd(ps1,..,psn): Gives the formal power series sum of the specified series

> subtract(ps1,ps2): Gives the formal power series subtraction of the specified series

> negative (pserie): Gives the additive inverse of the specified power series (i.e. changes its sign)

> multconst (pserie, expression): Multiplies each coefficient of the specified power series by the given expression

> multiply (ps1, ps2): Gives the product of the two specified power series

> quotient (ps1, ps2): Gives the quotient of the two specified power series

> powsqrt (pserie): Gives the square root of the specified power series

> powexp (pserie): Gives the exponential of the specified power series

> powlog (pserie): Gives the natural logarithm of the specified power series

> powsin (pserie): Gives the sine of the specified power series

> powcos (pserie): Gives the cosine of the specified power series

> powdiff (pserie): Gives the derivative of the specified power series

> powint (pserie): Gives the indefinite integral of the specified power series

compose (ps1, ps2): Composes the specified power series

reversion (ps1, ps2): Calculates the reversion of the power series ps1 with respect to the power series ps2 (reversion is the inverse of composition)

inverse (pserie): Calculates the multiplicative inverse of the given series

evalpow (exprseries): Returns the power series obtained by evaluating the expression *exprseries*, where the latter is any arithmetic expression involving formal power series, polynomials, or functions that is accepted by the power series package

tpsform (pserie, variable, n): Transforms the formal power series *pserie* into a series of order *n* in the given variable

tpsform (pserie, variable): Transforms the formal series *pserie* into a series in the given variable with order defined by the global variable *Order*

op (pserie): Returns the internal structure of the formal power series *pserie* and gives access to its operands

op (op (pserie) 4): Returns a table that defines all the coefficients of the formal power series *pserie*. Any operand can be replaced with *subsop*.

Here are some examples:

```
>> maple('with(powseries):powcreate(t(n)=1/n!,t(0)=1):')
>> pretty(simple(sym(maple('tpsform(t, x, 7)'))))
```

$$1 + x + 1/2\ x^2 + 1/6\ x^3 + 1/24\ x^4 + 1/120\ x^5 + 1/720\ x^6 + O(x^7)$$

```
>> maple('powcreate(v(n)=(v(n-1)+v(n-2))/4,v(0)=4,v(1)=2): ')
>> pretty(simple(sym(maple('tpsform(v, x) '))))
```

$$4 + 2\ x + 3/2\ x^2 + 7/8\ x^3 + \frac{19}{32}\ x^4 + \frac{47}{128}\ x^5 + O(x^6)$$

```
>> maple('with(powseries): ')
>> maple('t:=powpoly(2*x^5+4*x^4-x+5, x): ')
>> pretty(simple(sym(maple('tpsform(t, s, 5) '))))
```

$$5 - s + 4\ s^4 + O(s^5)$$

```
>> pretty(simple(sym(maple('tpsform(t, s, 4)'))))
```

$$5 - s + O(s^4)$$

```
>> maple('powcreate(t(n)=t(n-1)/n,t(0)=1): ')
>> maple('powcreate(v(n)=v(n-1)/2,v(0)=1): ')
>> maple('s := powadd(t, v): ')
>> pretty(simple(sym(maple('tpsform(s, x, 7) '))))
```

$$2 + 3/2\ x + 3/4\ x^2 + 7/24\ x^3 + 5/48\ x^4 + \frac{19}{480}\ x^5 + \frac{49}{2880}\ x^6 + O(x^7)$$

```
>> maple('s := multiply(t, v): ')
>> pretty(simple(sym(maple('tpsform(s, x) '))))
```

$$1 + 3/2\ x + 5/4\ x^2 + \frac{19}{24}\ x^3 + 7/16\ x^4 + \frac{109}{480}\ x^5 + O(x^6)$$

```
>> maple('s := powexp(x): ')
>> pretty(simple(sym(maple('tpsform(s, x, 7) '))))
```

$$1 + x + 1/2\ x^2 + 1/6\ x^3 + 1/24\ x^4 + 1/120\ x^5 + 1/720\ x^6 + O(x^7)$$

```
>> maple('t := powexp( exp(x) ): ')
>> pretty(simple(sym(maple('tpsform(t, x, 4) '))))
```

$$exp\ (1) + exp\ (1)\ x + exp\ (1)\ x^2 + 5/6\ exp\ (1)\ x^3 + or\ (x^4)$$

```
>> maple('u := powexp( powdiff( powlog(1+x) ) ): ')
>> pretty(simple(sym(maple('tpsform(u, x, 5) '))))
```

$$xp(1) - exp(1)\ x + 3/2\ exp(1)\ x^2 - 13/6\ exp(1)\ x^3 + \frac{73}{24}\ exp(1)\ x^4 + O(x^5)$$

```
> maple('powcreate(t(n)=t(n-1)/n,t(0)=0,t(1)=1): ')
> maple('powcreate(v(n)=v(n-1)/2,v(0)=0,v(1)=1): ')
> maple('s := reversion(t,v): ')
> pretty(simple(sym(maple('tpsform(s,x,11) '))))
```

$$+ 1/12\ x^3 + 1/80\ x^5 + 1/448\ x^7 + 1/2304\ x^9 + O(x^{11})$$

```
> maple('ts := compose(t,s): ')
> pretty(simple(sym(maple('tpsform(ts,x) '))))
```

$$+ 1/2\ x^2 + 1/4\ x^3 + 1/8\ x^4 + 1/16\ x^5 + O(x^6)$$

```
> pretty(simple(sym(maple('tpsform(v,x) '))))
```

$$+ 1/2\ x^2 + 1/4\ x^3 + 1/8\ x^4 + 1/16\ x^5 + O(x^6)$$

```
  maple('powcreate(f(n)=f(n-1)/n,f(0)=1): ')
  maple('powcreate(g(n)=g(n-1)/2,g(0)=0,g(1)=1): ')
  maple('powcreate(h(n)=h(n-1)/5,h(0)=1): ')
  maple('k:=evalpow(f^3+g-quotient(h,f)): ')
  pretty(simple(sym(maple('tpsform(k,x,5) '))))
```

```
        233   2   7273   3   52171   4       5
24/5 x + --- x + ---- x + ----- x + O (x)
         50        1500       15000
```

3.6 Power Series Expansions and Functions

A local approximation of a real function of a real variable at a point replaces the definition of the function in a neighborhood of the point by a simpler function. The most commonly used local approximations replace an arbitrary function $f(x)$ by a polynomial $p(x)$ (a truncated power series), so that for any x close to the point, $f(x)$ is close to $p(x)$.

MATLAB implements several commands which can be used to work with local approximations. The command *maple* must first be used. The syntax of these commands is presented below:

> **series(expr,var=a): Returns a truncated power series expansion of expr in a neighborhood of the point *a*. The series is truncated in the order specified by the global variable *Order*. The expansion can be Taylor, Laurent or other more generalized series. The expansion may have fractional exponents, in which case the series will be represented in ordinary sum-of-products form.**

> **series (expr, var): Equivalent to the above with $a = 0$**

> **series (int (expr, var) var = a): Returns a generalized series expansion of the specified integral in a neighborhood of the point *a***

> **series (leadterm (expr), var = a): Returns the smallest degree term in the generalized series expansion of *expr* in a neighborhood of *a***

> **series(expr,var=a,n): Returns the generalized series expansion of *expr* in a neighborhood of *a* up to order *n*. In order to evaluate the expansion at some input, it must first be converted to a polynomial using the command *convert (polynom).***

> **convert (s, polynom): Converts the series *s* to a polynomial, eliminating the order term**

> **convert (s, ratpoly): Converts the series *s* to a rational polynomial expression. If *s* is a Taylor or Laurent series, then the rational polynomial expression is the Padé approximation. If *s* is a Chebyshev series, then the rational polynomial expression is the Chebishev-Padé approximation.**

> **convert(s,ratpoly,m,n): Converts the series *s* to a rational polynomial where the numerator polynomial has degree *m* and the denominator polynomial has degree *n***

> **op (s): Shows the internal structure of the series *s* and allows access to its operands. It returns a sequence of *2n* operands where *n* is the number of terms of the series, including the order. The ith coefficient is the $2i$-1th term and the ith exponent is the $2i^{th}$ term. If the expansion is in a neighborhood of $x = a$, *op(0,series)* extracts the expression *var = a*. Any operand can be substituted with *subsop*.**

> **order (s): Determines the order of the truncated expansion of the series *s***

> **Order: = n sets the global variable *Order* to the value *n*. By default, the value is 6. This variable determines the order of all future truncated series expansions.**

> **Order returns the current value of the order at which all truncated series expansions are given. The default order is 6.**

> **type (expr, series): Determines whether the expression is a series**

type (expr, taylor): Determines whether the expression is a Taylor series

type (expr, laurent): Determines whether the expression is a Laurent series

Here are some examples:

```
>> pretty(simple(sym(maple('series(x/(1-x-x^2), x=0) '))))
```

$$x + x^2 + 2 x^3 + 3 x^4 + 5 x^5 + O(x^6)$$

```
>> pretty(simple(sym(maple('series(exp(x)/x, x=0, 8 ) '))))
```

$$x^{-1} + 1 + 1/2 \, x + 1/6 \, x^2 + 1/24 \, x^3 + 1/120 \, x^4 + 1/720x^5 + 1/5040 \, x^6 + O(x^7)$$

```
>> pretty(simple(sym(maple('series(GAMMA(x), x=0, 2 ) '))))
```

$$x^{-1} - gamma + (1/12 \, Pi^2 + 1/2 \, gamma^2) \, x + O(x^2)$$

```
>> pretty(simple(sym(maple('series(x^3/(x^4+4*x-5),x=infinity) '))))
```

$$1/x - \frac{4}{x^4} + \frac{5}{x^5} + O(\frac{1}{x^7})$$

```
>> pretty(simple(sym(maple('int(exp(x^3), x ) : series(", x=0) '))))
```

$$x + 1/4 \, x^4 + O(x^7)$$

```
> pretty(simple(sym(maple('series(x^x, x=0, 3) '))))
```

$$1 + ln(x) \, x + 1/2 \, ln(x)^2 \, x^2 + O(x^3)$$

```
> pretty(simple(sym(maple('convert(" ,polynom) '))))
```

$$1 + ln(x) \, x + 1/2 \, ln(x)^2 \, x^2$$

```
> pretty(simple(sym(maple('series(exp(x), x) '))))
```

$$1 + x + 1/2 \, x^2 + 1/6 \, x^3 + 1/24 \, x^4 + 1/120 \, x^5 + O(x^6)$$

```
>> pretty(simple(sym(maple('convert(", ratpoly) '))))
```

$$\frac{1 + 3/5\ x + 3/20\ x^2 + 1/60\ x^3}{1 - 2/5\ x + 1/20\ x^2}$$

3.7 Taylor, Laurent, Padé and Chebyshev Expansions

Taylor's theorem gives us a way of approximating a function $f(x)$ by a polynomial at a point $x = x_0$. The series that is truncated to give such a polynomial is called the Taylor series of the function $f(x)$ at the point $x = x_0$. The Taylor series of $f(x)$ at $x = 0$ is called the MacLaurin series of $f(x)$.

Taylor's theorem says that if $f(x)$ is an $n + 1$ times differentiable function defined on an interval that *contains the point a*, then $f(x)$ can be approximated in a neighborhood of a by the following polynomial:

$$f(x) = \sum_{k=0}^{n} \frac{f^{(k)}(a)}{k!}(x-a)^k + \frac{f^{(n+1)}(z)}{(n+1)!}(x-a)^{n+1}$$

where z is a number between a and x.

The above expression is the Taylor series expansion of $f(x)$ at the point $x = a$. The last term of the expression is the remainder term, and represents a measure of the error of the approximation.

The Laurent expansion allows a finite number of negative powers in the series expansion of a function.

The Padé expansion approximates the function as a ratio of polynomials whose numerator and denominator have fixed degrees m and n.

The Chebyshev expansion approximates the function using Chebyshev polynomials. The *Chebyshev-Padé expansion* mixes both types.

When you use the command "series", without further specification, MATLAB uses by default the type of expansion most suitable in each case. There are commands that allow you to specify which type of expansion should be used (all require the prior use of the *maple* command). The syntax is as follows:

taylor(expr,var=a): Returns the Taylor series expansion of the expression expr at the point *a* where the order is determined by the global variable *Order*

taylor (expr, variable): Returns the Taylor series expansion of the expression expr in a neighborhood of the origin (i.e. the MacLaurin expansion)

taylor(expr,var=a,n): Returns the Taylor expansion of expr at *a* up to order *n*.

taylor(int,var=a): Returns the Taylor expansion of the indefinite integral int in a neighborhood of *a*

taylor(leadterm(expr),var=a): Returns the lowest degree term in the Taylor series expansion of expr in a neighborhood of *a*

readlib (mtaylor): Loads into the memory a package that allows you to work with multivariate Taylor expansions

mtaylor (expression, [var1,..., varn] or mtaylor(expression,{var1,...,varn})):

Returns the multivariate Taylor expansion of *expr* given in the specified variables up to the order determined by the global variable *Order*

mtaylor(expression,[var1,...,varn],n):

Returns the multivariate Taylor expansion of the specified expression up to order n

mtaylor(expression,[var1,...,varn],n,[w1,...,wn]):

Returns the multivariate Taylor expansion of the given expression by assigning weights $w1$ to wn to the variables. The default weight is 1. A weight of 2 will halve the order of the corresponding variable to which the expansion is given.

readlib (coeftayl): Loads into the memory a package that allows you to find coefficients of Taylor expansions

coeftayl(expr,variable=a,n): Returns the coefficient of x^n in the Taylor expansion of *expr* in a neighborhood of the point a.

coeftayl(expr,[var1,..,varm]=[a1,...,an],[n1,...,nm]):

Returns the coefficient of the term $(var1-a1)^{n1} ... (varm-am)^{nm}$ in the Taylor expansion of *expr* in a neighborhood of the point $(a1,..., am)$

readlib (poisson): Loads into the memory a package that allows you to work with multivariate Taylor series in Poisson form

poisson(expression,[var1,...,varn]) or poisson(expr,{var1,...,varn}):

Returns the multivariate Taylor expansion of the expression in Poisson form. The Poisson form combines the terms of the series in terms of sines and cosines, forming the Fourier canonical form. The order of the expansion is specified by the global variable *Order*.

poisson(expr,[var1,...,varn],n):

Returns the multivariate Taylor expansion of *expr* in Poisson form up to order n

poisson(expr,[var1,...,varn],n,[w1,...,wn]):

Returns the multivariate Taylor expansion of order n of *expr* in Poisson form using the specified weights

chebyshev(expr,var=a..b):

Returns the Chebyshev expansion of an analytical expression *expr* in the interval $[a, b]$. The result is a sum based on orthogonal Chebyshev polynomials in t. The orthopoly package needs to be loaded via the command *with(orthopoly,t)* before applying the Chebyshev command.

chebyshev(expr,var): Returns the Chebyshev expansion of an analytical expression *expr* in the interval $[- 1,1]$

chebyshev(expr,var=a..b, error):

Returns the Chebyshev expansion with the specified tolerance, which by default is $10 \wedge (-Digits)$

asymt (expr, var): Returns the asymptotic expansion $(var \rightarrow infinity)$ of the given expression expr up to the order specified by the global variable *Order*

asymt (expr, var, n): Returns the asymptotic expansion $(var \rightarrow infinity)$ of the given expression expr up to order n

with (numapprox): Loads into the memory a package that allows you to work with Padé, Padé-Chebyshev and Laurent expansions

chebdeg (series): Returns the degree of the specified Chebyshev series

chebmult (s1, s2): Returns the product of the two specified Chebychev series in the same variable

chebpade(expr,var=a..b,[n,d]): Finds the Chebyshev-Padé approximation of the given expression *expr* in the specified variable, in the interval *[a, b]*, with numerator and denominator polynomials of degrees *n* and *d* respectively

chebpade(expr,var,[n,d]): Returns the Chebyshev-Padé approximation of the given expression *expr* in the specified variable, in the interval *[- 1,1]*, with numerator and denominator polynomials of degrees *n* and *d* respectively

chebpade(expr,var=a.. b, [n, 0]) or chebpade(expr,var=a..b, n): Simply returns the Chebyshev polynomial of degree *n* in *[a, b]*

chebsort (series): Orders the terms of the given Chebyshev series

pade(expr,var=a,[n,d]): Returns the Padé approximation of the given expression *expr* in the specified variable at the point *a*, with numerator and denominator polynomials of degrees *n* and *d* respectively

pade(expr,var,[n,d]): Returns the Padé approximation of the given expression *expr* in the specified variable, at 0, with numerator and denominator polynomials of degrees *n* and *d* respectively

pade(expr,var=a,[n,0]) or pade(expr,var=a,n):

Simply returns the Taylor series expansion up to order n of the expression at the given point

laurent(expr,var=a,n):

Returns the Laurent series of the given expression *expr* at the given point up to order *n*

laurent(expr,var,n): Returns the Laurent series of the given expression *expr* at the point 0 up to order *n*

readlib (eulermac) loads into the memory a package whose commands allow you to find Euler-MacLaurin expansions

eulermac(expr,var,n): Finds the Euler-MacLaurin expansion of the given expression up to degree *n* in the given variable

eulermac (expr, var): Finds the Euler-MacLaurin expansion of the given expression up to the degree specified by the global variable *Order*

EXERCISE 3-13

Find the Taylor series up to 13th order of *sinh (x)* at the point $x = 0$. Also find the Taylor expansion of 1 /(1+*x*) up to 10th order at the point $x = 0$. Find the corresponding Laurent and Euler-McLaurin series. Find the Chebychev-Padé approximation of degree (4,3) in the interval [0,1].

```
>> pretty(simple(sym(maple('taylor(sinh(x),x=0,13) '))))
```

$$x + 1/6\ x^3 + 1/120\ x^5 + 1/5040\ x^7 + 1/362880\ x^9 + 1/39916800\ x^{11} + O(x^{13})$$

```
>> pretty(simple(sym(maple('taylor(1/(1+x),x=0,10) '))))
```

$$1 - x + x^2 - x^3 + x^4 - x^5 + x^6 - x^7 + x^8 - x^9 + O(x^{10})$$

```
>> maple('with(numapprox): ')
>> pretty(simple(sym(maple('laurent(sinh(x),x=0,13) '))))
```

$$x + 1/6\ x^3 + 1/120\ x^5 + 1/5040\ x^7 + 1/362880\ x^9 + 1/39916800\ x^{11} + O(x^{13})$$

```
>> pretty(simple(sym(maple('laurent(1/(1+x),x=0,10) '))))
```

$$1 - x + x^2 - x^3 + x^4 - x^5 + x^6 - x^7 + x^8 - x^9 + O(x^{10})$$

Note that the Laurent and Taylor series agree in this case.

```
>> maple('readlib(eulermac) : ')
>> pretty(simple(sym(maple('eulermac(sinh(x),x,13) '))))
```

$$\frac{314416268077}{290594304000}\ cosh(x) - 1/2\ sinh(x) + O(cosh(x))$$

```
>> pretty(simple(sym(maple('eulermac(1/(1+x),x,10) '))))
```

$$ln(1 + x) - 1/2\ \frac{1}{1 + x} - 1/12\ \frac{1}{(1 + x)^2} + 1/120\ \frac{1}{(1 + x)^4}$$

$$- 1/252\ \frac{1}{(1 + x)^6} + 1/240\ \frac{1}{(1 + x)^8} - 1/132\ \frac{1}{(1 + x)^{10}} + O\left(\frac{1}{(1 + x)^{12}}\right)$$

```
>> maple(' with(numapprox): ')
>> pretty(simple(sym(maple(' with(orthopoly,T):chebpade(sinh(x),x=0..1,[4,3]) '))))
```

$$(.03672350156 + .9734745062\ x - .02546155828\ (2.\ x - 1.)^2$$

$$+ .009531362262\ (2.\ x - 1.)^3 - .001730582994\ (2.\ x - 1.)^4)\ /$$

$$(1.157361890 - .3056450150\ x - .009078765811\ (2.\ x - 1.)^2$$

$$+ .001929812884\ (2.\ x - 1.)^3)$$

```
>> pretty(simple(sym(maple('with(orthopoly,T):chebpade(1/(1+x),x=0..1,[4,3]) '))))
```

```
         .6666666665
------------------------------
.6666666666 + .6666666668 x
```

EXERCISE 3-14

Find the Laurent expansion of 1 / *(x sin (x))* at the point $x = 0$ up to degree 10. Also find the Padé approximation of degree (3,4) at the same point and the Taylor expansion of *log (x)* at the point $x = 2$ up to degree 5.

```
>> pretty(simple(sym(maple('with(numapprox):laurent(1/(x*sin(x)),x=0,10) '))))
```

```
  -2                2    31     4    127     6        7
 x    + 1/6 + 7/360 x  + ----- x  + ------ x  + O(x )
                         15120      604800
```

```
>> pretty(simple(sym(maple('with(numapprox):pade(1/(x*sin(x)),x=0,[3,4]) '))))
```

```
            2
  -60 - 3 x
  ------------
      4      2
   7 x  - 60 x
```

```
>> pretty(simple(sym(maple('taylor(log(x),x=2,4) '))))
```

```
                         2            3           4
 ln(2) + 1/2 (x - 2) - 1/8 (x - 2) + 1/24 (x - 2) + O((x - 2) )
```

EXERCISE 3-15

Find the Taylor series at the origin, both in its normal form and in its Poisson form, up to order 5, of the function:

$$f(x, y) = e^{x+y^2}$$

```
>> maple('readlib(mtaylor): ')
>> pretty(simple(sym(maple('mtaylor(exp(x+y^2),[x,y],5) '))))
```

```
         2       2     2        3        4       2 2        4
 1 + x + y + 1/2 x + x y + 1/6 x + 1/2 y + 1/2 y  x + 1/24 x
```

```
>> maple('readlib(poisson): ')
>> pretty(simple(sym(maple('poisson(exp(x+y^2),[x,y],5) '))))
```

$$+ x + y^2 + 1/2\ x^2 + x\ y^2 + 1/6\ x^3 + 1/2\ y^4 + 1/2\ y^2\ x^2 + 1/24\ x^4$$

see that the two forms coincide.

EXERCISE 3-16

Find the Taylor expansion of the function $1/(2-x)$ at the point $x = 1$ up to order 10. Also find the Taylor expansion of $sin(x)$ at $pi/2$ up to order 8, and the same for the function $log(x)$ at the point $x = 2$ up to degree 5.

```
>> pretty(simple(sym(maple('taylor(1/(2-x),x=1,10)'))))
```

$$1 + x - 1 + (x - 1)^2 + (x - 1)^3 + (x - 1)^4 + (x - 1)^5 + (x - 1)^6 + (x - 1)^7 +$$

$$(x - 1)^8 + (x - 1)^9 + O((x - 1)^{10})$$

```
>> pretty(simple(sym(maple('taylor(sin(x),x=pi/2,8)'))))
```

$$1 - 1/2(x - 1/2\ pi)^2 + 1/24(x - 1/2\ pi)^4 - 1/720(x - 1/2\ pi)^6 + O((x - 1/2\ pi)^8)$$

```
>> pretty(simple(sym(maple('taylor(log(x),x=2,5)'))))
```

$$log(2) + 1/2\ (x - 2) - 1/8\ (x - 2)^2 + 1/24\ (x - 2)^3 - 1/64\ (x - 2)^4 + O((x - 2)^5)$$

CHAPTER 4

■ ■ ■

Derivatives and Applications. One and Several Variables

4.1 The Concept of the Derivative

The derivative of a real function at a point is the instantaneous rate of change of that function in a neighborhood of the point; i.e., it is a measure of how the dependent variable changes as a result of a small change in the independent variable.

Geometrically, the derivative of a function at a point represents the gradient of the tangent to the function at the point. The origin of the idea of the derivative comes precisely from the attempt to draw the tangent line at a given point on a curve.

A function $f(x)$ defined in a neighborhood of a point $x = a$ is *differentiable* at a if the following limit exists:

$$\lim_{h \to 0} \frac{f(a+h) - f(a)}{h} = f'(a)$$

The value of the limit, if it exists, is denoted by $f'(a)$, and *is called the derivative of the function f at the point a.* If f is differentiable at every point of its domain, it is simply said to be differentiable.

The continuity of a function is a necessary condition for its differentiablity, and all differentiable functions are continuous.

MATLAB can make use of the Maple library is *differentiable*, whose commands allow you to analyze the differentiability of a function, and calculate the points where it is not differentiable. The syntax is as follows:

readlib (isdifferentiable): isdifferentiable (expression, var, n, name)

This determines whether the given expression is differentiable to order *n* in the variable *var*. The expression can contain piecewise-defined functions. The optional variable *name* stores the sequence of points where the expression is not differentiable.

EXERCISE 4-1

Study the differentiability of the function:

$$f(x) = x \sin\left(\frac{1}{x}\right) \text{ if } x \neq 0 \text{ and } f(x) = 0 \text{ if } x = 0.$$

we study the differentiability at the point $x = 0$:

```
h, limit((h*sin(1/h) - 0)/h,h,0)
```

. 1

The limit does not exist, since in any neighborhood of 0 the function $\sin\dfrac{1}{x}$ takes both values - 1 and 1 infinitely many times. Hence MATLAB responds to the calculation of this limit with -1..1.

Let's see what happens at a non-zero point $x = a$:

```
>> maple ('f: = x - > x * sin (1)');
>> maple('limit((f(a+h)-f(a))/h,h=a)')
```

ans =

*2 * sin(1/2/a) - sin (1/a)*

Thus we have found the value of the derivative for any non-zero point $x = a$. The function is plotted in Figure 4-1:

```
>> fplot ('x * sin (x)', [-1/10.1/10])
```

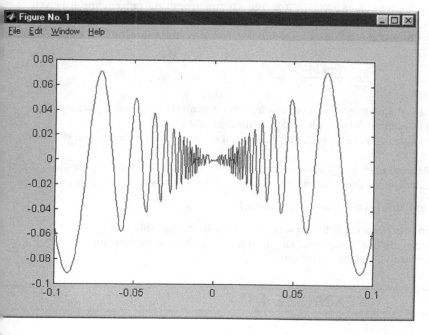

Figure 4-1.

0

You can also determine whether the function is differentiable using the following:

```
>> maple('readlib(isdifferentiable):')
>> maple('isdifferentiable(piecewise(x=0,0,x*sin(1/x)),x,0)')
```

ans =

false

EXERCISE 4-2

Study the differentiability of the function:

$$f(x) = \frac{x^3}{|x|} \text{ if } x \neq 0 \text{ and } f(x) = 0 \text{ if } x = 0.$$

```
>> maple('f:=x->x^3/abs(x)');
>> maple('limit((f(0+h)- 0)/h,h=0,left)')
```

ans =

0

```
>> maple('limit((f(0+h)- 0)/h,h=0,right)')
```

ans =

0

Thus we see that the derivative at zero exists and has the value zero. The function is plotted in Figure 4-2, from which we see that it appears to be differentiable at all points of its domain:

```
>> fplot('x^3/abs(x)',[-1/10,1/10])
```

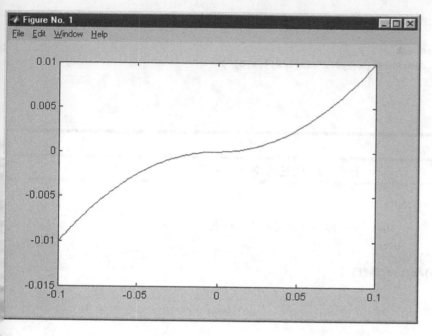

Figure 4-2.

4.2 Calculating Derivatives

MATLAB provides several commands that allow you to calculate derivatives. We have:

diff('f', 'x') is the derivative of the function *f* with respect to *x*

syms x, diff(f,x) is the derivative of the function *f* with respect to *x*

diff('f', 'x', n) is the nth derivative of the function *f* with respect to *x*

syms x, diff(f, x, n) is the nth derivative of the function *f* with respect to *x*

The following commands can also be used for differentiation, but to use them it is necessary to prepend the command ***maple***.

D (function) returns the derivative of the given expression or function

D (function) (num) returns the value of the derivative of the function at the point *num*

D (var -> expression) returns the partial derivative of the expression with respect to the given variable

D [n] (function) returns the partial derivative of the function with respect to its nth argument

D [n1, n2] (function) returns the partial derivative of the function, first with respect to its $n1^{th}$ argument and then with respect to its $n2^{th}$ argument

(D@@n)(function) returns the nth derivative of the function

(D@@n)(f)(num) returns the value of the nth derivative of f at the point *num*

diff (expr, var) returns the derivative of *expr* with respect to the specified variable

diff (expr, var$ n) returns the derivative of order n of *expr* with respect to the specified variable

diff(expr,var1,var2,...,varn):

Returns the partial derivative of *expr* with respect to the variables *var1* to *varn* in this order

Diff(expr,var) returns the inert derivative of *expr* with respect to the variable *var*

Diff(expr,var1,..,varn) returns the inert partial derivative of *expr* with respect to *var1* to *varn* in this order

op (Diff (expr, var)) shows the internal structure of *Diff* and allows access to its operands

op (n, Diff(expr,var)) extracts the nth operand (the first is *expr*, the second is *var*, the 3rd, 4th,... are the variables). You can replace any operand with *subsop*.

convert (expr, D) converts an expression of the form *diff* ($f(x)$, x) to the form D (f) (x)

convert (expr, diff) converts an expression of the form D (f) (x) to *diff* ($f(x)$, x)

implicitdiff (equation, vardep, varind) returns the derivative (dy/dx) of the implicit function specified by the given equation

implicitdiff (equation, vardep, varind, n) returns the derivative of order n ($d\,y^n / dx^n$) of the implicit function defined by the given equation

implicitdiff(equation,vardep,varind1,...,varindn) returns the derivative ($d^n y/dx1...dxn$) of the implicit function defined by the given equation

implicitdiff (expression, vardep, varindp) returns the derivative of the implicit function defined by the equation *expression = 0*

readlib(isdiffentiable):isdifferentiable(expression,var,n): This determines if the expression is differentiable to order n in the variable *var*. The expression can contain piecewise defined functions.

EXERCISE 4-3

Calculate the derivative with respect to x of the following functions:

$$\log(\sin(2x)), \; x^{\tan(x)}, \; \frac{4}{3}\sqrt{\frac{x^2-1}{x^2+2}}, \; \log\left(x+\sqrt{x^2+1}\right).$$

```
>> pretty(simple(diff('log(sin(2*x))','x')))
```

$$\frac{2}{\tan(2\ x)}$$

```
>> pretty(simple(diff('x^tanx','x')))
```

$$\frac{x \quad \dfrac{tanx}{x}}{x} \quad tanx$$

```
>> pretty(simple(diff('(4/3)*sqrt((x^2-1)/(x^2+2))','x')))
```

$$4 \; \frac{x}{(x^2 - 1)^{1/2} \, (x^2 + 2)^{3/2}}$$

```
>> pretty(simple(diff('log(x+(x^2+1)^(1/2))','x')))
```

$$\frac{1}{(x^2 + 1)^{1/2}}$$

EXERCISE 4-4

Calculate the nth derivative of the following functions:

$$\frac{1}{x}, \; e^{x/2}, \; \frac{1+x}{1-x}$$

```
>> f='1/x';
>> [diff(f),diff(f,2),diff(f,3),diff(f,4),diff(f,5)]
```

ans =

-1/x ^ 2   2/x ^ 3   - 6/x ^ 4   24/x ^ 5   - 120/x ^ 6

We see from the pattern here that the nth derivative is given by $\dfrac{(-1)^n n!}{x^{n+1}}$.

```
>> f='exp(x/2)';
>> [diff(f),diff(f,2),diff(f,3),diff(f,4),diff(f,5)]
```

ans =

1/2*exp(1/2*x)   1/4*exp(1/2*x)   1/8*exp(1/2*x)   1/16*exp(1/2*x)   1/32*exp(1/2*x)

Thus the nth derivative is $\dfrac{e^{x/2}}{2^n}$.

```
>> f='(1+x)/(1-x)';
>> [simple(diff(f)),simple(diff(f,2)),simple(diff(f,3)),simple(diff(f,4))]
```

ans =

2 /(-1+x) ^ 2-4 /(-1+x) ^ 3 12 /(-1+x) ^ 4-48 /(-1+x) ^ 5

Thus, the nth derivative is given by $\dfrac{2(n!)}{(1-x)^{n+1}}$.

4.3 Tangents, Asymptotes, Concavity, Convexity, Maxima and Minima, Inflection Points and Growth

If f is a function which is differentiable at x_0, then $f'(x_0)$ is the slope of the tangent line to the curve $y = f(x)$ at the point $(x_0, f(x_0))$. The equation of the tangent will be $y - f(x_0) = f'(x_0)(x - x_0)$.

The horizontal asymptotes of the curve $y = f(x)$ are limit tangents, as $x_0 \to \infty$, which are horizontal. They are defined by the equation $y = \lim_{x_0 \to \infty} f(x_0)$.

The vertical asymptotes of the curve $y = f(x)$ are limit tangents, as $f(x_0) \to \infty$, which are vertical. They are defined by the equation $x = x_0$, where x_0 is a value such that $\lim_{x \to x_0} f(x) = \infty$.

The oblique asymptotes to the curve $y = f(x)$ at the point $x = x_0$ have the equation $y = mx + n$, where

$$m = \lim_{x \to \infty} \frac{y}{x} \text{ and } n = \lim_{x \to \infty}(y - mx) .$$

If f is a function for which $f'(x_0)$ and $f''(x_0)$ both exist, then, if $f'(x_0) = 0$ and $f''(x_0) < 0$, the function f has a local maximum at the point $(x_0, f(x_0))$.

If f is a function for which $f'(x_0)$ and $f''(x_0)$ both exist, then, if $f'(x_0) = 0$ and $f''(x0) > 0$, the function f has a local minimum at the point $(x0, f(x0))$.

If f is a function for which $f'(x_0), f''(x_0)$ and $f'''(x_0)$ exist, then, if $f'(x_0) = 0$ and $f''(x_0) = 0$ and $f'''(x_0) \neq 0$, the function f has a turning point at the point $(x_0, f(x_0))$.

If f is differentiable, then the values of x for which the function f is increasing are those for which $f'(x)$ is greater than zero.

If f is differentiable, then the values of x for which the function f is decreasing are those for which $f'(x)$ is less than zero.

If f is twice differentiable, then the values of x for which the function f is concave are those for which $f''(x)$ is greater than zero.

If f is twice differentiable, then the values of x for which the function f is convex are those for which $f''(x)$ is less than zero.

EXERCISE 4-5

Find the equation of the tangent to the curve:

$$f(x) = 2x^3 + 3x^2 - 12x + 7 \text{ at } x = -1.$$

Also find the x for which the tangents to the curve $g(x) = \dfrac{x^2 - x - 4}{x - 1}$ are horizontal and vertical. Find their asymptotes.

```
>> f ='2 * x ^ 3 + 3 * x ^ 2-12 * x + 7';
>> g = diff (f)

g =

6*x^2+6*x-12

>> subs(g,-1)
```

ans =

-12

>> subs(f,-1)

ans =

20

Thus the slope of the tangent line at the point $x = -1$ is -12, and the function at $x = -1$ has the value 20. Therefore the equation of the tangent to the curve at the point $(-1, 20)$ is:

$$y - 20 = -12\,(x - (-1))$$

We plot the curve and its tangent on the same axes (see Figure 4-3):

>> fplot('[2*x^3+3*x^2-12*x+7, 20-12*(x - (-1))]',[-4,4])

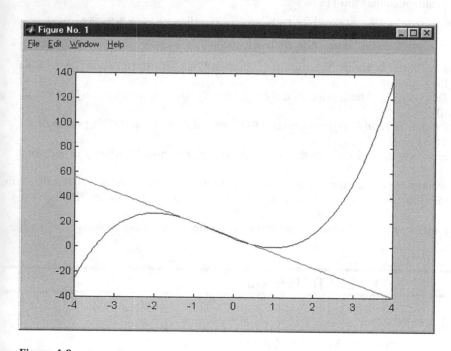

Figure 4-3.

To calculate the horizontal tangent to the curve $y = f(x)$, we find the values x_0 for which $f'(x_0) = 0$. The equation of this tangent will then be $y = f(x_0)$.

To calculate the vertical tangent to the curve $y = f(x)$, we find the values x_0 for which $f'(x_0) = \infty$. The equation of this tangent will then be $x = x_0$.

```
>> g ='(x^2-x+4) /(x-1)'
>> solve(diff(g))
```

ans =

[3]
[-1]

```
>> subs(g,3)
```

ans =

5

```
>> subs(g,-1)
```

ans =

-3

The two horizontal tangents will have equations:

$$y = g'[-1] (x + 1) - 3, \text{ that is, } y = -3$$
$$y = g'[3] (x - 3) + 5, \text{ that is, } y = 5$$

The horizontal tangents are not asymptotes because the corresponding values of x_0 are finite (they are - 1 and 3).

We now find the vertical tangents. To do this, we calculate the values of x for which $g'(x) = \infty$ (i.e. values for which the denominator of g' is zero, but does not cancel with the numerator):

```
>> solve('x-1')
```

ans =

1

Therefore, the vertical tangent has equation $x = 1$.

For $x = 1$, the value of $g(x)$ is infinite (see below), so the vertical tangent is a vertical asymptote.

```
subs(g,1)
```

Error, division by zero

As $\lim\limits_{x \to \infty} g(x) = \infty$, there are no horizontal asymptotes.

Now let us see if there are any oblique asymptotes:

```
>> syms x,limit(((x^2-x+4)/(x-1))/x,x,inf)
```

ans =

1

```
>> syms x,limit(((x^2-x+4)/(x-1) - x)/x,x,inf)
```

ans =

0

Thus, the diagonal $y = x$ is an asymptote.

We plot the curve with its asymptotes and tangents:

Using the default command *plot*, we represent on the same axes (see Figure 4-4) the curve whose equation is $g(x) = (x^2 - x + 4)/(x-1)$, the horizontal tangents with equations $y = -3$ and $y = 5$, and the oblique asymptote with equation $y = x$.

```
>> fplot('[(x^2-x+4)/(x-1),-3,5,x]',[-10,10,-20,20])
```

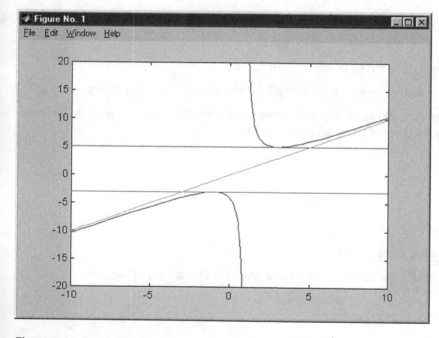

Figure 4-4.

EXERCISE 4-6

Find the asymptotes, maxima, minima, inflection points, intervals of growth and decrease and intervals of concavity and convexity for the function:

$$f(x) = \frac{x^3}{x^2 - 1}$$

```
>> f='x^3/(x^2-1)'
```

f =

x^3/(x^2-1)

```
>> syms x, limit(x^3/(x^2-1),x,inf)
```

ans =

NaN

Therefore, there are no horizontal asymptotes. To see if there are any vertical asymptotes, let us look at the values of x that make y infinite:

```
>> solve('x^2-1')
```

ans =

[1]
[-1]

Thus the vertical asymptotes are the lines $x = 1$ and $x = -1$. Now let us see if there are any oblique asymptotes:

```
>> limit(x^3/(x^2-1)/x,x,inf)
```

ans =

1

```
>> limit(x^3/(x^2-1)-x,x,inf)
```

ans =

0

The line $y = x$ is an oblique asymptote. Now we shall find the maxima and minima, inflection points and intervals of concavity:

```
>> solve (diff (f))
```

```
ans =

[        0]
[        0]
[3 ^(1/2)]
[^(1/2) - 3]
```

The first derivative vanishes at $x = 0$, $x = \sqrt{3}$ and $x = -\sqrt{3}$. These include maximum and minimum candidates. To verify if they are maxima or minima, we find the value of the second derivative at these points:

```
>> [numeric(subs(diff(f,2),0)),numeric(subs(diff(f,2),sqrt(3))),
numeric(subs(diff(f,2),-sqrt(3)))]

ans =

0 2.5981 - 2.5981
```

Therefore, at $x = -\sqrt{3}$ there is a maximum and at $x = \sqrt{3}$ there is a minimum. At $x = 0$ we know nothing:

```
>> [numeric (subs (f, sqrt (3))), numeric (subs (f, - sqrt (3)))]

ans =

2.5981 - 2.5981
```

Therefore, the maximum point is $(-\sqrt{3}, -2.5981)$ and the minimum point is $(\sqrt{3}, 2.5981)$.

We will now analyze the points of inflection:

```
>> solve(diff(f,2))

[           0]
[  i*3^(1/2)]
[-i*3^(1/2)]
```

The only possible turning point occurs at $x = 0$, and as $f(0) = 0$, the possible turning point is (0,0):

```
>> subs (diff(f,3), 0)

ans =

-6
```

As the third derivative at $x = 0$ is non-zero, the origin really is a turning point:

```
>> pretty(simple(diff(f)))
```

$$\frac{x^2 (x^2 - 3)}{(x^2 - 1)^2}$$

The curve is increasing when $y' > 0$, i.e., in the intervals $(-\infty, -\sqrt{3})$ and $(\sqrt{3}, \infty)$.

The curve is decreasing when $y' < 0$, i.e., in the intervals

$(-\sqrt{3}, -1)$, $(-1, 0)$, $(0, 1)$ and $(1, \sqrt{3})$.

```
>> pretty(simple(diff(f,2)))
```

$$2 \, \frac{x \, (x^2 + 3)}{(x^2 - 1)^3}$$

The curve will be concave when $y'' > 0$, i.e., in the intervals $(-1, 0)$ and $(1, \infty)$.

The curve is convex when $y'' < 0$, i.e. in the intervals $(0, 1)$ and $(-\infty, -1)$.

The curve has a horizontal tangent at the three points at which the first derivative is zero. The equations of the horizontal tangents are $y = 0$, $y = -2.5981$ and $y = 2.5981$.

The curve has vertical tangents at the points that make the first derivative infinite. These are $x = 1$ and $x = -1$. Therefore, the vertical tangents coincide with the two vertical asymptotes.

We plot the curve together with its asymptotes (see Figure 4-5):

```
>> fplot('[x^3/(x^2-1),x]',[-5,5,-5,5])
```

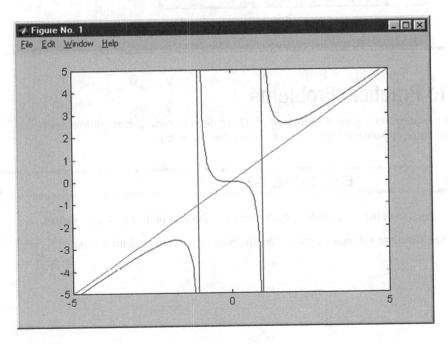

Figure 4-5.

We can also represent the curve, its asymptotes and its horizontal and vertical tangents in the same graph (Figure 4-6):

```
>> fplot('[x^3/(x^2-1),x,2.5981,-2.5981]',[-5,5,-5,5])
```

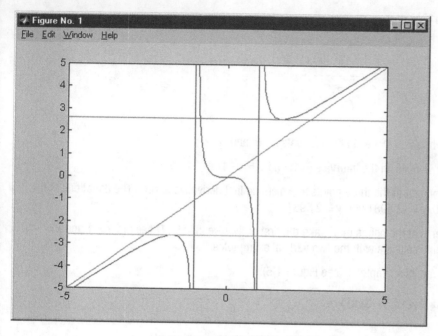

Figure 4-6.

4.4 Applications to Practical Problems

Many practical problems can be expressed in terms of a function which we need to maximize or minimize, where these maxima and minima have some applied interpretation. Let's see some examples:

EXERCISE 4-7

Write a positive number *a* as the sum of two summands in such a way that the sum of their cubes is minimal.

Let *x* be one of the summands. The other will be $a-x$. We require the sum $x^3 + (a-x)^3$ to be minimized.

```
>> f='x^3+(a-x)^3'
```

f =

```
x^3+(a-x)^3
```

```
>> solve(diff(f,'x'))
```

ans =

1/2 * a

The possible maximum or minimum is at $x = a/2$. We use the second derivative to verify that it is indeed a minimum:

```
>> subs(diff(f,'x',2),'a/2')
```

ans =

3 * a

As $a > 0$ (by hypothesis), $3a > 0$, which means $x = a/2$ is a minimum.

Therefore the two summands must be equal to $a/2$.

EXERCISE 4-8

Suppose you want to purchase a rectangular plot of 1600 square meters and then fence it. Knowing that the fence costs 200 cents per meter, what dimensions must the plot of land have to ensure that the fencing is most economical?

If the surface area is 1600 square feet and one of its dimensions, unknown, is x, and the other will be $1600/x$.

The perimeter of the rectangle is $p(x) = 2x + 2(1600/x)$, and the cost is given by $f(x) = 200 \, p(x)$:

```
>> f ='200 * (2 * x + 2 *(1600/x))'
```

f =

200 * (2 * x + 2 *(1600/x))

This is the function to minimize:

```
>> solve (diff (f))
```

 ans =

[40]
[-40]

The possible maxima and minima are presented for $x = -40$ and $x = 40$. To determine their nature, we look at the second derivative at these points.

```
>> [subs (diff(f,2), 40), subs (diff(f,2), - 40)]
```

ans =

20   -20

$x = 40$ is a minimum, and $x = -40$ is a maximum. Thus, one of the sides of the rectangular field must be 40 meters, and the other will measure $1600/40 = 40$ meters. Therefore the optimal rectangle is a square with sides of 40 meters.

4.5 Partial Derivatives

As we know, MATLAB can differentiate functions with the command *diff*, but we can also make use of the differentiation operator *D*, which calculates derivatives of functions, as well as partial derivatives for functions that depend on more than one variable.

If you define a function *maple('f:=x->...')*, to calculate its derivative with respect to the single variable *x* you can use the command *maple ('D (f)')*. To find the value of the derivative at the point $x = x_0$, i.e., the slope of the function at the point $x = x_0$, we use the command *maple ('D (f)(x_0)')*.

We also know that to calculate the derivative of order *n* of the function *f* with respect to *x*, we can use, apart from the command *diff*, *@* operators and *D*, writing *maple ('(D@@n) (f)')*.

If a function depends on several variables (for simplicity, we shall restrict ourselves to a function of two variables, *x* and *y*) we can write it as *maple ('g:=(x,y) ->...')*. In this case, the partial derivatives of the function *g* can be calculated in the following way:

g'_x : **maple('D[1](g)');**

g'_y : **maple('D[2](g)');**

g''_{xx} : **maple('D[1,1](g)');**

g''_{xy} : **maple('D[1,2](g)');**

g''_{yy} : **maple('D[2,2](g)');**

g^{iv}_{xxyy} : **maple('D[1,1,2,2](g)').**

This notation is generalizable to *n* variables.

EXERCISE 4-9

Given the function $f(x,y) = \sin(xy) + \cos(xy^2)$, calculate:

$\partial f/\partial x, \partial f/\partial y, \partial^2 f/\partial x^2, \partial^2 f/\partial y^2, \partial^2 f/\partial x\partial y, \partial^2 f/\partial y\partial x$ and $\partial^4 f/\partial^2 x\partial^2 y$.

```
>> maple ('f:=(x,y) - > sin(x*y) + cos(x*y^2)');

>> pretty(sym(maple('D[1](f)')))
```
$$(x,y) \to \cos(x\ y)\ y - \sin(x\ y^2)\ y^2$$

```
>> pretty(sym(maple('D[2](f)')))
```
$$(x,y) \to \cos(x\ y)\ x - 2\ \sin(x\ y^2)\ x\ y$$

```
>> pretty(sym(maple('D[1,1](f)')))
```
$$(x,y) \to -\sin(x\ y)\ y^2 - \cos(x\ y^2)\ y^4$$

```
>> pretty(sym(maple('D[2,2](f)')))
```
$$(x,y) \rightarrow -\sin(x\ y)\ x^2 - 4\cos(x\ y^2)\ x^2\ y^2 - 2\sin(x\ y^2)\ x$$

```
>> pretty(sym(maple('D[1,2](f)')))
```
$$(x,y) \rightarrow -\sin(x\ y)\ y\ x + \cos(x\ y) - 2\cos(x\ y^2)\ y^3\ x^2 - 2\sin(x\ y^2)\ y$$

```
>> pretty(sym(maple('D[2,1](f)')))
```
$$(x,y) \rightarrow -\sin(x\ y)\ y\ x + \cos(x\ y) - 2\cos(x\ y^3)\ y^2\ x - 2\sin(x\ y^2)\ y$$

```
>> pretty(sym(maple('D[1,1,2,2](f)')))
```
$$(x,y) \rightarrow \sin(x\ y)\ y^2\ x^2 - 4\cos(x\ y)\ y\ x - 2\sin(x\ y) + 4\cos(x\ y^2)\ y^6\ x^2$$
$$+ 18\sin(x\ y^2)\ y^4\ x - 12\cos(x\ y^2)\ y^2$$

4.6 Implicit Differentiation

The differential operator *D* allows you to find derivatives of functions defined implicitly by an equation. Alternatively, we can use the command *implicitdiff*, which we introduced at the beginning of the chapter.

EXERCISE 4-10

Calculate the implicit derivative of *y* with respect to *x*, where *x* and *y* satisfy the following equation:

$$x^3 + 3\ x^2 y^3 + 5xy + 6y^3 = 8$$

First, we will use the operator *D* to differentiate the equation:

```
>> pretty (sym (maple ('D(x^3+3*x^2*y^3+5*x*y+6*y^3=8)')))
```

$$3\ D(x)\ x^2 + 6\ D(x)\ x\ y^3 + 9\ x^2\ D(y)\ y^2 + 5\ D(x)\ y + 5\ x\ D(y) + 18\ D(y)\ y^2 = 0$$

Now we replace *D (x)* with 1 and solve for *D (y)*:

```
>> pretty (sym (maple ('subs (D (x) = 1, D(x^3+3*x^2*y^3+5*x*y+6*y^3=8))')))
```

$$3\ x^2 + 6\ x\ y^3 + 9\ x^2\ D(y)\ y^2 + 5\ y + 5\ x\ D(y) + 18\ D(y)\ y^2 = 0$$

```
>> pretty (sym (maple ('solve (3 * x ^ 2 + 6 * x * y ^ 3 + 9 * x ^ 2 * D (y) * y ^ 2 + 5 *
y + 5 * x * D (y) + + 18 * D (y) * y ^ 2 = 0, D (y))')))
```

$$
-\frac{3\ x^2\ +\ 6\ x\ y^3\ +\ 5\ y}{9\ x^2\ y^2\ +\ 5\ x\ +\ 18\ y^2}
$$

A faster and easier way to find implicit first and second order derivatives is to use the command *implicitdiff* in the following way:

```
>> pretty (sym (maple ('implicitdiff(x^3+3*x^2*y^3+5*x*y+6*y^3=8,y,x)')))
```

$$
-\frac{3\ x^2\ +\ 6\ x\ y^3\ +\ 5\ y}{9\ x^2\ y^2\ +\ 5\ x\ +\ 18\ y^2}
$$

```
>> pretty (sym (maple ('implicitdiff(x^3+3*x^2*y^3+5*x*y+6*y^3=8,y,x$2)')))
```

$$
-2\ y\ (810\ x^2\ y^3 + 648\ x^3\ y^3 + 135\ y\ x^4 + 81\ x^5\ y^3 + 972\ x^3\ y - 810\ x^3\ y^4
$$

$$
-\ 405\ x^4\ y^6\ -\ 525\ x^2\ y^2\ -\ 324\ x^2\ y^6\ -\ 540\ x^4\ y\ -\ 125\ x^6\ +\ 972\ y^6\ +\ 162\ x^4
$$

$$
+\ 81\ x^6\ )\ /\ (1350\ x^2\ y^2\ +\ 4860\ x\ y^4\ +\ 125\ x^3\ +\ 8748\ x^2\ y^6\ +\ 4860\ x^3\ y^4
$$

$$
+\ 729\ x^6\ y^6\ +\ 1215\ x^5\ y^4\ +\ 4374\ x^4\ y^6\ +\ 675\ x^4\ y^2\ +\ 5832\ y^6\ )
$$

EXERCISE 4-11

Find the tangents to the ellipse $2\ x^2 - 2xy + y^2 + x + 2y + 1 = 0$ at the point $x = -3/2$.

The slope of the tangent is determined by $y'\ (-3/2)$:

```
>> pretty(sym(maple('subs(D(x)=1,D(2*x^2 -2*x*y+y^2+x+2*y+1=0 ))')))
```

$$
4\ x - 2\ y - 2\ x\ D(y) + 2\ D(y)\ y + 1 + 2\ D(y) = 0
$$

```
>> pretty(sym(maple('solve(4*x-2*y-2*x*D(y)+2*D(y)*y+1+2*D(y) = 0,D(y))')))
```

$$
1/2\ \frac{4\ x - 2\ y + 1}{x - y - 1}
$$

Alternatively, the implicit derivative can be calculated as follows:

```
>> pretty(sym(maple('implicitdiff(2*x^2-2*x*y+y^2+x+2*y+1,y,x )')))
                         4 x - 2 y + 1
             1/2  -------------
                         x - y - 1
```

Now, to find the values y for which (x, y) is a point on the ellipse with $x = -3/2$, we substitute $x = -3/2$ into the equation of the ellipse and solve for y.

```
>> maple ('solve (subs(x=-3/2,2*x^2-2*x*y+y^2+x+2*y+1=0), y)')
```

ans =

-1, - 4

The points of contact of the two tangents will be (-3/2,-1) and (-3/2, - 4). Now let's calculate the slopes of the two possible tangents:

```
(((>> maple('subs(x=-3/2,y=-1,-(4*x-2*y+1)/(-2*x+2*y+2))')
```

ans =

1

```
(((>> maple('subs(x=-3/2,y=-4,-(4*x-2*y+1)/(-2*x+2*y+2))')
```

ans =

1

The equations of the two tangents to the curve at $x = -3/2$ are then:

$$y + 1 = x + 3/2 \text{ and } y + 4 = x + 3/2.$$

We graphically represent the ellipse, the tangents and the coordinate axes (see Figure 4-7). As the curve is given in implicit coordinates, we first modify it. To do this, we try to complete the squares in order to find a trigonometric parameterization that eliminates possible fractional powers arising when trying to separate a variable.

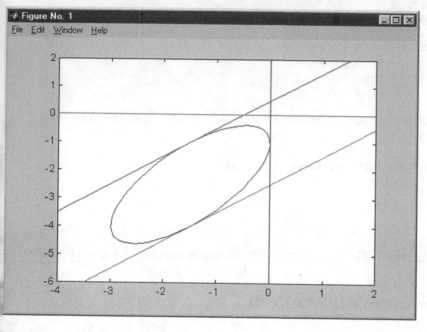

Figure 4-7.

MATLAB has the command *maple('completesquare'),* implemented in the *student* library, which allows you to complete the square of an expression with respect to a specified variable.

We complete the square of the defining expression of the ellipse with respect to the variable *y* as follows:

```
>> pretty(maple('completesquare(2*x^2-2*x*y+y^2+x+2*y+1,y)'))
```

$$(y - x + 1)^2 + x^2 + 3 x$$

Now, it is trivial to separate the variable *y* for the given equation: $y = x - 1 + \sqrt{-x^2 - 3x}$. But we have an expression within a square root, which we rewrite as follows:

```
>> pretty(maple('completesquare(-x^2-3*x,x)'))
```

$$- (x + 3/2)^2 + 9/4$$

We obtain the equation of the curve

$$y = x - 1 + \sqrt{-\left(x + \frac{3}{2}\right)^2 + 9/4}$$

which is easily parametrized by putting $x + 3/2 = 3/2 \sin (t)$, so that $x = \frac{3}{2} * (sin(t) - 1)$, $y = 3/2 * (\sin (t) + \cos (t)) - 5/2$.

Now we can create the graph of the curve, the asymptotes and the coordinate axes (the *OY* axis is represented in parametric form as *x* = 0, *y* = *t*).

```
>> fplot('[x+3/2-1,x+3/2-4,0]',[-4,2,-6,2]);
>> hold on;
>> t=(0:.1:2*pi);
>> x=3/2*(sin(t)-1);
>> y=3/2*(sin(t)+cos(t))-5/2;
>> plot(x,y);
>> t=(-6:.1:2);
>> x=zeros(size(t));
>> y=t;
>> plot(x,y)
```

4.7 Differentiation of Functions of Several Variables

We now present some of the features that MATLAB offers to treat differentiation of functions of several variables.

Given a function $f: R^2 \to R$, the *partial derivative of f* with respect to the variable x at the point (a, b) is defined as follows:

$$\frac{\partial f}{\partial x}(a,b) = \lim_{h \to 0} \frac{f(a+h,b) - f(a,b)}{h}$$

Similarly, the partial derivative of f with respect to the variable y at the point (a, b) is defined as:

$$\frac{\partial f}{\partial y}(a,b) = \lim_{h \to 0} \frac{f(a,b+h) - f(a,b)}{h}$$

Generally speaking, we can define the partial derivative with respect to any variable for a function of n variables. Given the function $f: R^n \to R$, the partial derivative of f with respect to the variable x_i ($i = 1, 2,..., n$) at the point $(a_1, a_2, ..., a_n)$ is defined as follows:

$$\frac{\partial f}{\partial x_i}(a_1,a_2,...,a_n) = \lim_{h \to 0} \frac{f(a_1,a_2,...,a_i+h,...,a_n) - f(u_1,u_2,...,a_n)}{h}$$

The function f is differentiable if all partial derivatives with respect to x_i ($i = 1, 2,..., n$) exist and are continuous. All differentiable functions are continuous, and if a function is not continuous, it cannot be differentiable.

The *directional derivative of the function f* with respect to the vector $v = (v_1, v_2,..., v_n)$ is defined as the following scalar product:

$$(Df)v = \left(\frac{\partial f}{\partial x_1}, \frac{\partial f}{\partial x_2},..., \frac{\partial f}{\partial x_n} \right) \bullet (v_1, v_2,..., v_n) = (\nabla f) \bullet v$$

$$\nabla f - \left(\frac{\partial f}{\partial x_1}, \frac{\partial f}{\partial x_2},..., \frac{\partial f}{\partial x_n} \right) \text{ is called the } \textit{gradient vector of } f.$$

The directional derivative of the function f with respect to the vector $v = (dx_1, dx_2,..., dx_n)$ is called the *total differential of f*. Its value is:

$$Df = \left(\frac{\partial f}{\partial x_1} dx_1 + \frac{\partial f}{\partial x_2} dx_2 +...+ \frac{\partial f}{\partial x_n} dx_n \right)$$

At the beginning of the chapter (under the heading "Calculating derivatives") we defined the functions that MATLAB implements to find partial derivatives. Using these functions, we have the following:

$$\text{diff (f (x, y, z...), x)} = \frac{\partial f}{\partial x} = \text{maple ('D [1] (f)(x,y,z,...)')} = \text{maple ('diff (f(x,y,z,...), x)')}$$

$$\text{diff (f(x,y,...), x, n)} = \frac{\partial^n f}{\partial x^n} = \text{maple('D[1,1,...1]} \overset{n)}{(f)(x,y,...)'}) = \text{maple ('diff (f(x,y,...), x\$n)')}$$

$$\text{diff(f(x1,x2,...),xj)} = \frac{\partial f}{\partial xj} \quad \text{maple('D[j](f)(x1,x2,...)')} = \text{maple('diff(f(x1,x2,..), xj)')}$$

$$\text{diff(f(x1,...),xj,n)} = \frac{\partial^n f}{\partial xj^n} = \text{maple('D[j, j,...j](f)(x1,...)')} \overset{n)}{=} \text{maple('diff(f(x1,...), xj \$n)')}$$

$$\text{maple ('diff (f(x,y,z,...), x, y, z,...)')} = \frac{\partial\partial\partial}{\partial x\ \partial y\ \partial z} \ ...f = \text{maple('D[1,2,3..])(f)(x,y,z,...)')}$$

$$\text{maple ('diff (f(x,y), x, y)')} = \frac{\partial^2 f}{\partial x \partial y} = \text{maple ('D [1,2] (f)(x,y)')}$$

$$\text{maple('diff(f(x1,...),xn,xm,xp)')} = \frac{\partial^{(k)} f}{\partial x_n \partial x_m \partial x_p\ ...} = \text{maple('D[n,m,p,...](f)(x1,x2,...)')}$$
$$\text{(k = number of variables)}$$

EXERCISE 4-12

Given the real-valued two-variable function f defined by:
$$f(x,y) = \frac{xy}{x^2+y^2} \text{ if } x^2+y^2 \neq 0 \text{ and } f(x,y) = 0 \text{ if } x^2+y^2 = 0$$
calculate the partial derivatives of f at the origin. Study the differentiability of f.

```
>> maple ('f:=(x,y) - >(x*y) /(x^2+y^2)');
```

To find $\partial f/\partial x$ and $\partial f/\partial y$ at the point (0,0), we directly apply the definition of a partial derivative at a point:

```
>> maple('(f(h,0)-0)/h')
```

ans =

0

```
>> maple('(f(0,k)-0)/k')
```

ans =

0

The limits of the two previous expressions as $h \to 0$ and $k \to 0$, respectively, are both zero.

We see that the two partial derivatives at the origin are the same and have value zero. But the function is not differentiable at the origin, because it is not continuous at (0,0), since there is no limit as (x, y) tends to $(0,0)$:

```
>> maple('limit((m*x)^2/(x^2+(m*x)^2),x=0)')
```

ans =

m ^ 2 /(1+m^2)

The limit does not exist at (0,0), because approaching the origin along different straight lines $y = mx$ yields different results depending on the parameter *m*.

EXERCISE 4-13

Study the differentiability of the following function:

$$f(x,y) = \frac{2xy}{\sqrt{x^2 + y^2}} \text{ if } (x, y) \neq (0,0) \text{ and } f(0,0) = 0.$$

The function is differentiable if it has continuous partial derivatives at every point. We will consider any point other than the origin and calculate the partial derivative with respect to the variable x:

```
>> maple('f:=(x,y)->(2*x*y)/(x^2+y^2)^(1/2)');
>> pretty(simple(sym(maple('D[1](f)(x,y)'))))
```

$$
\begin{array}{c}
3 \\
y \\
2\ \text{-------------} \\
2\quad 2\ 3/2 \\
(x\ +\ y\ )
\end{array}
$$

Now, let's see if this partial derivative is continuous at the origin:

```
>> maple('limit(2*(m*x)^3/(x^2+(m*x)^2)^(3/2),x=0)')
```

ans =

2*m^3/(1+m^2)^(3/2)

The limit does not exist at (0,0), because approaching the origin along different straight lines $y = mx$ yields different results depending on the parameter *m*. Therefore, the partial derivative is not continuous at the origin.

We conclude that the function is not differentiable.

However, the function is continuous, since the only problematic point is the origin, and the limit of the function at the origin is $0 = f(0,0)$:

```
>> maple('limit(limit(f(x,y),x=0),y=0)')
```

ans =

0

```
>> maple('limit(limit(f(x,y),y=0),x=0)')
```

ans =

0

```
>> maple('limit(f(x,(m*x)),x=0)')
```

ans =

0

```
>> maple('limit(f(x,(m*x)^(1/2)),x=0)')
```

ans =

0

```
>> maple('limit(f((r*cos(a)),(r*sin(a))),r=0)')
```

ans =

0

The iterated limits and the directional limits are all zero, and by changing the function to polar coordinates, the limit at the origin turns out to be zero, which coincides with the value of the function at the origin.

This is therefore an example of a non-differentiable continuous function.

EXERCISE 4-14

Calculate the total differential of the following functions:
$$3 + x^3 - 2x^2 y, e^{ax} \cos(by).$$

```
>> maple('f:=(x,y)->x^3-2*x^2*y+3');
```

```
>> pretty(simplify(sym('D(f(x,y))')))
```

$$3\ D(x)\ x^2\ -\ 4\ D(x)\ x\ y\ -\ 2\ x^2\ D(y)$$

Grouping the terms together, we obtain the expression of the total differential:

```
>> pretty(sym(maple('collect(D(f(x,y)),D(x))')))
```

$$(3 \ x^2 \ - \ 4 \ x \ y) \ D(x) \ - \ 2 \ x^2 \ D(y)$$

```
>> maple('g:=(x,y)->exp(a*x)*cos(b*y)');
>> pretty(sym(maple('dotprod([D[1](g)(x,y),D[2](g)(x,y)],[dx,dy])')))
```

$$a \ exp(a \ x) \ cos(b \ y) \ dx \ - \ exp(a \ x) \ sin(b \ y) \ b \ dy$$

EXERCISE 4-15

Verify that if $f(x,y,z) = \dfrac{1}{\sqrt{x^2+y^2+z^2}}$ then $\dfrac{\partial^2 f}{\partial x^2} + \dfrac{\partial^2 f}{\partial y^2} + \dfrac{\partial^2 f}{\partial z^2} = 0$.

```
>> f='1/(x^2+y^2+z^2)^(1/2)';
>> simplify(symop(diff(f,'x',2),'+',diff(f,'y',2),'+',diff(f,'z',2)))
```

ans =

0

Another path would be the following:

```
>> maple('f:=x->1/(x^2+y^2+z^2)^(1/2)');
>> simplify(sym('diff(f(x,y,z),x$2)+diff(f(x,y,z),y$2)+diff(f(x,y,z),z$2)'))
```

ans =

0

Alternatively, another way to do the same is as follows:

```
>> maple('simplify(D[1,1](f)(x,y,z)+D[2,2](f)(x,y,z)+D[3,3](f)(x,y,z))')
```

ans =

0

EXERCISE 4-16

Find the directional derivative of the function:

$$f(x,y,z) = \dfrac{1}{\sqrt{x^2+y^2+z^2}}$$

at the point (2,1,1), with respect to the vector $v = (1,1,0)$.

```
>> maple('f:=(x,y,z)->1/(x^2+y^2+z^2)^(1/2)');
>> maple('dotprod([D[1](f)(2,1,1),D[2](f)(2,1,1),D[3](f)(2,1,1)],[1,1,0])')
```

ans =

*-1/12*6^(1/2)*

EXERCISE 4-17

Given the function:

$$f(x,y)=e^{-\frac{x^2+y^2}{8}}\left[\cos^2(x)+\sin^2(y)\right]$$

calculate:

$$\frac{\partial f}{\partial x},\frac{\partial f}{\partial y},\frac{\partial^2 f}{\partial x\,\partial y},\frac{\partial^2 f}{\partial x^2},\frac{\partial^2 f}{\partial y^2},\frac{\partial^3 f}{\partial x\,\partial y^2},\frac{\partial^4 f}{\partial x^2\,\partial y^2}\text{ and }\frac{\partial^5 f}{\partial x^3\,\partial y^2}$$

and find its value at the point $(3\pi, 6\pi)$.

```
>> maple('f:=(x,y)->exp(-(x^2+y^2)/8)*(cos(x)^2+sin(y)^2)');
>> pretty(factor(sym('D[1](f)(x,y)')))
```

$$- 1/4 \; exp(- 1/8 \; x^2 - 1/8 \; y^2) \; (x \; cos(x)^2 + x \; sin(y)^2 + 8 \; cos(x) \; sin(x))$$

```
>> pretty(factor(sym('D[1](f)(pi/3,pi/6)')))
```

$$- 1/24 \; exp(- 5/288 \; pi^2) \; (pi + 12 \; 3^{1/2})$$

If an approximation is required, we can find it as follows:

```
>> numeric('D[1](f)(pi/3,pi/6)')
```

ans =

  -0.8399

```
>> pretty(factor(sym('D[2](f)(x,y)')))
```

$$- 1/4 \; exp(- 1/8 \; x^2 - 1/8 \; y^2) \; (y \; cos(x)^2 + y \; sin(y)^2 - 8 \; sin(y) \; cos(y))$$

```
>> pretty(factor(sym('D[2](f)(pi/3,pi/6)')))
```

$$- 1/48 \; exp(- 5/288 \; pi^2) \; (pi - 24 \; 3^{1/2})$$

```
>> numeric('D[2](f)(pi/3,pi/6)')
```

ans =

    0.6745

```
>> pretty(factor(sym('D[1,2](f)(x,y)')))
```

$$1/16 \ exp(- \ 1/8 \ x^2 \ - \ 1/8 \ y^2)$$

$$(y \ x \ cos(x)^2 \ + \ y \ x \ sin(y)^2 \ + \ 8 \ y \ cos(x) \ sin(x) \ - \ 8 \ x \ sin(y) \ cos(y))$$

```
>> pretty(factor(sym('D[1,2](f)(pi/3,pi/6)')))
```

$$1/576 \ pi \ exp(- \ 5/288 \ pi^2 \ ) \ (pi \ - \ 12 \ 3^{1/2} \ )$$

```
>> numeric('D[1,2](f)(pi/3,pi/6)')
```

ans =

    -0.0811

```
>> pretty(factor(sym('D[2,1](f)(x,y)')))
```

$$1/16 \ exp(- \ 1/8 \ x^2 \ - \ 1/8 \ y^2 \ )$$

$$(y \ x \ cos(x)^2 \ + \ y \ x \ sin(y)^2 \ + \ 8 \ y \ cos(x) \ sin(x) \ - \ 8 \ x \ sin(y) \ cos(y))$$

```
>> pretty(factor(sym('D[2,1](f)(pi/3,pi/6)')))
```

$$1/576 \ pi \ exp(- \ 5/288 \ pi^2 \ ) \ (pi \ - \ 12 \ 3^{1/2} \ )$$

```
>> numeric('D[2,1](f)(pi/3,pi/6)')
```

ans =

    -0.0811

```
>> pretty(factor(sym('D[1,1](f)(x,y)')))
```

$$1/16 \ exp(- \ 1/8 \ x^2 \ - \ 1/8 \ y^2 \ ) \ (- \ 36 \ cos(x)^2 \ - \ 4 \ sin(y)^2 \ + \ x^2 \ cos(x)^2 \ + \ x^2 \ sin(y)^2$$

$$+ \ 16 \ x \ cos(x) \ sin(x) \ + \ 32 \ sin(x)^2 \ )$$

```
>> pretty(factor(sym('D[1,1](f)(pi/3,pi/6)')))
```

$$1/288\ exp(-\ 5/288\ pi^2)\ (252 + pi^2 + 24\ pi\ 3^{1/2})$$

```
>> numeric('D[1,1](f)(pi/3,pi/6)')
```

ans =

   1.1481

```
>> pretty(factor(sym('D[2,2](f)(x,y)')))
```

$$1/16\ exp(-\ 1/8\ x^2 - 1/8\ y^2)\ (-\ 4\ cos(x)^2 - 36\ sin(y)^2 + y^2\ cos(x)^2 + y^2\ sin(y)^2$$

$$-\ 16\ y\ sin(y)\ cos(y) + 32\ cos(y)^2)$$

```
>> pretty(factor(sym('D[2,2](f)(pi/3,pi/6)')))
```

$$-\ 1/1152\ exp(-\ 5/288\ pi^2)\ (-\ 1008 - pi^2 + 48\ pi\ 3^{1/2})$$

```
>> numeric('D[2,2](f)(pi/3,pi/6)')
```

ans =

   0.5534

```
>> pretty(factor(sym('D[1,1,1,2](f)(x,y)')))
```

$$1/256\ exp(-\ 1/8\ x^2 - 1/8\ y^2)\ (-\ 108\ y\ x\ cos(x)^2 - 12\ y\ x\ sin(y)^2$$

$$-\ 608\ y\ cos(x)\ sin(x) + y\ x^3\ cos(x)^2 + y\ x^3\ sin(y)^2$$

$$+\ 24\ y\ x^2\ cos(x)\ sin(x) + 96\ y\ x\ sin(x)^2 + 96\ x\ sin(y)\ cos(y)$$

$$-\ 8\ x^3\ sin(y)\ cos(y))$$

```
>> pretty(factor(sym('D[1,1,1,2](f)(pi/3,pi/6)')))
```

$$1/82944\ pi\ exp(-\ 5/288\ pi^2)\ (pi^2 + 12\ 3^{1/2}\ pi^2 + 756\ pi - 5616\ 3^{1/2})$$

```
>> numeric('D[1,1,1,2](f)(pi/3,pi/6)')
```

ans =

  -0.2271

>> **pretty(factor(sym('D[1,1,2,2](f)(x,y)')))**

$$1/256 \; exp(- 1/8 \; x^2 - 1/8 \; y^2) \; (144 \; cos(x)^2 + 144 \; sin(y)^2 - 4 \; x^2 \; cos(x)^2$$

$$- 36 \; x^2 \; sin(y)^2 - 64 \; x \; cos(x) \; sin(x) - 128 \; sin(x)^2 - 36 \; y^2 \; cos(x)^2$$

$$- 4 \; y^2 \; sin(y)^2 + y^2 \; x^2 \; cos(x)^2 + y^2 \; x^2 \; sin(y)^2 + 16 \; y^2 \; x \; cos(x) \; sin(x)$$

$$+ 32 \; y^2 \; sin(x)^2 + 64 \; y \; sin(y) \; cos(y) - 16 \; y \; x^2 \; sin(y) \; cos(y) - 128 \; cos(y)^2$$

$$+ 32 \; x^2 \; cos(y)^2 \;)$$

>> **pretty(factor(sym('D[1,1,2,2](f)(pi/3,pi/6)')))**

$$1/165888*$$
$$exp(- 5/288 \; pi^2) \; (- 77760 + 1260 \; pi^2 - 1728 \; pi^{1/2} \; 3^4 + pi^4 - 24 \; pi^3 \; 3^{1/2} \;)$$

>> **numeric('D[1,1,2,2](f)(pi/3,pi/6)')**

ans =

  -0.3856

>> **pretty(factor(sym('D[1,1,1,2,2](f)(x,y)')))**

$$- 1/1024 \; exp(- 1/8 \; x^2 - 1/8 \; y^2) \; (2432 \; cos(x) \; sin(x) + 432 \; x \; cos(x)^2$$

$$+ 432 \; x \; sin(y)^2 - 384 \; x \; sin(x)^2 - 4 \; x^3 \; cos(x)^2 - 36 \; x^3 \; sin(y)^2$$

$$+ 192 \; y \; x \; sin(y) \; cos(y) + 96 \; y^2 \; x \; sin(x)^2 - 108 \; y^2 \; x \; cos(x)^2$$

$$+ y^2 \; x^3 \; cos(x)^2 + y^2 \; x^3 \; sin(y)^2 + 24 \; y^2 \; x^2 \; cos(x) \; sin(x) - 12 \; y^2 \; x \; sin(y)^2$$

$$- 608 \; y^2 \; cos(x) \; sin(x) - 96 \; x^2 \; cos(x) \; sin(x) + 32 \; x^3 \; cos(y)^2$$

$$- 384 \; x \; cos(y)^2 - 16 \; y \; x^3 \; sin(y) \; cos(y))$$

```
>> pretty(factor(sym('D[1,1,1,2,2](f)(pi/3,pi/6)')))
```

```
                  2
1/1990656 exp(- 5/288 pi )*
```

```
          1/2                      3          2 1/2        4 1/2       5
  (- 1181952 3    + 233280 pi - 1764 pi  + 8208 pi  3   + 12 pi  3    - pi )
```

```
>> numeric('D[1,1,1,2,2](f)(pi/3,pi/6)')
```

```
ans =
```

```
  -0.5193
```

The advantage of using the operator *D* instead of the command *diff* is that it is much faster at directly calculating the value of the derivative at a point.

4.8 Maxima and Minima of Functions of Several Variables

A function $f: R^n \rightarrow R$, which maps the point $(x_1, x_2, ..., x_n) \in R$ to $f(x_1, x_2, ..., x_n) \in R$, has an extreme point at $(a_1, a_2, ..., a_n)$ if the gradient vector $\nabla f = \left(\dfrac{\partial f}{\partial x_1}, \dfrac{\partial f}{\partial x_2}, ..., \dfrac{\partial f}{\partial x_n} \right)$ is zero at $(a_1, a_2, ..., a_n)$.

By setting all the first order partial derivatives equal to zero and solving the resulting system, we can find the possible maxima and minima.

To determine the nature of the extreme point, it is necessary to construct the ***Hessian matrix***, which is defined as follows:

$$H = \begin{bmatrix} \dfrac{\partial^2 f}{\partial x_1^2} & \dfrac{\partial^2 f}{\partial x_1 \partial x_2} & .... & \dfrac{\partial^2 f}{\partial x_1 \partial x_n} \\ \dfrac{\partial^2 f}{\partial x_1 \partial x_2} & \dfrac{\partial^2 f}{\partial x_2^2} & .... & \dfrac{\partial^2 f}{\partial x_2 \partial x_n} \\ .... & .... & .... & .... \\ \dfrac{\partial^2 f}{\partial x_1 \partial x_n} & \dfrac{\partial^2 f}{\partial x_2 \partial x_n} & .... & \dfrac{\partial^2 f}{\partial x_n^2} \end{bmatrix}$$

First, suppose that the determinant of *H* is non-zero at the point $(a_1, a_2, ..., a_n)$. In this case, we say that the point is non-degenerate and, in addition, we can determine the nature of the extreme point via the following conditions:

If the Hessian matrix at the point $(a_1, a_2, ..., a_n)$ is positive definite, then the function has a minimum at that point.
If the Hessian matrix at the point $(a_1, a_2, ..., a_n)$ is negative definite, then the function has a maximum at that point.
In any other case, the function has a saddle point at $(a_1, a_2, ..., a_n)$.
If the determinant of H is zero at the point $(a_1, a_2, ..., a_n)$, we say that the point is degenerate.
MATLAB includes a specific function which calculates the determinant of the Hessian of a function of several variables. Its syntax is:

```
aple ('hessian(function, [x1,x2,..., xn])')
```

MATLAB also includes a function which calculates the gradient of a function of several variables. Its syntax is as follows:

```
maple ('grad(function, [x1,x2,..., xn])')
```

EXERCISE 4-18

Find and classify the extreme points of the function:

$$f(x,y)=-120x^3-30x^4+18x^5+5x^6+30xy^2.$$

First, we find the extreme points, setting the partial derivatives (the components of the gradient vector of f) to zero and solving the resulting system:

```
>> maple('f:=(x,y)->-120*x^3-30*x^4+18*x^5+5*x^6+30*x* y^2 ');
>> maple('solve({diff(f(x,y),x)=0,diff(f(x,y),y)=0},{x,y})')
```

ans =

{x = 0, y = 0}, {y = 0, x = 2}, {y = 0, x = -3}, {y = 0, x = -2}

Thus, the extreme points are: (– 2,0), (2,0), (0,0) and (– 3.0).

Alternatively, we can find the gradient vector and solve the system obtained by setting it equal to zero:

```
>> pretty(sym(maple('grad(f(x,y),[x,y])')))
```

[-360*x^2-120*x^3+90*x^4+30*x^5+30*y^2, 60*x*y]

```
>> maple('solve({-360*x^2-120*x^3+90*x^4+30*x^5+30*y^2=0, 60*x*y=0},{x,y})')
```

ans =

{x = 0, y = 0}, {y = 0, x = 2}, {y = 0, x = -3}, {y = 0, x = -2}

To classify the extreme points, we construct the Hessian matrix, and calculate its value at each point:

```
>> pretty(sym(maple('hessian(-120*x^3-30*x^4+18*x^5+5*x^6+30*x* y^2,[x,y])')))
```

[-720*x-360*x^2+360*x^3+150*x^4, 60*y]
[60*y, 60*x]

You can also find the Hessian matrix in the following way:

```
>> pretty(sym(maple('array([[D[1,1](f)(x,y),D[1,2](f)(x,y)],[D[1,2](f)(x,y),
   D[2,2](f)(x,y)]])')))
```

[-720*x-360*x^2+360*x^3+150*x^4, 60*y]
[60*y, 60*x]

But what we need is the Hessian matrix *M* as a function of *x* and *y* so we can evaluate it at certain points:

```
>> maple ('m:=(x,y) - >
                hessian(-120*x^3-30*x^4+18*x^5+5*x^6+30*x* y^2,[x,y])');
>> pretty (sym (maple ('subs (x = 0, y = 0, M(x,y))')))
```

$$[0, 0]$$
$$[0, 0]$$

The origin turns out to be a degenerate point, as the determinant of the Hessian matrix is zero at (0,0).

```
>> pretty (sym (maple ('subs (x =-2, y = 0, M(x,y))')))
```

$$[- 480, 0]$$
$$[0, - 120]$$

```
>> maple ('H: = subs (x =-2, y = 0, M(x,y))');
>> maple('det(H)')
```

ans =

57600

```
>> maple('eigenvals(H)')
```

ans =

-480, - 120

The Hessian matrix at the point (– 2,0) has non-zero determinant, and is also negative definite, because all its eigenvalues are negative. Therefore, the point (– 2,0) is a maximum of the function.

```
>> H = sym (maple ('subs (x = 2, y = 0, M(x,y))'))
```

H =

[2400,   0]
[0, 120]

```
>> determ(H)
```

ans =

288000

```
>> eigensys(H)
```

ans =

[120].
[2400].

The Hessian matrix at the point (2,0) has non-zero determinant, and is furthermore positive definite, because all its eigenvalues are positive. Therefore, the point (2,0) is a minimum of the function.

```
>> H = sym (maple ('subs (x = 3, y = 0, M(x,y))'))
```

H =

```
[1350,    0]
[   0, -180]
```

```
>> determ(H)
```

ans =

-243000

```
>> eigensys(H)
```

ans =

```
[-180.]
[1350]
```

The Hessian matrix at the point (– 3,0) has non-zero determinant, and, in addition, is neither positive definite nor negative definite, because its eigenvalues are not all positive or all negative. Therefore (– 3.0) is a saddle point of the function.

EXERCISE 4-19

Find and classify the extreme points of the function:

$$f(x,y,z) = x^2 + xy + y^2 + z^2$$

First, we set the partial derivatives (the components of the gradient vector of f) to zero and solve the resulting system:

```
>> maple ('f:=(x,y) - > x ^ 2 + y ^ 2 + z ^ 2 + x * y ');
>> maple ('solve ({diff (f (x, y, z), x) = 0, diff (f (x, y, z), y) = 0, diff (f (x, y, z),
   z)}, {x, y, z})')
```

ans =

{z = 0, y = 0, x = 0}

The single extreme point is the origin (0,0,0). We determine what kind of extreme point it is. To do this, we calculate the Hessian matrix and express it as a function of x, y and z:

```
>> maple ('h:=(x,y,z) - > hessian (f (x, y, z), [x, y, z])');
>> M = maple ('H (x, y, z)')
```

M =

```
[2, 1, 0]
[1, 2, 0]
[0, 0, 2]
```

>> determ(M)

ans =

6

We see that the Hessian matrix is constant (it does not depend on the point (x,y,z)), therefore its value at the origin is already found. The determinant is non-zero, so the origin is non-degenerate.

>> eigensys (M)

ans =

```
[1]
[2]
[3]
```

The Hessian matrix at the origin is positive definite, because all its eigenvalues are positive. Thus we conclude that the origin is a minimum of the function.

4.9 Conditional Minima and Maxima. The Method of "Lagrange Multipliers"

Suppose we want to optimize (i.e. maximize or minimize) the function $f(x_1,x_2,...,x_n)$, called the objective function, but subject to certain restrictions given by the equations:

$$g_1(x_1,x_2...,x_n) = 0$$

$$g_2(x_1,x_2...,x_n) = 0$$

$$........................$$

$$g_k(x_1,x_2...,x_n) = 0$$

This is the setting in which the Lagrangian is introduced. The Lagrangian is a linear combination of the objective function and the constraints, and has the following form:

$$L(x_1,x_2,...,x_n,\lambda) = f(x_1,x_2,...,x_n) + \sum_{i=1}^{k} \lambda_i g_i(x_1,x_2,...,x_n)$$

The extreme points are found by solving the system by setting the components of the gradient vector of L to zero, that is, $\nabla L(x_1,x_2,...,x_n,\lambda) = (0,0,...,0)$. Which translates into:

$$\nabla L = \left(\frac{\partial L}{\partial x_1}, \frac{\partial L}{\partial x_2}, ..., \frac{\partial L}{\partial x_n}, \frac{\partial L}{\partial \lambda_1}, \frac{\partial L}{\partial \lambda_2}, ..., \frac{\partial L}{\partial \lambda_n} \right) = (0,0,......,0)$$

By setting the partial derivatives to zero and solving the resulting system, we obtain the values of $x_1, x_2, ..., x_n, \lambda_1, \lambda_2, ..., \lambda_k$ corresponding to possible maxima and minima.

To determine the nature of the points $(x_1, x_2, ..., x_n)$ found above, the following bordered Hessian matrix is used:

$$\begin{bmatrix} \dfrac{\partial^2 f}{\partial x_1^2} & \dfrac{\partial^2 f}{\partial x_1 \partial x_2} & .... & \dfrac{\partial^2 f}{\partial x_1 \partial x_n} & \dfrac{\partial g_i}{\partial x_1} \\[2mm] \dfrac{\partial^2 f}{\partial x_1 \partial x_2} & \dfrac{\partial^2 f}{\partial x_2^2} & .... & \dfrac{\partial^2 f}{\partial x_2 \partial x_n} & \dfrac{\partial g_i}{\partial x_2} \\[2mm] .... & .... & .... & .... & .... \\[2mm] \dfrac{\partial^2 f}{\partial x_1 \partial x_n} & \dfrac{\partial^2 f}{\partial x_2 \partial x_n} & .... & \dfrac{\partial^2 f}{\partial x_n^2} & \dfrac{\partial g_i}{\partial x_n} \\[2mm] \dfrac{\partial g_i}{\partial x_1} & \dfrac{\partial g_i}{\partial x_2} & .... & \dfrac{\partial g_i}{\partial x_n} & 0 \end{bmatrix}$$

The nature of extreme points can be determined by studying the set of bordered Hessian matrices:

$$H1 = \begin{bmatrix} \dfrac{\partial f}{\partial x_1^2} & \dfrac{\partial g_i}{\partial x_1} \\[2mm] \dfrac{\partial g_i}{\partial x_1} & 0 \end{bmatrix} \qquad H2 = \begin{bmatrix} \dfrac{\partial^2 f}{\partial x_1^2} & \dfrac{\partial^2 f}{\partial x_1 \partial x_2} & \dfrac{\partial g_i}{\partial x_1} \\[2mm] \dfrac{\partial^2 f}{\partial x_1 \partial x_2} & \dfrac{\partial^2 f}{\partial x_2^2} & \dfrac{\partial g_i}{\partial x_2} \\[2mm] \dfrac{\partial g_i}{\partial x_1} & \dfrac{\partial g_i}{\partial x_2} & 0 \end{bmatrix} \cdots Hn = H$$

For a single restriction g_1, if H1 < 0, H2 < 0, H3 < 0,..., H < 0, then the extreme point is a minimum.

For a single restriction g_1, if H1 > 0, H2 < 0, H3 > 0, H4 < 0, H5 > 0, ... then the extreme point is a maximum.

For a collection of restrictions $g_i(x_1, ..., x_n)$ (i = 1, 2,..., k) the lower right 0 will be a block of zeros and the conditions for a minimum will all have sign $(-1)^k$, while the conditions for a maximum will have alternating signs with H1 having sign $(-1)^{k+1}$. When considering several restrictions at the same time, it is easier to determine the nature of the extreme point by simple inspection.

MATLAB also offers some commands for function optimization, all of which require the prior use of the command *maple*. Among them are the following:

maximize (expression) is the maximum value of the given expression with respect to all of its variables

maximize(expression,{var1,...,varn}) is the maximum value of the given expression with respect to the specified variables

minimize (expression) is the minimum value of the given expression with respect to all of its variables

minimize(expression,{var1,...,varn}) is the minimum value of the given expression with respect to the specified variables

minimize(expression,{var1,...,varn},{a1..b1,..., an...bn}) is the minimum value of the given expression with respect to the specified variables, limiting the ranges of the variables *var1,..., varn* to the intervals [a1, b1],..., [an, bn] (by default the variable ranges are infinite)

In addition, MATLAB has the command *extrema*, which gives us the extreme points of a function (the objective function) subject to a few restrictions, determined by the method of Lagrange multipliers. Its syntax is as follows:

```
maple ('extrema(fobjective, {restrictions}, {variables},s)')
```

The variable *s* contains the list of candidate extreme points. To use this function one must read it from a Maple library using the command *maple ('readlib(extrema)')*. This library also includes the following commands (all require the prior use of the command *maple*):

> **readlib (extrema)** loads into the memory a library of commands for optimization with restrictions

> **extrema(expression,equation,var)** returns candidate extreme points for the function defined by the given expression in the specified variable under the constraint defined by the equation, using the method of Lagrange multipliers

> **extrema(expression,equation)** finds candidate extreme points of the expression for all variables subject to the restriction defined by the equation

> **extrema(expression, variable, {})** finds candidate extreme points for the expression in the given variable and without restrictions

> **extrema(expression,{equation1,...,equationn},{variable1,...,variablen})** finds candidate extreme points for the given expression with respect to the specified variables subject to the constraints given by *equation1,..., equationn*

> **extrema(expression,{equ1,...,equn},{variable1,...,variablen},n)** The variable *n* returns the set of values obtained by evaluating the expression (objective function) at every candidate extreme point. These values will be used to differentiate between minima and maxima.

EXERCISE 4-20

Find and classify the extreme points of the function:

$f(x, y, z) = x + z$ subject to the constraint $x^2 + y^2 + z^2 = 1$.

```
>> maple ('readlib (extrema)');
>> maple ('extrema(x+z,{x^2+y^2+z^2=1},{x,y,z},s)')
```

ans =

```
{2 ^(1/2), - 2 ^(1/2)}
```

The command *extrema* returns the values that the objective function takes at each extreme point and the variable *s* contains the extreme points.

```
>> maple ('s ')
```

ans =

```
{{z = 1/2 * 2 ^(1/2), x = 1/2 * 2 ^(1/2), y = 0}, {x = - 1/2 * 2 ^(1/2)}}
{{z = - 1/2 * 2 ^(1/2), y = 0}}
```

Thus the extreme points are:

($\sqrt{2}/2$, 0, $\sqrt{2}/2$) and ($-\sqrt{2}/2$, 0, $-\sqrt{2}/2$)

Now let's determine the nature of these extreme points. To do this, we evaluate the objective function at these points (we already know that the results are $\sqrt{2}$ and $-\sqrt{2}$).

```
>> maple ('obj:=(x,y,z) - > x+z');
>> maple('obj(sqrt(2)/2,0,sqrt(2)/2)')
```

ans =

```
2^(1/2)
```

```
>> maple('obj(-sqrt(2)/2,0,-sqrt(2)/2)')
```

ans =

```
-2 ^(1/2)
```

Then, at the point ($-\sqrt{2}/2$, 0, $-\sqrt{2}/2$) the function has a minimum, and there is a maximum at the point ($\sqrt{2}/2$, 0, $\sqrt{2}/2$).

EXERCISE 4-21

Find and classify the extreme points of the function:

$$f(x,y,z)=\sqrt{x^2+y^2}-z$$

subject to the restrictions: $x^2 + y^2 = 16$ and $x + y + z = 10$.

```
>> maple('f:= (x^2+y^2) ^(1/2)-z');
>> maple('g1:= x^2+y^2=16; g2:= x+y+z = 10');
>> maple('readlib(extrema)');
>> maple('allvalues(extrema(f,{g1,g2},{x,y,z},s))')
```

ans =

```
{-6+4*2^(1/2)}, {-6-4*2^(1/2)}
```

```
>> maple('allvalues(s)')
```

ans =

```
{{y = 2 * 2 ^ (1/2) x = 2 * 2 ^ (1/2), z = - 4 * 2 ^(1/2) + 10}},
{{y = - 2 * 2 ^ (1/2), x = - 2 * 2 ^ (1/2), z = 4 * 2 ^(1/2) + 10}}
```

Thus the extreme points are ($\sqrt{8}$, $\sqrt{8}$, $-2\sqrt{8} + 10$) and ($-\sqrt{8}$, $-\sqrt{8}$, $2\sqrt{8} + 10$). Now let's determine the nature of these points. To this end, we evaluate the objective function at these points:

```
>> maple ('obj:=(x,y,z) - >(x^2+y^2) ^(1/2)-z');
>> numeric(maple('obj(-sqrt(8),-sqrt(8),sqrt(8)+10)'))
```

ans =

-8.8284

```
>> numeric(maple('obj(sqrt(8),sqrt(8),-sqrt(8)+10)'))
```

ans =

-3.1716

Thus, the function has a minimum at the point ($-\sqrt{8}$, $-\sqrt{8}$, $2\sqrt{8} + 10$) and a maximum at the point ($\sqrt{8}$, $\sqrt{8}$, $-2\sqrt{8} + 10$).

4.10 Some Applications of Maxima and Minima in Several Variables

As in the case of a single variable, many practical problems involving several variables inevitably lead to the consideration of derivatives.

EXERCISE 4-22

Find the dimensions of the rectangular cuboid of maximum volume which has a surface area of 10 square meters.

If x, y, z are the dimensions of the block, its volume will be $V = xyz$. As we know that it has a surface area of 10 square meters, the restriction will be $2xy + 2xz + 2yz = 10$. We therefore have to maximize the objective function $V = xyz$ subject to the condition $2xy + 2xz + 2yz - 10 = 0$. We will use the method of Lagrange multipliers:

```
>> maple('func:=x*y*z');
>> maple('g1:=2*x*y+2*x*z+2*y*z-10');
>> maple ('readlib (extrema)');
>> maple ('allvalues (extrema(func,{g1},{x,y,z}, a))')
```

ans =

{5/9 * 15 ^(1/2)}, {- 5/9 * 15 ^(1/2)}

```
>> maple ('a')
```

ans =

{{z = 1/3 * 15 ^(1/2), y = 1/3 * 15 ^(1/2), x = 1/3 * 15 ^(1/2)}},
{{z = - 1/3 * 15 ^(1/2), y = - 1/3 * 15 ^ (1/2) x = - 1/3 * 15 ^(1/2)}}

Thus the extreme points are:

$(-\sqrt{15}/3, -\sqrt{15}/3, -\sqrt{15}/3)$ and $(\sqrt{15}/3, \sqrt{15}/3, \sqrt{15}/3)$.

The only point which is a meaningful solution is the second, because there can be no sides of negative length. But it remains to be confirmed that $(\sqrt{15}/3, \sqrt{15}/3, \sqrt{15}/3)$ is indeed a maximum:

```
>> maple ('obj:=(x,y,z) - > x * y * z');
```

```
>> numeric('[obj(-sqrt(15)/3,- sqrt(15)/3,- sqrt(15)/3), obj(sqrt(15)/3, sqrt(15)/3,
sqrt(15)/3)]')
```

ans =

```
-2.1517 2.1517
```

We see that the point is indeed a maximum, and so the maximal volume rectangular cuboid with fixed surface area is a cube ($x = y = z$).

CHAPTER 5

■■■

Vector Differential Calculus and Theorems in Several Variables

5.1 Concepts of Vector Differential Calculus

Consider a function $\bar{F}: R^m \to R^n$:

$$(x_1, x_2, \ldots, x_m) \to [F_1(x_1, x_2, \ldots, x_m), \ldots, F_n(x_1, x_2, \ldots, x_m)]$$

The vector function $\bar{F}$ is said to be differentiable at the point $a = (a_1, \ldots, a_m)$ if each of the component functions $F_1, F_2, \ldots, F_n$ is differentiable.

The Jacobian matrix of the above function is defined as:

$$J = \begin{bmatrix} \dfrac{\partial F_1}{\partial x_1} & \dfrac{\partial F_1}{\partial x_2} & \cdots\cdots & \dfrac{\partial F_1}{\partial x_n} \\[2mm] \dfrac{\partial F_2}{\partial x_1} & \dfrac{\partial F_2}{\partial x_2} & \cdots\cdots & \dfrac{\partial F_2}{\partial x_n} \\[2mm] \cdots\cdots & \cdots\cdots & \cdots\cdots & \cdots\cdots \\[2mm] \dfrac{\partial F_n}{\partial x_1} & \dfrac{\partial F_n}{\partial x_2} & \cdots\cdots & \dfrac{\partial F_n}{\partial x_n} \end{bmatrix} = \dfrac{\partial(F_1, F_2, \ldots, F_n)}{\partial(x_1, x_2, \ldots, x_n)}$$

The Jacobian of a vector function is an extension of the concept of a partial derivative for a single-component function.

MATLAB has the command *jacobian* which enables you to calculate the Jacobian matrix of a function:

maple ('jacobian([F1,F2,...,Fn],[x1,x2,...,xn])') returns $J = \dfrac{\partial(F_1, F_2, \ldots, F_n)}{\partial(x_1, x_2, \ldots, x_n)}$

EXERCISE 5-1

Calculate the Jacobian matrix for the following function:

$$f(x,y,z) = [e^x, \cos(y), \sin(z)]$$

and find its value at the point $(0, -\pi/2, 0)$.

```
>> sym (maple ('jacobian ([exp (x), cos (y), sin(z)], [x, y, z])'))

ans =

[exp (x), 0, 0]
[0,-sin (y), 0]
[0, 0, cos (z)]

>> maple ('m:=(x,y,z) - > array ([[exp(x), 0, 0], [0, -sin(y), 0], [0, 0, cos(z)]])');
>> sym(maple('m(0,-Pi/2,0)'))

ans =

[1, 0, 0]
[0, 1, 0]
[0, 0, 1]
```

We see that the Jacobian matrix evaluated at the given point is the identity matrix.

5.2 The Chain Rule

The chain rule allows you to differentiate the composition of vector functions. The chain rule is one of the most familiar rules of differential calculus. It is often first introduced in the case of single variable real functions, and is then generalized to vector functions. It says the following:

Suppose we have two vector functions

$$\bar{g}: U \subset R^n \to R^m \text{ and } \bar{f}: V \subset R^m \to R^p.$$

where U and V are open and consider the composite function $\bar{f} \circ \bar{g}: R^n \to R^p$.

If $\bar{g}$ is differentiable at $\bar{x}_0$ and $\bar{f}$ is differentiable at $\bar{y}_0 = \bar{g}(\bar{x}_0)$, then $\bar{f} \circ \bar{g}$ is differentiable at $\bar{x}_0$ and we have the following:

$$D(\bar{f} \circ \bar{g})(\bar{x}_0) = D\bar{f}(\bar{y}_0) D\bar{g}(\bar{x}_0)$$

MATLAB will directly apply the chain rule when instructed to differentiate composite functions.

EXERCISE 5-2

Consider the functions $f(x,y)=x^2+y$ and $\bar{h}(u)=[\sin(3u),\cos(8u)]$. If $g(u)=f[\bar{h}(u)]$ calculate $\dfrac{dg}{du}$ at $u=0$.

```
>> maple ('f:=(x,y) - > x ^ 2 + y ');
>> maple ('h: = u - > (sin(3*u), cos(8*u))');
>> maple ('g: = u - > (f@h) (u)');
>> pretty(sym(maple('diff(g(u),u)')))
```

$$6 \sin(3\ u)\ \cos(3\ u) - 8\ \sin(8\ u)$$

This is the derivative of the composite function. Now, we find the value of its derivative at $u = 0$, defining it first as a function of u:

```
>> maple ('dcomp: = u - > diff (g (u) u)');
```

$$dcomp: = u - > diff (g (u), u)$$

```
>> numeric (maple ('subs (u = 0, dcomp (u))'))
```

ans =

0

EXERCISE 5-3

Calculate $\dfrac{\partial z}{\partial x}$ and $\dfrac{\partial z}{\partial y}$ given that:

$$z=\frac{u^2+v^2}{u^2-v^2},\ \ u=e^{x-y} \text{ and } v=e^{xy}.$$

```
>> maple ('f:=(u,v) - >(u^2+v^2) /(u^2-v^2)');
```

Now we define the following vector function:

```
>> maple ('g:=(x,y) - > (exp(x-y), exp(x*y))');
```

We define the function z as the composite of the previous two functions:

```
>> maple ('z:=(x,y) - > (f@g)(x,y)');
```

11

Finally, we differentiate the composite function. MATLAB automatically differentiates composite functions via the usual syntax:

```
>> pretty(sym(maple('simplify(diff(z(x,y),x))')))
```

$$4 \frac{(-1+y)\ exp(2\ x - 2\ y + 2\ x\ y)}{(exp(2\ x - 2\ y) - exp(2\ x\ y))^2}$$

```
>> pretty(sym(maple('simplify(diff(z(x,y),y))')))
```

$$4 \frac{(1+x)\ exp(2\ x - 2\ y + 2\ x\ y)}{(exp(2\ x - 2\ y) - exp(2\ x\ y))^2}$$

Alternatively we could have directly calculated the composite function and differentiated it as follows:

```
>> pretty(sym(maple('simplify(f(g(x,y)))')))
```

$$\frac{exp(2\ x - 2\ y) + exp(2\ x\ y)}{exp(2\ x - 2\ y) - exp(2\ x\ y)}$$

Now, the problem would be reduced to finding the partial derivatives of this expression with respect to x and y, which is trivial with MATLAB.

```
>> maple('comp:=(x,y)->simplify(f(g(x,y)))');
>> pretty(sym(maple('simplify(diff(comp(x,y),x))')))
```

$$4 \frac{(-1+y)\ exp(2\ x - 2\ y + 2\ x\ y)}{(exp(2\ x - 2\ y) - exp(2\ x\ y))^2}$$

```
>> pretty(sym(maple('simplify(diff(comp(x,y),y))')))
```

$$4 \frac{(1+x)\ exp(2\ x - 2\ y + 2\ x\ y)}{(exp(2\ x - 2\ y) - exp(2\ x\ y))^2}$$

Obviously, the result obtained is the same.

5.3 The Implicit Function Theorem

Consider the vector function $\bar{F}: A \subset R^{n+m} \to R^m$ where A is an open subset of R^{n+m}

$$(\bar{x},\bar{y}) \xrightarrow{\ F\ } [F_1(\bar{x},\bar{y}),...,F_m(\bar{x},\bar{y})]$$

If F_i (i = 1, 2,..., m) are differentiable with continuous derivatives up to order r and the Jacobian matrix $J = \partial (F_1,..., F_m) / \partial (y_1,..., y_m)$ has non-zero determinant at a point $(\bar{x}_0,\bar{y}_0)$ such that $\bar{F}(\bar{x}_0,\bar{y}_0)=0$, then there is an open $U \subset R^n$ containing $\bar{x}_0$, an open $V \subset R^m$ containing $\bar{y}_0$ and a single-valued function $\bar{f}: U \to V$ such that $\bar{F}[\bar{x},\bar{f}(\bar{x})]=\bar{0}$ $\forall x \in U$ and $\bar{f}$ is differentiable of order r with continuous derivatives.

This theorem guarantees the existence of certain derivatives of implicit functions. MATLAB allows differentiation of implicit functions and offers the results in those cases where the hypothesis of the theorem are met.

EXERCISE 5-4

Find the conditions on x, y, z so that the surface defined by the following equation defines an implicit function z = z(x,y) where z is a differentiable function:

$$x^3 + 3y^2 + 8xz^2 - 3yz^3 = 1$$

Calculate:

$$\frac{\partial z}{\partial x}, \frac{\partial z}{\partial y}, \frac{\partial^2 z}{\partial x^2} \text{ and } \frac{\partial^2 z}{\partial y^2}.$$

```
>> maple('f:=(x,y,z)->x^3+3*y^2+8*x*z^2-3*z^3*y-1');
```

In order for the hypotheses of the implicit function theorem to be met, the partial derivative of f with respect to the variable z must be non-zero.

```
>> pretty(sym(maple('diff(f(x,y,z),z)')))
```

$$16\ x\ z\ -\ 9\ z^2\ y$$

Thus the required condition is $16xz \neq 9yz^2$.

Now we can calculate the partial derivatives, assuming that the above condition is met.

The implicit (total) derivative of f and D(z) are found as follows:

```
>> pretty(sym(maple('D(f(x,y,z)=0)')))
```

$$3\ D(x)\ x^2\ +\ 6\ D(y)\ y\ +\ 8\ D(x)\ z^2\ +\ 16\ x\ D(z)\ z\ -\ 9\ D(z)\ z^2\ y\ -\ 3\ z^3\ D(y)\ =\ 0$$

```
>> pretty(sym(maple('D(z):=-solve(D(f(x,y,z)=0),D(z))')))
>> pretty(sym(maple('D(z)')))
```

$$D(z)\ :=\ -\ \frac{3\ D(x)\ x^2\ +\ 6\ D(y)\ y\ +\ 8\ D(x)\ z^2\ -\ 3\ z^3\ D(y)}{16\ x\ z\ -\ 9\ z^2\ y}$$

11

As y does not depend on x (x and y are, by hypothesis, independent variables, and the variable z depends on x and y), we put $D(y) = 0$ in the expression for $D(z)/D(x)$:

```
>> pretty(sym(maple('simplify(subs(D(y)=0,D(z)/D(x)))')))
```

$$- \frac{3 x^2 + 8 z^2}{z (16 x - 9 z y)}$$

This gives the expression for $\partial z/\partial x$. For $\partial z/\partial y$, we similarly calculate the following:

```
>> pretty(sym(maple('simplify(subs(D(x)=0,D(z)/D(y)))')))
```

$$- 3 \frac{2 y - z^3}{z (16 x - 9 z y)}$$

To calculate $\partial^2 z / \partial x^2$, we find the partial derivative of $\partial z/\partial x$ with respect to x:

```
>> pretty(simple(sym(diff(maple('simplify(subs(D(y)=0,D(z)/D(x)))'),'x'))))
```

$$- 2 \frac{24 x^2 - 27 x z y - 64 z^2}{z (16 x - 9 z y)^2}$$

To calculate $\partial^2 z / \partial y^2$, we find the partial derivative of $\partial z/\partial y$ with respect to y:

```
>> pretty(simple(sym(diff(maple('simplify(subs(D(x)=0,D(z)/D(y)))'),'y'))))
```

$$- 3 \frac{32 x - 9 z^4}{z (16 x - 9 z y)^2}$$

EXERCISE 5-5

Show that near the point $(x, y, u, v) = (1,1,1,1)$ the system

$$xy + yvu^2 = 2$$

$$xu^3 + y^2 v^4 = 2$$

can be solved uniquely for u and v as functions of x and y ($u = u(x,y)$, $v = v(x,y)$).

First, we check that the hypotheses of the implicit function theorem are met at the point $(1,1,1,1)$.

The functions are differentiable and have continuous derivatives. We need to show that the corresponding Jacobian determinant is non-zero at the point (1,1,1,1):

```
>> maple('f1:=(x,y,u,v)-> x*y +y*v*u^2-2');
>> maple('f2:=(x,y,u,v)->x*u^3+y^2*v^4-2');
>> sym(maple('jacobian([f1(x,y,u,v),f2(x,y,u,v)],[u,v])'))
```

```
ans =
```

```
[2*y*v*u,      y*u^2]
[3*x*u^2,  4*y^2*v^3]
```

```
>> J=sym(maple('subs(x=1,y=1,u=1,v=1,jacobian([f1(x,y,u,v),f2(x,y,u,v)],[u,v]))'))
```

```
J =
```

```
[2, 1]
[3, 4]
```

```
>> determ(J)
```

```
ans =
```

```
5
```

Thus the assumptions of the implicit function theorem are met and the proposed system can be solved uniquely.

5.4 The Inverse Function Theorem

Consider the vector function $\bar{f} : U \subset R^n \to R^n$ where U is an open subset of R^n

$$(x_1, x_2,..., x_n) \to [f_1(x_1, x_2,..., x_n),..., f_n(x_1, x_2,..., x_n)]$$

and assume it is differentiable with continuous derivative.

If there is an $\bar{x}_0$ such that $|J| = |\partial(f_1,...,f_n) / \partial(x_1,...,x_n)| \neq 0$ at x_0, then there is an open set A containing $\bar{x}_0$ and an open set B containing $\bar{f}(\bar{x}_0)$ such that $\bar{f}(A) = B$ and $\bar{f}$ has an inverse function $\bar{f}^{-1} : B \to A$ that is differentiable with continuous derivative. In addition we have:

$$D\bar{f}^{-1}(y) = \left[D\bar{f}(\bar{x}) \right]^{-1} \text{ and if } J = \partial (f1,..., fn) / \partial (x_1,..., x_n) \text{ then } |J^{-1}| = 1 / |J|.$$

MATLAB automatically performs the calculations related to the inverse function theorem, provided that the assumptions are met.

EXERCISE 5-6

Given the vector function $(u(x,y), v(x,y))$ where:

$$u(x,y) = \frac{x^4 + y^4}{x}, v(x,y) = \sin(x) + \cos(y)$$

find the conditions under which the inverse vector function $(x(u,v), y(u,v))$ with $x = x(u, v)$ and $y = y(u,v)$ exists and find the derivative of the inverse transformation. Find its value at $(\pi/4, -\pi/4)$.

The conditions to be met are precisely the hypotheses of the inverse function theorem. The functions are differentiable with continuous derivatives, except perhaps at $x = 0$. Now let's consider the Jacobian of the transformation $\partial(u(x,y), v(x,y)) / \partial(x, y)$:

```
>> J=simple(sym(maple('jacobian([(x^4+y^4)/x,sin(x)+cos(y)],[x,y])')))

J =

[(3*x^4-y^4)/x^2, 4*y^3/x]
[        cos(x), -sin(y)]

>> pretty(sym(determ(J)))
```

$$-\frac{3 \sin(y) x^4 - \sin(y) y^4 + 4 y^3 \cos(x) x}{x^2}$$

Therefore, at the points where this expression is non-zero, x and y can be expressed in terms of u and v. In addition, we must have $x \neq 0$.

We calculate the derivative of the inverse function. Its value is the inverse of the Jacobian matrix and the determinant of the inverse Jacobian matrix is the reciprocal of the determinant of the Jacobian matrix:

```
>> I=simple(inv(J))

I =

[sin(y)/(3*sin(y)*x^4-sin(y)*y^4+4*y^3*cos(x)*x)*x^2,
4*y^3*x/(3*sin(y)*x^4-sin(y)*y^4+4*y^3*cos(x)*x)]
[cos(x)/(3*sin(y)*x^4-sin(y)*y^4+4*y^3*cos(x)*x)*x^2,
-(3*x^4-y^4)/(3*sin(y)*x^4-sin(y)*y^4+4*y^3*cos(x)*x)]

>> pretty(sym(simple(determ(inv(J)))))
```

$$\frac{x^2}{3 \sin(y) x^4 - \sin(y) y^4 + 4 y^3 \cos(x) x}$$

Observe that this is indeed the reciprocal of the determinant found above.

Next we find the value of the inverse Jacobian at the point $(\pi/4, -\pi/4)$:

```
>> numeric(subs(subs(determ(I),pi/4,'x'),-pi/4,'y'))
```

ans =

0.3821

```
>> numeric(subs(subs(symdiv(1,determ(J)),pi/4,'x'),-pi/4,'y'))
```

ans =

0.3821

Here it is clear that the determinant of the Jacobian of the inverse function is the reciprocal of the determinant of the Jacobian of the function.

EXERCISE 5-7

Demonstrate that the transformation between cartesian and polar coordinates complies with the assumptions of the inverse function theorem.

We know that the transformation equations are:

$$x = a\cos[b], y = a\sin[b]$$

Obviously, the functions have continuous partial derivatives. Let's see if the determinant of the Jacobian of the transformation is non-zero:

```
>> J = simple (sym (maple ('jacobian ([a * cos (b), a * sin (b)], [a, b])')))
```

J =

```
[cos (b),-a * sin (b)]
[sin(b),  a*cos(b)]
```

```
>> pretty(simple(sym(determ(J))))
```

a

We see that the Jacobian of the transformation is non-zero $(a \neq 0)$. Thus, the inverse function theorem is applicable. The determinant of the Jacobian of the inverse transformation will be *1/a*.

11

5.5 The Change of Variables Theorem

Suppose we have a function $f(x,y)$ that depends on the variables x and y, and that meets all the conditions of differentiation and continuity necessary for the inverse function theorem to hold. We introduce new variables u and v, relating to the above, regarding them as functions $u = u(x,y)$ and $v = v(x,y)$, so that u and v also fulfil the necessary conditions of differentiation and continuity (described by the inverse function theorem) to be able to express x and y as functions of u and v: $x=x(u,v)$ and $y=y(u,v)$.

Under the above conditions, it is possible to express the initial function f as a function of the new variables u and v using the expression:

$$f(u,v) = f(x(u,v), y(u,v))|J| \text{ where } J \text{ is the Jacobian } \partial(x(u, v), y(u,v))/\partial(u, v).$$

The theorem generalizes to vector functions of n components.

EXERCISE 5-8

Consider the function $f(x,y)=e^{x-y}$ and the transformation $u = u(x,y) = x + y$, $v = v(x,y) = x$. Calculate $f(u,v)$.

```
>> maple ('f:=(x,y) - > exp(x-y)');
```

This transformation fulfils the conditions of the inverse function theorem (continuous partial derivatives and a Jacobian with non-zero determinant).

We find the inverse transformation and its Jacobian to apply the change of variables theorem:

```
>> maple ('solve({u=x+y,v=x},{x,y})')
```

ans =

```
{x = v, y = u-v}
```

```
>> sym (maple ('jacobian([v,u-v],[u,v])'))
```

ans =

```
[0, 1]
[1, - 1]
```

```
>> pretty (simple (sym (maple ('f (v, u-v) * abs (det (jacobian([v,u-v],[u,v])))'))))
```

exp(2 v-u)

The requested function is $f(u,v)= e^{2v-u}$.

5.6 Taylor's Theorem with n Variables

Let $f:R^n \to R$, $(x_1,...,x_n) \to f(x_1,...,x_n)$, be differentiable k times with continuous partial derivatives. The Taylor series expansion of order k of $f(\bar{x})$ at the point $\bar{a}=(a_1,...,a_n)$ is as follows:

$$f(\bar{x})= f(\bar{a})+\sum_{i=1}^{n}\frac{\partial f}{\partial x_i}(\bar{a})t_i +\frac{1}{2!}\sum_{i=1}^{n}\sum_{j=1}^{n}\frac{\partial^2 f}{\partial x_i \partial x_j}(\bar{a})t_i t_j +$$

$$\frac{1}{3!}\sum_{i=1}^{n}\sum_{j=1}^{n}\sum_{k=1}^{n}\frac{\partial^3 f}{\partial x_i \partial x_j \partial x_k}(\bar{a})t_i t_j t_k +...+R(k+1)$$

Here

$$\bar{x}=(x_1,x_2...x_n), \bar{a}=(a_1,a_2...a_n), t_i=x_i-a_i(i=1,2,...n)$$

R = remainder.
Normally, the series are given up to order 2.

EXERCISE 5-9

Find the Taylor series of order 2 at the point (1,0) of the function:

$$f(x,y)=e^{(x-1)^2}\cos(y).$$

```
>> maple('f:=(x,y)->exp((x-1)^2)*cos(y)');

>> pretty(sym(maple('f(1,0)+D[1](f)(1,0)*(x-1)+D[2](f)(1,0)*(y)+
+(1/2!)*(D[1,1](f)(1,0)*(x-1)^2+ 2*D[1,2](f)(1,0)*( x-1)*y+D[2,2](f)(1,0)*(y)^2)')))
```

$$1 + (x - 1)^2 - 1/2\ y^2$$

EXERCISE 5-10

Find the Taylor series of order 2 at the origin of the function:

$$f(x,y)=e^{x+y^2}$$

```
>> maple('f:=(x,y)->exp(x+y^2)');
>> pretty(sym(maple('f(0,0)+D[1](f)(0,0)*(x)+D[2](f)(0,0)*(y)+
(1/2!)*(D[1,1](f)(0,0)*(x)^2+2*D[1,2](f)(0,0)*(x)*( y)+D[2,2](f)(0,0)*(y)^2)')))
```

$$1 + x + 1/2\ x^2 + y^2$$

5.7 Vector Fields. Curl, Divergence and the Laplacian

We recall some basic definitions:

Definition of gradient: If $h = f(x,y,z)$, then the gradient of f, which is denoted by $\Delta f(x,y,z)$, is the vector:

$$grad(f) = \Delta f(x,y,z) = \frac{\partial f(x,y,z)}{\partial x} i + \frac{\partial f(x,y,z)}{\partial y} j + \frac{\partial f(x,y,z)}{\partial z} k$$

Definition of a scalar potential of a vector field: A vector field $\overline{F}$ is called conservative if there is a differentiable function f such that $\overline{F} = \Delta f$. The function f is known as a scalar potential function for $\overline{F}$.

Definition of the curl of a vector field: The curl of a vector field $F(x,y,z) = Mi + Nj + Pk$ is the following:

$$curl\ F(x,y,z) = \Delta \times F(x,y,z) = \left(\frac{\partial P}{\partial y} - \frac{\partial N}{\partial z} \right) i - \left(\frac{\partial P}{\partial x} - \frac{\partial M}{\partial z} \right) j + \left(\frac{\partial N}{\partial x} - \frac{\partial M}{\partial y} \right) k$$

Definition of a vector potential of a vector field: A vector field F is a vector potential of another vector field G if $F = curl(G)$.

Definition of the divergence of a vector field: The divergence of the vector field $F(x,y,z) = Mi + Nj + Pk$ is the following:

$$diverge\ F(x,y,z) = \Delta \cdot F(x,y,z) = \frac{\partial M}{\partial x} + \frac{\partial N}{\partial y} + \frac{\partial P}{\partial z}$$

Definition of the Laplacian: The Laplacian is the differential operator defined by:

$$Laplacian = \Delta^2 = \Delta \cdot \Delta = \frac{\partial^2}{\partial x^2} + \frac{\partial^2}{\partial y^2} + \frac{\partial^2}{\partial z^2}$$

MATLAB provides the following commands for the above operations:

maple ('grad(f,[x1,...,xn])') calculates the gradient of f(x1,...,xn)

maple('potential([f1,...,fn],[x1,...,xn],p)') determines if the vector field with components [f1,..., fn] has a scalar potential (to do this, the vector field has to be irrotational or have zero curl). If so, p is the scalar potential.

maple ('curl([f1,...,fn],[x1,...,xn])') gives the rotational component of the vector field [f1,..., fn].

maple('vectpotent([f1,...,fn],[x1,...,xn],p)') determines if the vector field with components [f1,..., fn] has a vector potential (for this purpose, the vector field has to be incompressible or have zero divergence). If so, p is the vector potential.

maple ('diverge([f1,...,fn],[x1,...,xn])') gives the divergence of the vector field with components [f1,..., fn].

maple ('laplacian(f,[x1,...,xn])') computes the Laplacian of the function f.

EXERCISE 5-11

Calculate the gradient and Laplacian of the function

$$w = \frac{1}{\sqrt{1-x^2-y^2-z^2}} .$$

```
>> maple('w:=1/sqrt(1-x^2-y^2-z^2)');
>> pretty(simple(sym(maple('grad(w,[x,y,z])'))))
```

$$\left[\frac{x}{(1-x^2-y^2-z^2)^{3/2}}, \frac{y}{(1-x^2-y^2-z^2)^{3/2}}, \frac{z}{(1-x^2-y^2-z^2)^{3/2}}\right]$$

```
>> pretty(simple(sym(maple('laplacian(w,[x,y,z])'))))
```

$$\frac{3}{(1-x^2-y^2-z^2)^{5/2}}$$

EXERCISE 5-12

Calculate the scalar potential of the vector field $[1, 2y, 3z^2]$.

```
>> maple ('potential([1,2*y,3*z^2],[x,y,z],P)')
```

ans =

true

The response *true* is given because there is a scalar potential, i.e., because the curl of the given vector field is null:

```
>> sym (maple ('curl([1,2*y,3*z^2],[x,y,z])'))
```

ans =

[0, 0, 0]

The value of the scalar potential is contained in the variable P:

```
>> pretty(sym(maple('P')))
```

$$y^2 + x + z^3$$

12

If we calculate the gradient of this scalar potential, we get the initial vector field.

```
>> pretty(simple(maple('grad(y^2+x+z^3,[x,y,z])')))
```

$$[1, \ 2\ y, \ 3\ z^2\ ]$$

EXERCISE 5-13

Calculate the curl and the divergence of the vector field:

$$\bar{F}(x,y,z)=\tan^{-1}\frac{x}{y}\bar{i}+\ln\sqrt{x^2+y^2}\bar{j}+\bar{k}.$$

```
>> pretty(simple(sym(maple('curl([arctan(x/y),ln(sqrt(x^2+y^2)),1],[x,y,z])'))))
```

$$[0, \ 0, \ 2\ \frac{x}{x^2 + y^2}]$$

```
>> pretty(simple(sym(maple('diverge([arctan(x/y),ln(sqrt(x^2+y^2)),1],[x,y,z])'))))
```

$$2\ \frac{y}{x^2 + y^2}$$

EXERCISE 5-14

Calculate the vector potential of the following vector fields:

$$F=[xz,-yz,y],\ G=[xe^y,\ x\cos(z),-ze^y],\ H=[x\cos(y),-\sin(y),\sin(x)].$$

```
>> maple ('vecpotent([x*z,-y*z,y],[x,y,z],Q)')
```

ans =

true

Thus, we know that there is a vector potential, and the divergence of the vector field is zero:

```
>> sym (maple ('diverge([x*z,-y*z,y],[x,y,z])'))
```

ans =

0

The value of the vector potential is contained in the variable Q:

```
>> pretty(simple(sym(maple('print(Q)'))))
```

$$[- 1/2 \ y \ (z^2 + y), \ - \ 1/2 \ x \ z^2 \ , \ 0]$$

If we calculate the curl of the previous result, we obtain the initial vector field:

```
>> pretty (sym (maple ('curl ([-1/2 * y *(z^2+y), - 1/2 * x * z ^ 2, 0], [x, y, z])')))
```

$$[x \ z, - \ y \ z, \ y]$$

Now, we calculate the vector potential of the other two fields:

```
>> pretty(simple(sym(maple('print(Q)'))))
```

$$[- 1/2 \ y \ (z^2 + y), \ - \ 1/2 \ x \ z^2 \ , \ 0]$$
$$[-z \ sin \ (y) - y \ sin \ (x), \ - \ x \ z \ cos(y), \ 0]$$

If we calculate the curl of these vector potentials, we obtain the initial vector fields:

```
>> pretty(sym(maple('curl([- sin(z)*x, - x*exp(y)*z, 0],[x,y,z])')))
```

$$[x \ exp(y), \ - \ x \ cos(z), \ - \ z \ exp(y)]$$

```
>> pretty(sym(maple('curl([- sin(y)*z - sin(x)*y, - x*cos(y)*z, 0],[x,y,z])')))
```

$$[x \ cos(y), \ - \ sin(y), \ sin(x)]$$

5.8 Coordinate Transformation

In this section we will see how to convert cylindrical and spherical coordinates to rectangular coordinates, cylindrical coordinates to spherical coordinates, and their inverse transformations. Given the simplicity of the functions we will define them ourselves.

First we recall the definitions of cylindrical and spherical coordinates:

In a *cylindrical coordinate* system, a point P in the space is represented by a triplet (r, θ, z), where:

r is the distance from the origin (O) to the projection P' of P in the XY plane

θ is the angle between the X axis and the segment OP'

z is the distance PP'

In a *spherical coordinate* system, a point P in the space is represented by a triplet (ρ, θ, ϕ), where:

ρ is the distance from P to the origin

θ is the same angle as the one used in cylindrical coordinates

ϕ is the angle between the positive Z axis and the segment OP

The following conversion equations are easily found:
Cylindrical to rectangular:

$$x = r\cos\theta$$
$$y = r\sin\theta$$
$$z = z$$

Rectangular to cylindrical:

$$r = \sqrt{x^2 + y^2}$$
$$\theta = \tan^{-1}\frac{y}{x}$$
$$z = z$$

Spherical to rectangular:

$$x = \rho\sin\phi\cos\theta$$
$$y = \rho\sin\phi\sin\theta$$
$$z = \rho\cos\phi$$

Rectangular to spherical:

$$\rho = \sqrt{x^2 + y^2 + z^2}$$
$$\theta = \tan^{-1}\frac{y}{x}$$
$$\phi = \cos^{-1}\frac{z}{\sqrt{x^2 + y^2 + z^2}}$$

Therefore, in MATLAB we can define the following functions:

```
> maple ('sphrec:=(r,t,f) - > [r * sin (f) * cos (t), r * sin (f) * sin (t), r * cos (f)]');

> maple ('cylrec:=(r,t,z) - > [r * cos (t), r *sin (t), z]');
> maple ('recsph:=(x,y,z) - > (sqrt(x^2+y^2+z^2), arctan (y/x), arccos (z/sqrt(x^2+y^2+z^2)))');

> maple ('reccyl:=(x,y,z) - > [sqrt(x^2+y^2), arctan (y/x), z]');
```

EXERCISE 5-15

Express the point given in spherical coordinates by $(4, \pi/6, \pi/4)$ in rectangular and cylindrical coordinates.

```
>> maple ('sphrec(4,pi/6,pi/4)')
```

ans =

```
[2 ^(1/2) * 3 ^(1/2), 2 ^(1/2), 2 * 2 ^(1/2)]
```

Now, we convert the rectangular to cylindrical coordinates:

```
>> maple ('reccyl (2 ^(1/2) * 3 ^(1/2), 2 ^(1/2), 2 * 2 ^(1/2))')
```

ans =

*[2 * 2 ^ (1/2), 1/6 * pi, 2 * 2 ^(1/2)]*

EXERCISE 5-16

Express the point given in cylindrical coordinates by $(4, 5\pi/6, 3)$ in rectangular and spherical coordinates.

```
>> maple('cylrec(4,5*Pi/6,3)')
```

ans =

*[- 2 * 3 ^ (1/2), 2, 3]*

Now, we convert the rectangular to spherical coordinates:

```
>> maple ('recsph (- 2 * 3 ^ (1/2), 2, 3)')
```

ans =

*5, - 1/6 * pi, acos(3/5)*

EXERCISE 5-17

Express the equations of the surfaces $xz = 1$ and $x^2 + y^2 + z^2 = 1$ in spherical coordinates.

```
>> pretty(sym(maple('subs(x=r*sin(a)*cos(t),y=r*sin(a)*sin(t),z=r*cos(a), x*z=1)')))
```

$$r^2 \sin(a) \cos(t) \cos(a) = 1$$

```
>> pretty(simple(sym(maple('subs(x=r*sin(a)*cos(t),y=r*sin(a)*sin(t),
   z=r*cos(a), x^2+y^2-z^2=1)'))))
```

$$- r^2 \cos(2\,a) = 1$$

12

EXERCISE 5-18

Express in cartesian and spherical coordinates the equation of the surface which in cylindrical coordinates is given by $z = r^2 (1 + \sin(t))$.

```
>> pretty(sym(maple('expand(simplify(subs(r=sqrt(x^2+y^2),t=arctan(y/x),
   z=z, z=r^2*(1+sin(t))),symbolic))')))
```

$$z = x^2 + y^2 + (x^2 + y^2)^{1/2}\, y$$

Now let us convert the cartesian to spherical coordinates:

```
>> pretty(sym(maple('assume(t,real):expand(simplify(subs(x=r*sin(a)*cos(t),
   y=r*sin(a)*sin(t), z=r*cos(a), z=(x^2+y^2)*(1+sin(atan(y/x)))),symbolic))')))
```

$$r\cos(a) = r^2 \sin(t) - r^2 \cos(a)\ \sin(t) + r^2 - r^2 \cos(a)$$

EXERCISE 5-19

Find the unit tangent, the unit normal, and the unit binormal vectors of the twisted cubic: $x = t, y = t^2, z = t^3$.

We begin by restricting the variable t to the real field:

```
>> maple('assume(t,real)') ;
```

We define the symbolic vector V as follows:

```
>> syms t, V=[t,t^2,t^3]
```

$V =$

$[t,\ t\mathbin{\char`\^}2,\ t\mathbin{\char`\^}3]$

The tangent vector is calculated by:

```
>> tang= diff (V)
```

$tang =$

$[1,\ 2\,{*},\ 3\,{*}\,t\mathbin{\char`\^}2]$

The unit tangent vector will be:

```
>> ut = simple (tang / sqrt (dot(tan,tan)))
```

ut =

[1/(1+4*t^2+9*t^4)^(1/2),2*t/(1+4*t^2+9*t^4)^(1/2),3*t^2/(1+4*t^2+9*t^4)^(1/2)]

To find the unit normal vector we calcuate $((v' \wedge v'') \wedge v') /(|v' \wedge v''| \, |v'|)$:

```
>> v1=cross(diff(V),diff(V,2)) ;
>> un=simple(cross(v1,tang)/(sqrt(dot(v1,v1))*sqrt(dot(tang,tang))))
```

un =

[(-2*t-9*t^3)/(9*t^4+9*t^2+1)^(1/2)/(1+4*t^2+9*t^4)^(1/2),
(1-9*t^4)/(9*t^4+9*t^2+1)^(1/2)/(1+4*t^2+9*t^4)^(1/2),
(6*t^3+3*t)/(9*t^4+9*t^2+1)^(1/2)/(1+4*t^2+9*t^4)^(1/2)]

The unit binormal vector is the vector product of the tangent vector and the unit normal vector.

```
>> ub=simple(cross(ut,un))
```

ub =

[3*t^2/(9*t^4+9*t^2+1)^(1/2),-3*t/(9*t^4+9*t^2+1)^(1/2),1/(9*t^4+9*t^2+1)^(1/2)]

The unit binormal vector can also be calculated via $(v' \wedge v'') / |v' \wedge v''|$ as follows:

```
>> ub=simple(v1/sqrt(dot(v1,v1)))
```

ub =

[3*t^2/(9*t^4+9*t^2+1)^(1/2),-3*t/(9*t^4+9*t^2+1)^(1/2),1/(9*t^4+9*t^2+1)^(1/2)]

We have calculated the Frenet frame for a twisted cubic.

CHAPTER 6

■ ■ ■

Integration and Applications

MATLAB works with integral calculus in a clear and simple way. The number of functions that enables you to work in this area is not very high, but they are very efficient in solving integration problems. You can calculate the indefinite integral of most integrable functions whose structure is not very complicated; for example, functions that involve simple logarithms, exponentials, rational, trigonometric functions, inverse trigonometric functions, etc. Definite and improper integrals do not present problems for MATLAB. Double integrals, triple integrals and n-fold integrals are also easily found.

The most commonly used MATLAB commands for integral calculus are:

syms x, int(f(x), x) or int('f(x)', 'x')

$$\text{Computes the indefinite integral } \int f(x)dx$$

int (int ('f(x,y)', 'x'), 'y')

$$\text{Computes the double integral } \iint f(x,y)dxdy$$

syms x y int (int (f(x,y), x), y)

$$\text{Computes the double integral } \iint f(x,y)dxdy$$

int(int(int(...int('f(x,y...z)', 'x'), 'y')...), 'z')

$$\text{Computes } \iint ... \int f(x,y,...,z)dxdy...dz$$

syms x y z, int(int(int(...int(f(x,y...z), x), y)...), z)

$$\text{Computes } \iint ... \int f(x,y,...,z)dxdy...dz$$

syms x a b, int(f(x), x, a, b)

$$\text{Computes the definite integral } \int_a^b f(x)dx$$

int ('f (x)', 'x', 'a', 'b')

$$\text{Computes the definite integral } \int_a^b f(x)dx$$

int(int('f(x,y)', 'x', 'a', 'b'), 'y', 'c', 'd'))

$$\text{Computes the definite double integral } \int_a^b \int_c^d f(x,y)dxdy$$

syms x y b c d, int (int (f(x,y), x, a, b), y, c, d)

$$\text{Computes the definite double integral } \int_a^b \int_c^d f(x,y)dxdy$$

int(int(int(....int('f(x,y,...,z)', 'x', 'a', 'b'), 'y', 'c', 'd'),...), 'z', 'e', 'f')

$$\text{Computes } \int_a^b \int_c^d ... \int_e^f f(x,y,...,z)dxdy...dz$$

Syms x y z a b c d e f, int (int (int (... int (f(x,y,...,z), x, a, b), y, c, d),...), z, e, f)

Computes $\int_a^b \int_c^d ... \int_e^f f(x,y,...,z)\,dxdy...dz$

In addition, with the prior use of the command *maple*, the following commands can be used for integration:

int (f (x), x)

Computes the indefinite integral $\int f(x)dx$

int (f (x), x = a...b)

Computes the definite integral $\int_a^b f(x)dx$

int(f(x), x = a..b, continuous)

Computes the definite integral removing the check for continuity of the function in the interval (a, b)

residue (f(x), x = a)

Returns the algebraic residue of $f(x)$ at the point a. Used to solve integrals by the method of residues. The algebraic residue is the coefficient of x^{-1} in the Laurent expansion of $f(x)$ at a.

readlib (singular):singular(f(x))

Returns the singularities of the function $f(x)$

readlib (singular): singular (f (x), x)

Returns the singularities of the function $f(x)$ treating all variables other than x as constants

readlib (singular): singular (f(x, y, z,...), {x, y,z,...})

Returns the singularities of the function $f(x,y,z,...)$ treating all variables other than $x, y,z,...$ as constants

op (Int (f (x), x))

Shows the internal structure of the *Int* command and allows access to its operands

op (n, Int (f (x), x)

Removes the n-th operand of int. The first operand is the integrand, the second operand is the variable of integration or $x = a...b$ for definite integrals, and the third operand is *continuous*, if it is being used. The operands can be replaced with the command *subsop*.

int (int (f(x,y), x), y) computes the indefinite integral $\iint f(x,y)dxdy$

int(int(int(...int(f(x,y,...,z), x), y),...), z)

Computes $\iint ... \int f(x,y,...,z)\,dxdy...dz$

int(int(f(x,y),x=a..b),y=c..d)

Computes the definite integral $\int_a^b \int_c^d f(x,y)dxdy$

int (int (int (... int (f(x,y,...,z), x = a...b), y = c...d),...), z = e...f)

Computes $\int_a^b \int_c^d ... \int_e^f f(x,y,...,z)\,dxdy...dz$

Here are some examples:

```
>> int('1/(x^2-1)','x')
```

ans =

-atanh(x)

```
>> pretty(simple(int('a*log(1+b*x)','x')))
```

$$\frac{a\ (log(1 + b\ x)\ -\ 1)\ (1 + b\ x)}{B}$$

```
>> syms x a b, pretty(simple(int(a*log(1+b*x),x)))
```

$$\frac{a\ (log(1 + b\ x)\ -\ 1)\ (1 + b\ x)}{B}$$

```
>> pretty(int('x^n','x'))
```

$$\frac{x^{(n + 1)}}{n + 1}$$

We have seen how MATLAB allows you to include parameters in the integrals, which are treated as generic constants:

```
>> pretty(simple(int(int('x^3+y^3','x',0,'a'),'y',0,'b')))
```

$$1/4\ a^4\ b + 1/4\ a\ b^4$$

```
>> syms x y a b, pretty(simple(int(int(x^3+y^3,x,0,a),y,0,b)))
```

$$1/4\ a^4\ b + 1/4\ a\ b^4$$

```
>> pretty(simple(int(int('x^3+y^3','x',0,'a'),'y',0,'x')))
```

$$1/4\ a^4\ x + 1/4\ a\ x^4$$

In these last examples definite integrals have been solved, one of which has a variable limit of integration, which is perfectly valid with MATLAB.

6.1 Indefinite Integrals

In the examples that follow, we demonstrate the ease with which MATLAB can find integrals that are not so obvious using classical techniques. MATLAB is able to find indefinite integrals involving şimple, rational, exponential, logarithmic, trigonometric and inverse trigonometric functions.

EXERCISE 6-1

Find the following integrals:

$$\int \sec(x)\csc(x)\,dx, \int x\cos(x)\,dx, \int \cos^{-1}(2x)\,dx.$$

```
>> pretty(simple(int('sec(x)*csc(x)')))
```

$$log(tan(x))$$

```
>> pretty(simple(int('x*cos(x)')))
```

$$cos(x) + x\ sin(x)$$

```
>> pretty(simple(int('acos(2*x)')))
```

$$
x\ acos(2\ x) - 1/2\ (1 - 4\ x^{2})^{1/2}
$$

EXERCISE 6-2

Find the following integrals:

$$\int \frac{1}{\sqrt{x^2+1}}\,dx, \int \frac{\ln(x)}{\sqrt{x}}, \int \frac{1}{(2+x)\sqrt{1+x}}\,dx, \int x^3\sqrt{1+x^4}\,dx$$

```
>> pretty(simple(int('1/sqrt(x^2+1)')))
```

$$asinh(x)$$

```
>> pretty(simple(int('log(x)/x^(1/2)')))
```

$$
x^{1/2}\ (4\ log(x^{1/2}) - 4)
$$

```
>> pretty(simple(int('1/((2+x)*(1+x)^(1/2))')))
```

$$
2\ atan((x + 1)^{1/2})
$$

```
>> pretty(simple(int('x^3*sqrt(1+x^4)')))
```

$$
1/6\ (1 + x^{4})^{3/2}
$$

6.2 Integration by Substitution (or Change of Variables)

Integration by substitution is used to solve integrals $\int f(x)dx$ where a direct solution is not immediate and where other techniques fail.

The method is to find a function $x = g(t)$ which replaces x under the integral sign, converting the integral into another simpler integral in the variable t. The new integrand will in the majority of cases be immediately integrable or will be a rational function.

The substitution $x = g(t)$ must meet the following conditions:

1. $g(t)$ is differentiable:

$$\frac{dx}{dt} = g'(t).$$

2. $x = g(t)$ must be invertible, supporting an inverse function $t = h(x)$.

Once the transformed integral has been calculated as a function of t, we must substitute $t = h(x)$ to give the final solution as a function of x.

The substitution method is one of the most wide ranging of integral calculus, because of the great variety of substitutions that can be used, depending on the type of function that appears under the integral sign. However, it can easily go wrong in the sense that the transformed integral may be more difficult than the original integral, so some care is needed to choose an appropriate substitution.

MATLAB provides the function *maple('changevar')* in the *student* library (which has to be previously loaded via the command *with (student)*). This allows you to solve integrals by substitution. Its syntax is as follows:

> maple ('changevar(expr_vnew=expr_vold, integral, v_new))

> > **This performs the change of variable (as specified by the expression in the new variable equal to the expression in the old variable) for the given integral using the new variable**

As an example, we calculate the integral of the function $1 / (1 + e^x)$ via the change of variable $t = e^x$:

```
>> maple('with(student)');
>> pretty(simple(sym(maple('changevar(t=exp(x),int(1/(1+exp(x)),x),t)'))))
```

$$-log\ (1 + exp\ (x)) + x$$

EXERCISE 6-3

Solve the following integrals by substitution:

$$\int \frac{\tan^{-1}\left(\dfrac{x}{2}\right)}{x^2 + 4}dx,\ \int \frac{a\sin(x)}{(1-x^2)^{3/2}}dx,\ \int \frac{\cos^3(x)}{\sqrt{\sin(x)}}dx.$$

```
>> maple('with(student)');
>> pretty(simple(sym(maple('changevar(t=atan(x/2),int(atan(x/2)/(4+x^2),x),t)'))))
```

$$1/16\ log(1 + 1/2\ i\ x)^2 + 1/8\ log(2)\ log(1/16\ x^2 + 1/4)$$

$$-\ 1/8\ dilog(1/2 + 1/4\ i\ x) - 1/16\ log(1 - 1/2\ i\ x)^2$$

$$-\ 1/8\ dilog(1/2 - 1/4\ i\ x)$$

13

Results can easily be found by using the integral operator in inert mode, i.e. *Int*, making the substitution and finding the value of the integral later with *value* as follows:

```
>> pretty(sym(maple('value(simplify(changevar(t=arctan(x/2),
   Int(arctan(x/2)/(4+x^2),x),t)))')
```
$$1/4 \ t^2$$

Now we undo the change of variable to obtain the final result:

```
>> pretty(subs('1/4*t^2','atan(x/2)'))
```
$$1/4 \ atan(1/2 \ x)^2$$

```
>> pretty(simple(sym(maple('changevar(t=asin(x), Int(asin(x)/(1-x^2)^(3/2),x),t)'))))
```

$$t \ tan(t) + log(cos(t))$$

Now we reverse the change of variable:

```
>> pretty(subs('t*tan(t)+t*log(t)','asin(x)'))
```

$$\frac{asin(x) \ x}{(1 - x^2)^{1/2}} + asin(x) \ log(asin(x))$$

```
>> pretty(simple(sym(maple('changevar(t=sin(x), Int(cos(x)^3/sin(x)^(1/2),x),t)'))))
```

$$- 2/5 \ t^{1/2} \ (t^2 - 5)$$

```
>> pretty(subs('-2/5*t^(1/2)*(t^2-5)','sin(x)'))
```

$$- 2/5 \ sin(x)^{1/2} \ (sin(x)^2 - 5)$$

EXERCISE 6-4

Solve the following integrals:

$$\int \frac{dx}{x^3\sqrt{x^2+3x-1}}, \quad \int \frac{\sqrt{9-4x^2}}{x}\,dx, \quad \int x^8\left(3+5x^3\right)^{\frac{1}{4}}dx$$

For the first integral we use the change of variable $1/x = t$.

```
>> maple('with(student)');
>> pretty(simple(sym(maple('changevar(t=1/x, int(x^(-3)*(x^2+3*x-1)^(-1/2),x),t)'))))
```

$$1/2\ \frac{(x^2+3x-1)^{1/2}}{x^2} + 9/4\ \frac{(x^2+3x-1)^{1/2}}{x} + 31/8\ asin(1/13\ \frac{(3x-2)13^{1/2}}{x})$$

For the second integral, we use the change of variable $x = 3/2\sin(t)$, or equivalently, $t = \arcsin(2x/3)$:

```
>> pretty(simple(sym(maple('changevar(t=asin(2*x/3), int(x^(-1)* (9-4*x^2)^(-1/2), x),t)'))))
```

$$-\ 1/3\ atanh(\frac{3}{(9-4x^2)^{1/2}})$$

For the third integral, we use the change of variable $3 + 5x^3 = t^4$:

```
>> pretty(simple(sym(maple('changevar(t=(3+5*x^3)^(1/4),int(x^8* (3+5*x^3)^(1/4),x),t)'))))
```

$$4/73125\ (288 - 120\ x^3 + 125\ x^6 + 1875\ x^9)\ (3 + 5\ x^3)^{1/4}$$

6.3 Integration by Parts

Let $u = f(x)$ and $v = g(x)$ be two differentiable functions of x. The formula for the derivative of a product of functions is: d (u.v) = u.dv + v.du, which we rearrange as: u.dv = d (u.v) – v.du. Integrating both sides of this equation gives us: $\int u.dv = \int d(u.v) - \int v.du$, so we have:

$$\int u.dv = u.v - \int v.du$$

We have u = f (x) $\Rightarrow$ du = f'(x) dx, and v = g (x) $\Rightarrow$ dv = g'(x) dx, so the final expression of the integral will be:

$$\int f(x).g'(x)dx = f(x).g(x) - \int g(x).f'(x)dx$$

This gives us a method of finding the integral of a product of two functions which can potentially reduce the integral to a simpler integral.

MATLAB incorporates the command *maple('intparts')* which allows you to find an integral directly by parts. This command belongs to the *student* library, which has to be previously loaded into the memory with the command *maple ('with(student)')*. The syntax is as follows:

maple ('intparts (int (f (x), x), u (x))')

> Finds the integral of *f(x)* by parts, where *u(x)* is a factor of *f(x)* which will be differentiated when calculating the integral.

As an example, we calculate the integral of the function $(3x^2 + 2x - 7)\cos(x)$:

```
>> maple('with(student)');
>> pretty(simple(sym(maple('intparts(int((3*x^2+2*x-7)*cos(x),x),3*x^2+2*x-7)'))))
```

$$3 x^2 \sin(x) - 13 \sin(x) + 6 \cos(x) x + 2 \cos(x) + 2 x \sin(x)$$

EXERCISE 6-5

Solve the following integrals:

$$\int \left(5x^2 - 3\right) 4^{3x+1}\, dx, \ \int e^x \cos(x)\, dx, \ \int \sin\left[\ln(x)\right] x^2 dx.$$

For the first integral we put $u(x) = 5x^2 - 3$:

```
>> maple('with(student)');
>> pretty(simple(sym(maple('intparts(int((5*x^2-3)*4^(3*x+1),x),5*x^2-3)'))))
```

$$\frac{1}{27} \cdot \frac{64^x \left(5 - 54 \log(2) - 30 x \log(2)^2 + 90 x^2 \log(2)^2\right)}{\log(2)^3}$$

For the second integral we put $u(x) = e^x$:

```
>> pretty(simple(sym(maple('intparts(int(exp(x)*cos(x),x),exp(x))'))))
```

$$1/2 \exp (x) (\cos (x) + \sin (x))$$

For the third integral we put $u(x) = x$:

```
>> pretty(simple(sym(maple('intparts(int(sin(ln(x))*x^2,x),x)'))))
```

$$\frac{1}{10} \cdot \frac{x^3 \left(-1 + 6 \tan(1/2 \log(x)) + \tan(1/2 \log(x))^2\right)}{1 + \tan(1/2 \log(x))^2}$$

6.4 Integration by Reduction and Cyclic Integration

Integration by reduction (reduction formulas) is used to integrate functions involving large integer exponents. It reduces the integral to a similar integral where the value of the exponent has been reduced. Repeating this procedure we obtain the value of the original integral.

The usual procedure is to perform integration by parts. This will lead to the sum of an integrated part and an integral of a similar form to the original, but with a reduced exponent.

Cyclic integration is similar except we end up with the same integral that we had at the beginning, except for constants. The resulting equation can be rearranged to give the original integral.

In both cases the problem lies in the proper choice of the function $u(x)$ in the integration by parts.

MATLAB directly calculates the value of this type of integral in the majority of cases. In the worst case, the final value of the integral can be found after one to three applications of integration by parts.

EXERCISE 6-6

Solve the following integrals:

$$\int \sin^{13}(x)\cos^{15}(x)\,dx, \int x^7(m+nx)^{1/2}\,dx, \int e^{12x}\cos^{11}(x)\,dx.$$

We solve the first integral by parts by putting $u(x) = (\sin(x))^{12}$:

```
>> maple('with(student)');
>> pretty(simple(sym(maple('intparts(int(sin(x)^13*cos(x)^15,x),sin(x)^12)'))))
```

$$- \frac{1}{48048} \cos(x)^{16}\,(1716\,\sin(x)^{12} + 792\,\sin(x)^{10} + 330\,\sin(x)^8 + 120\,\sin(x)^6$$

$$+ 36\,\sin(x)^4 + 8\,\sin(x)^2 + 1)$$

We solve the second integral by putting $u(x) = x^7$:

```
>> pretty(simple(sym(maple('intparts(int(x^7*sqrt(m+n*x),x),x^7)'))))
```

$$\frac{2}{109395}\,(m + n\,x)^{3/2}\,(-2048\,m^7 + 6435\,n^7\,x^7 + 4480\,m^4\,n^3\,x^3 - 3840\,m^5\,n^2\,x^2$$

$$+ 3072\,m^6\,n\,x + 5544\,m^2\,n^5\,x^5 - 5040\,m^3\,n^4\,x^4 - 6006\,m\,n^6\,x^6)\,/\,n^8$$

We solve the third integral by putting $u(x) = (cos(x))^{10}$:

```
>> pretty(simple(sym(maple('intparts(int(exp(12*x)*cos(x)^11,x),cos(x)^10)'))))
```

$1/63918719475 \, exp(12\,x) \, (2894432580 \, cos(x)^{11} + 2653229865 \, cos(x)^{10} \, sin(x)$

$+ 1415055928 \, cos(x)^9 + 1061291946 \, cos(x)^8 \, sin(x) + 527896512 \, cos(x)^7$

$+ 307939632 \, cos(x)^6 \, sin(x) + 131193216 \, cos(x)^5 + 54663840 \, cos(x)^4 \, sin(x)$

$+ 17149440 \, cos(x)^3 + 4287360 \, cos(x)^2 \, sin(x) + 709632 \, cos(x) + 59136 \, sin(x))$

6.5 Definite Integrals

The definite integral acquires its strength when it comes to applying the techniques of integration to practical problems. Here we present some of the most common applications.

6.6 Curve Arc Length

One of the most common applications of integral calculus is to find lengths of arcs of a curve.

For a planar curve with equation $y = f(x)$, the arc length of the curve between points with coordinates $x = a$ and $x = b$ is given by the expression:

$$L = \int_a^b \sqrt{1 + f'(x)^2} \, dx$$

For a planar curve with parametric coordinates $x = x(t)$ and $y = y(t)$, the arc length of the curve between the points corresponding to the values $t = t_0$ and $t = t_1$ of the parameter is given by the expression:

$$L = \int_{t_0}^{t_1} \sqrt{x'(t)^2 + y'(t)^2} \, dt$$

For a curve in polar coordinates with equation $r = f(a)$, the arc length of the curve between the points corresponding to the parameter values $a = t_0$ and $a = t_1$ is given by the expression:

$$L = \int_{a_0}^{a_1} \sqrt{r^2 + r'(a)^2} \, dr$$

For a space curve with parametric coordinates $x = x(t)$, $y = y(t)$, $z = z(t)$, the arc length of the curve between the points corresponding to the parameter values $t = t_0$ and $t = t_1$ is given by the expression:

$$L = \int_{t_0}^{t_1} \sqrt{x'(t)^2 + y'(t)^2 + z'(t)^2} \, dt$$

For a space curve in cylindrical coordinates with equations $x = r \cdot cos(a)$, $y = r \cdot sin(a)$, $z = z$, the arc length of the curve between the points corresponding to the parameter values $a = a_0$ and $a = a_1$ is given by the expression:

$$L = \int_{a_0}^{a_1} \sqrt{r^2 + r'^2 + z'^2} \, dr$$

For a space curve in spherical coordinates with equations given by $x = r \cdot \sin(a) \cdot \cos(b)$, $y = r \cdot \sin(a) \cdot \sin(b)$, $z = r \cdot \cos(a)$, the arc length of the curve between the points corresponding to the values $a = a_0$ and $a = a_1$ is given by the expression:

$$L = \int_{a_0}^{a_1} \sqrt{dr^2 + r^2 da^2 + r^2 \sin^2(a) db^2}\, dr^2$$

EXERCISE 6-7

An electrical cable hangs between two towers which are 80 meters apart. The cable adopts the shape of a catenary whose equation is:

$$y = 100 \cosh \frac{x}{100}$$

Calculate the arc length of the cable between the two towers.

Given the symmetry of the curve with respect to the y-axis, the limits of integration will be −40 and 40:

```
>> f ='100*cosh(x/100)';
>> diff(f,'x')

ans =

sinh(1/100*x)

>> pretty(simple(int('(1+sinh(1/100*x)^2)^(1/2)','x','-40','40')))

100 exp (2/5) - 100 exp(-2/5)
```

If we want the approximate result, we use the command *numeric*:

```
>> numeric(simple(int('(1+sinh(1/100*x)^2)^(1/2)','x','-40','40')))

ans =

82.1505
```

Result: 82.1505 m.

EXERCISE 6-8

Calculate the arc length of the space curve represented by the parametric equations:

$$x = t \quad y = \frac{4}{3} t^{3/2} \quad z = \frac{t^2}{2} 6$$

between $t = 0$ and $t = 2$.

```
>> pretty(simple(int('(diff(t,t)^2+diff((4/3)*t^(3/2),t)^2+diff((1/2)*t^2,t)^2)^(1/2)',
   't','0','2')))
```

$$2 \quad 13^{1/2} \quad - 3/2 \ log(13^{1/2} + 4) - 1 + 3/2 \ log(3)$$

Now we approximate the result:

```
>> numeric(simple(int('(diff(t,t)^2+diff((4/3)*t^(3/2),t)^2+diff((1/2)*t^2,t)^2)^(1/2)',
   't','0','2')))
```

ans =

   4.8157

Result: 4.8157.

EXERCISE 6-9

Find the arc length for values from $a = 0$ to $a = 2pi$ of the cardioid given in polar coordinates by $r = 3-3\cos(a)$.

```
>> r = '3-3*cos(a)';
```

```
>> diff(r,'a')
```

ans =

*3 * sin (a)*

```
>> R = simple (int ('((3-3 * cos (a)) ^ 2 + (3 * sin (a)) ^ 2) ^(1/2) ',' a ', ' 0','2 * pi'))
```

R =

24

Result: 24.

6.7 The Area Enclosed between Curves

The area enclosed between a curve with equation $y = f(x)$ and the x-axis is given, in general, by the integral:

$$S = \left| \int_a^b f(x)\, dx \right|$$

where $x = a$ and $x = b$ are the abscissas of the end points of the curve.

If the curve is given in parametric coordinates $x = x(t)$ and $y = y(t)$, the area is given by the integral:

$$S = \left| \int_a^b y(t)\, x'(t)\, dt \right|$$

where values of the parameter $t = a$ and $t = b$ correspond to the end points of the curve.

If the curve is given in polar coordinates $r = f(a)$, the area is given by the integral:

$$S = \frac{1}{2} \int_{a_0}^{a_1} f(a)^2\, da$$

for the parameter values $a = a_0$ and $a = a_1$ corresponding to the end points of the curve.

To calculate the area between two curves with equations $y = f(x)$ and $y = g(x)$, we use the integral:

$$S = \int_a^b |f(x) - g(x)|\, dx$$

where $x = a$ and $x = b$ are the abscissas of the end points of the two curves.

When calculating these areas it is very important to take into account the sign of the functions involved since the integral of a negative portion of a curve will be negative. One must divide the region of integration so that positive and negative values are not computed simultaneously. For the negative parts one takes the modulus.

EXERCISE 6-10

Find the area of the region bounded by the curves defined below:

$$f(x) = 2 - x^2 \text{ and } g(x) = x.$$

We will have to find the abscissas of the points where the curves meet. Consider the equation:

$$2 - x^2 = x$$

```
>> solve('2-x^2=x')
```

ans =

```
[-2]
[1]
```

Now, we can already find the area that we have to calculate:

```
>> int('2-x^2-x','x',-2,1)
```

ans =

```
9/2
```

Result: 4.5 square units:

The graph in Figure 6-1 illustrates the area that we had to calculate:

```
>> fplot('[2-x^2,x]',[-2,1])
```

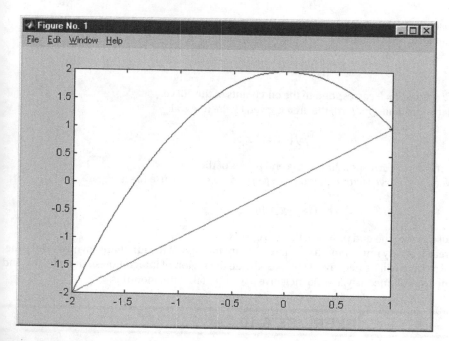

Figure 6-1.

EXERCISE 6-11

Calculate the area under the normal curve between the limits -1.96 and 1.96.

We need to calculate the integral $\int_{-1.96}^{1.96} \frac{e^{x^2/2}}{\sqrt{2\pi}}\,dx$.

```
numeric(int('exp(-x^2/2)/(2*pi)^(1/2)','x',-1.96,1.96))
```

ans =

0.9500

EXERCISE 6-12

Calculate the area of the ellipse with major and minor axes of length a and b.

As is well known, the equation of this ellipse is: $\dfrac{x^2}{a^2} + \dfrac{y^2}{b^2} = 1$

Rearranging this equation for y and assuming the positive root, we obtain $y = \dfrac{b}{a}\sqrt{a^2 - x^2}$.

By the symmetry of the ellipse, the area will be four times the integral of this expression between 0 and a.

Therefore we calculate: $\displaystyle\int_0^a \frac{4b\sqrt{a^2 - x^2}}{a}\,dx$.

```
>> pretty(int('(4*b*(a^2-x^2)^(1/2))/a','x',0,'a'))
```

pi a b

The requested result is therefore πab.

EXERCISE 6-13

Calculate the length of the perimeter and the area enclosed by the curves:

$$x(t) = \frac{\cos(t)[2 - \cos(2t)]}{4}, \quad y(t) = \frac{\sin(t)[2 + \cos(2t)]}{4}.$$

First, in order to get an idea of what the problem is, we graphically represent the curve (see Figure 6-2):

```
>> x = (0:.1:2*pi);
>> t = (0:.1:2*pi);
>> x = cos(t).*(2-cos(2*t))./4;
>> y = sin(t).*(2+cos(2*t))./4;
>> plot(x,y)
```

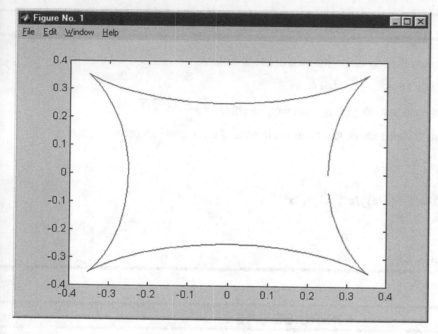

Figure 6-2.

We see that as the parameter ranges between 0 and 2π the curve described is closed. We can then calculate its length and the area that it encloses.

```
>> A = simple (diff ('cos (t) * (2-cos(2*t)) / 4'))
```

A =

*-3/8 * sin (t) + 3/8 * sin(3*t)*

```
>> B = simple (diff (' sin (t) * (2 + cos(2*t)) / 4'))
```

B =

*3/8 * cos (t) + 3/8 * cos(3*t)*

Now we apply the formula for the length of a curve in parametric coordinates (considering only half a quadrant):

```
>> int ('sqrt ((-3/8 * sin (t) + 3/8 * sin(3*t)) ^ 2 + (3/8 * cos (t) + 3/8 * cos(3*t)) ^ 2)',
't', 0, pi/4)
```

ans =

3/8

In total there are 8 semi-quadrants, so we have that $L = 8 * (3/8) = 3$.

The length of the curve is 3 units. To calculate the area, we divide it into four equal pieces (to prevent positive and negative cancellation), where t varies between 0 and 2π. The area of each piece will be the absolute value of the integral between 0 and 2π of the product $y(t) * x'(t)$:

```
>> S = simple(int('(sin(t)*(2+cos(2*t))/4)*(-3/8*sin(t)+3/8*sin(3*t))','t',0,pi/2))
```

```
S =
```

```
-3/128 * pi
```

Thus, the area enclosed by the curve is $3\pi/32$ square units.

EXERCISE 6-14

Calculate the length and the area enclosed by each of the following curves given in polar coordinates:

$$r = \sqrt{\cos(2a)} \quad \text{and} \quad r = \sin(2a).$$

We begin by representing both curves on the same graph (see Figure 6-3).

```
>> a = 0:.1:2*pi;
>> subplot(1,2,1)
>> r = sqrt(cos(2*a));
>> polar(a,r)
>> title(' r = (cos(2a))¹ᐟ²')
>> subplot (1,2,2)
>> r = sin(2*a);
>> polar (a, r)
>> title(' r = sin(2a)')
```

14

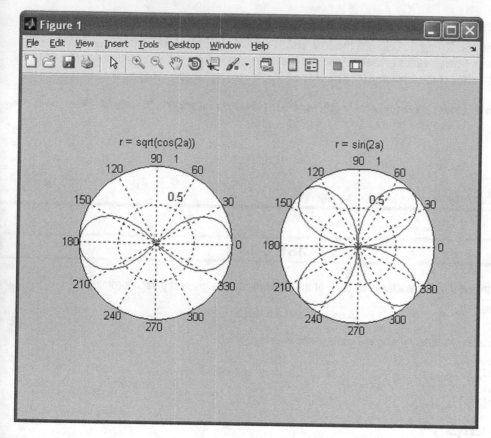

Figure 6-3.

Now, we calculate the arc lengths and the areas enclosed by both curves. The first curve repeats the structure for *a* between 0 and $\pi/4$ four times, and the second for *a* between 0 and $\pi/2$:

```
>> r = 'sqrt(cos(2*a))';
>> A = simple(diff(r,'a'))
```

A =

-1/cos(2*a) ^(1/2) * sin(2*a)

We calculate the area S1 enclosed by the first curve. The area under the curve in the first quadrant is:

```
>> I = simple(int('(sqrt(cos(2*a)))^2','a',0,pi/4))
```

I =

1/2

We have that $S1 = 4 * (1/2) * I = 1$ square units.

Now, we find the arc length $L1$ of the first curve:

```
>> integral = simple (sym ('sqrt ((sqrt (cos(2*a)) ^ 2 + (-1/cos(2*a) ^(1/2) * sin(2*a)) ^ 2))'))
```

integral =

1/cos(2*a)^(1/2)

```
>> I = numeric(int('1/cos(2*a)^(1/2)','a',0,pi/4))
```

I =

1.3110

Then, L1 = 4 * I = 4 * 1.3110 = 5.244 units.

Now, we find the area enclosed by the second curve:

```
>> r = 'sin(2*a)';
>> B = simple (diff (r))
```

B =

2 * cos(2*a)

```
>> I = simple (int ('sin(2*a) ^ 2', 'a', 0, pi/2))
```

I =

1/4 * pi

The area will be S2 = 4 * (1/2) * I = π /2 square units.

Lastly we find the arc length L2 of the second curve:

```
>> I = numeric(int('sqrt(sin(2*a)^2+(2*cos(2*a))^2)','a',0,pi/2))
```

I =

2.4221

We have that L2 = 4 * 2.4221 = 9.6884 units.

EXERCISE 6-15

Calculate the area enclosed by the curve $y = sin(x)$ and $y = cos(x)$ for x varying between 0 and 2π.

Figure 6-4 shows the graph of both curves on the same axis, so we can see the points of intersection and the region between the curves.

```
>> fplot ('[sin (x), cos (x)], [0, 2 * pi])
```

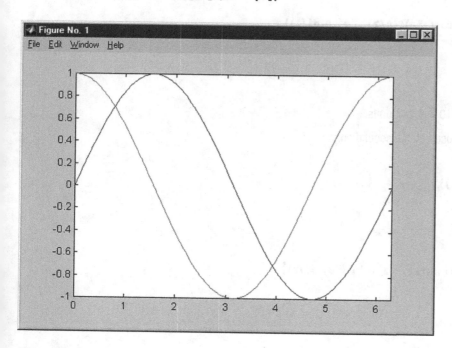

Figure 6-4.

We need to know the coordinates of the points of intersection of the two curves. To do this, we solve the system formed by their two defining equations. The command *solve* does not solve the problem. Therefore, since the graph indicates that there are solutions in the intervals (0,1) and (1,2π), we will use the command *maple('fsolve')* to find these solutions:

```
>> maple ('fsolve (sin (x) = cos (x), x, 0.. 1)')
```

ans =

.7853981633974483

```
>> maple ('fsolve (sin (x) = cos (x), x, 1.. 2 * pi)')
```

ans =

3.926990816987242

Now, we calculate the area between the two curves as follows:

```
>> S1=numeric(int('cos(x)-sin(x)','x',0,0.785398))
```

S1 =

0.4142

```
>> S2=numeric(int('cos(x)-sin(x)','x',0.785398,3.92699))
```

S2 =

-2.8284

```
>> S3=numeric(int('cos(x)-sin(x)','x',3.92699,2*pi))
```

S3 =

2.4142

We have $I = S1 + abs(S2) + S3 = 5.6569$ square units.

6.8 Surfaces of Revolution

The area of the surface generated by rotating the curve with equation $y = f(x)$ around the x-axis is given by the integral:

$$S = 2\pi \int_a^b f(x)\sqrt{1 + f'(x)^2}\, dx$$

where $x = a$ and $x = b$ are the x-coordinates of the end points of the revolving curve. If the curve is given in parametric coordinates $x = x(t)$ and $y = y(t)$ and the end points of the curve correspond to $t = t_0$ and $t = t_1$ then the rotational surface area is given by the integral:

$$S = 2\pi \int_{t_0}^{t_1} y(t)\sqrt{x'(t) + y'(x)^2}\, dt$$

The area of the surface generated by rotating the curve with equation $x = f(y)$ around the y axis is given by the integral:

$$S = 2\pi \int_a^b f(y)\sqrt{1 + f'(y)^2}\, dy$$

where $y = a$ and $y = b$ are the y-coordinates of the end points of the rotating curve.

14

EXERCISE 6-16

Calculate the area of the surface generated by rotating the cubic $y = 12x - 9x^2 + 2x^3$ around the OX axis, for x between 0 and 5/2.

The surface of revolution has equation $y^2 + z^2 = (12x - 9x^2 + 2x^3)^2$, and for the purposes of producing the graph shown in Figure 6-5, we can parameterize the surface as follows:

$$x = t, \; y = \cos(u)\left(12t - 9t^2 + 2t^3\right), \; z = \sin(u)(12t - 9t^2 + 2t^3)$$

```
>> t = (0:.1:5/2);
>> u = (0:.5:2*pi);
>> x = ones (size (u))'* t;
>> y = cos (u)'*(12*t-9*t.^2+2*t.^3);
>> z (u) = sin(u)'*(12*t-9*t.^2+2*t.^3);
>> surf (x, y, z)
```

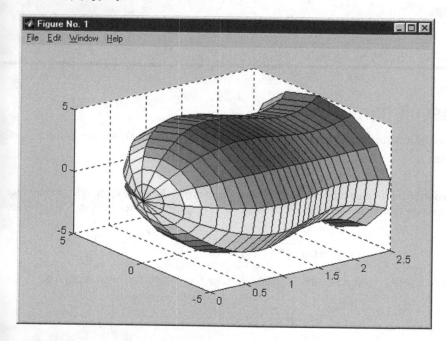

Figure 6-5.

Now we find the surface of revolution by integration:

```
>> I = numeric(int('(2*x^3-9*x^2+12*x)*sqrt(1+(6*x^2-18*x+12)^2)','x',0,5/2))
```

$I =$

0.8656

Thus the surface of revolution has area $2\pi(0.8656) = 1.7312\pi$ square units.

EXERCISE 6-17

Calculate the area of the surface of revolution given by rotating the parametric curve defined by $x(t) = t - \sin(t)$ and $y(t) = 1 - \cos(t)$ around the OX axis, for t between 0 and 2π.

```
>> x = 't - sin (t)';
>> y = '1 - cos (t)';
>> [diff(x),diff(y)]
```

ans =

[1-cos (t), sin (t)]

Now, we find the requested surface area by integration:

```
>> I = numeric(int('(1-cos(t))*sqrt(abs((1-cos(t))^2+sin(t)^2))','t',0,2*pi))
```

I =

10.6667

The area will be $2\pi(10.6667) = 21.3334\pi$ square units.

6.9 Volumes of Revolution

The volume generated by rotating the curve with equation $y = f(x)$ around the x-axis is given by the integral:

$$V = \pi \int_a^b f(x)^2\, dx$$

where $x = a$ and $x = b$ are the x-coordinates of the end points of the rotating curve.

The volume generated by rotating the curve with equation $x = f(y)$ around the y-axis is given by the integral:

$$V = \pi \int_a^b f(y)^2\, dy$$

where $y = a$ and $y = b$ are the y-coordinates of the end points of the rotating curve.

If one cuts a volume by planes parallel to one of the three coordinate planes (for example, the plane $z = 0$) and if the equation $S(z)$ of the curve given by the cross section is given in terms of the distance of the plane from the origin (in this case, z) then the volume is given by:

$$V = \int_{z_1}^{z_2} S(z)\, dz$$

EXERCISE 6-18

Calculate the volume generated by rotating the ellipse $\dfrac{x^2}{4}+\dfrac{y^2}{9}=1$ around the *OX* axis and around the *OY* axis.

We depict half of each of the generated surfaces of revolution next to each other in Figure 6-6. The final volume will therefore be twice that of the represented figure. The equation of the surface of revolution around the

OX axis is $y^2+z^2=9\left(1-\dfrac{x^2}{4}\right)$, which can be parameterized as follows:

$$x=t,\; y=3\cos(u)\left(1-\frac{t^2}{4}\right)^{\frac{1}{2}},\; z=3\sin(u)\left(1-\frac{t^2}{4}\right)^{\frac{1}{2}}$$

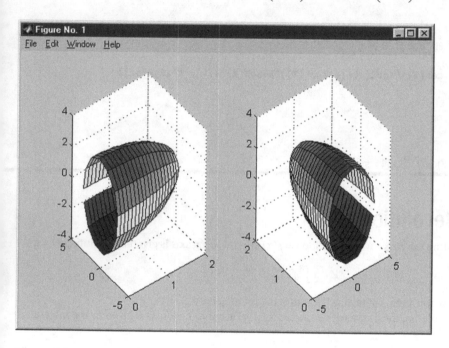

Figure 6-6.

The equation of the surface of revolution around the *OY* axis is $x^2+z^2=4\left(1-\dfrac{y^2}{9}\right)$, which can be parameterized as follows:

$$x=2\cos(u)\left(1-\frac{t^2}{9}\right)^{\frac{1}{2}},\; y=t,\; z=2\sin(u)\left(1-\frac{t^2}{9}\right)^{\frac{1}{2}}$$

```
>> t = (0:.1:2);
>> u = (0:.5:2*pi);
>> x = ones (size (u))'* t;
>> y = cos(u)'*3*(1-t.^2/4).^(1/2);
>> z = sin(u)'*3*(1-t.^2/4).^(1/2);
>> subplot(1,2,1)
>> surf(x,y,z)
```

```
>> subplot(1,2,2)
>> x = cos(u)'*2*(1-t.^2/9).^(1/2);
>> y = ones (size (u))'* t;
>> z = sin(u)'*2*(1-t.^2/9).^(1/2);
>> surf (x, y, z)
```

Now we calculate the generated volumes by integration:

```
>> V1 = int('pi*9*(1-x^2/4)','x',-2,2)
```

V1 =

24*pi

```
>> V2 = int('pi*4*(1-y^2/9)','y',-3,3)
```

V2 =

16*pi

EXERCISE 6-19

Calculate the volume generated by rotating the curve given in polar coordinates by $r = 1 + cos(a)$ about the OX axis.

The curve is given in polar coordinates, but there is no problem in calculating the values of $x(a)$ and $y(a)$ needed to implement the volume formula in cartesian coordinates. We have:

$x (a) = r (a) \cos (a) = (1 + \cos (a)) \cos (a)$

$y (a) = r (a) \sin (a) = (1 + \cos (a)) \sin (a)$

```
>> x ='(1 + cos (a)) * cos (a)';
   y ='(1 + cos (a)) * sin (a)';
>> A = simple(diff(x))
```

A =

-sin(2*a) - sin (a)

```
>> I = int ('((1 + cos (a)) * sin (a)) ^ 2 * (- sin(2*a) - sin (a))', 'a', 0, pi)
```

I =

-8/3

The required volume is $\pi \ (abs \ (I)) = 8\pi/3$ cubic units.

6.10 Curvilinear Integrals

Let $\bar{F}$ be a continuous vector field in R^3 and $c: [a, b] \to R^3$ be a continuous differentiable curve in R^3. We define $\int_c \bar{F} \cdot ds$, and call it the integral of $\bar{F}$ along the curve c, as follows:

$$\int_c \bar{F} \cdot ds = \int_a^b \bar{F}[c(t)] \cdot c'(t) \, dt$$

EXERCISE 6-20

Consider the curve $c(t) = [\sin(t), \cos(t), t]$ with $0 < t < 2\pi$, and the vector field $\bar{F}(x, y, z) = x\bar{i} + y\bar{j} + z\bar{k}$. Calculate $\int_c \bar{F} \cdot ds$.

derivC = [diff ('sin (t)'), diff('cos (t)'), diff ('t')]

derivC =

[cos (t),-sin(t), 1]

**>> pretty (int ('dotprod (vector ([sin (t), cos (t), t]), vector ([cos (t),-sin(t), 1]))
', ', 0, 2 * pi))**

```
        2
2 pi
```

EXERCISE 6-21

Consider the curve c defined by the parametric equations:

$$x = \cos^3(a), \; y = \sin^3(a), \; z = a, \; 0 < a < \frac{7\pi}{2}$$

Calculate $\int_c [\sin(z)dx + \cos(z)dy - \sqrt[3]{xy}dz]$.

derivC = [diff ('cos (a) ^ 3'), diff (' sin (a) ^ 3'), diff('a')]

derivC =

*[- 3 * cos (a) ^ 2 * sin (a) 3 * sin (a) ^ 2 * cos (a) 1]*

**>> pretty (sym (numeric (int ('dotprod (vector ([sin (a), cos (a) - sin (a) ^ 3 *
cos (a) ^ 3]), vector ([- 3 * cos (a) ^ 2 * sin (a), 3 * sin (a) ^ 2 * cos (a), 1]))
^(1/3)', 'a', 0, 7 * pi/2))))**

```
      1/2
5/2 + 3i
```

EXERCISE 6-22

Let the curve c be the circle of radius a: $x^2 + y^2 = a^2$. Calculate the value of $\int_c x^3 dy - y^3 dx$.

First, the circle can be parameterized ($x = a\cos(t)$, $y = a\sin(t)$) and we can then calculate the integral as follows:

```
>> pretty(int('a*cos(t)^3*diff(a*sin(t),t)-a*sin(t)^3*diff(a*cos(t),t)','t',0,2*pi))
```

$$\frac{3}{2}\ a\ pi^2$$

        2
  3/2 a pi

6.11 Approximate Numerical Integration

If it is not possible to solve an integral algebraically then MATLAB offers several techniques for numerical approximation, including such classical algorithms as the Newton-Cotes, Simpson, Chebyshev and trapezoidal methods. Opening the Maple *student* library (with the command *with(student)*), the available functions are the following (all must be preceded with the command *maple*):

> **evalf (int(expr,var=#..#) uses the Chebychev method (or if that fails, the Newton-Cotes method) to approximate the given integral**

> **readlib('evalf/int'): 'evalf/int'(expr,var=#..#) approximates the given integral using the Newton-Cotes method**

> **simpson(expr,var=a... b) evaluates the integral of the expression using Simpson's method with 4 equal size intervals**

> **simpson(expr,var=a..b, n) evaluates the integral of the expression using Simpson's method with n equal size intervals**

> **trapezoid(expr,var=a..b) evaluates the integral of the expression using the trapezoid method with 4 equal size intervals**

> **trapezoid(expr,var=a..b, n) evaluates the integral of the expression using the trapezoid method with n equal size intervals**

As an example, we calculate the integral of $x*Ln\ (x)$ between 1 and 3 using the Simpson and trapezoid methods with 4 equal intervals.

```
>> maple('with(student)');
>> maple('simpson(x^k*ln(x), x=1..3)')
```

uns =

1/6*3^k*log(3)+2/3*Sum((1/2+i)^k*log(1/2+i),i = 1 .. 2)+1/3*Sum((1+i)^k*log(1+i),i = 1 .. 1)

This expression can be written as:

$$\frac{1}{6}3^k \ln(3) + \frac{2}{3}\left(\sum_{i=1}^{2}\left(\frac{1}{2}+i\right)^k \ln\left(\frac{1}{2}+i\right)\right) + \frac{1}{3}\left(\sum_{i=1}^{1}(1+i)^k \ln(1+i)\right)$$

```
>> maple('trapezoid(x^k*ln(x), x = 1..3)')
```

```
ans =
```

```
1/2*Sum((1+1/2*i)^k*log(1+1/2*i),i = 1 .. 3)+1/4*3^k*log(3)
```

This expression can be written as:

$$\frac{1}{2}\left(\sum_{i=1}^{3}\left(1+\frac{1}{2}i\right)^k \ln\left(1+\frac{1}{2}i\right)\right) + \frac{1}{4}3^k \ln(3)$$

6.12 Improper Integrals

MATLAB works with improper integrals in the same way as it works with any other type of definite integral. We will not discuss theoretical issues concerning the convergence of improper integrals here, but within the class of improper integrals we will distinguish two types:

1. **Integrals with infinite limits**: the domain of definition of the integrand is a half-line $[(a,\infty)$ or $(-\infty, a)]$ or the entire line $(-\infty,\infty)$.

2. **Integrals of discontinuous functions**: the given function is continuous in an interval $[a, b]$ except at finitely many so-called isolated singularities.

Complicated combinations of these two cases may also occur. One can also generalize this to the more general setting of Stieltjes integrals, but to discuss this would require a course in mathematical analysis.

EXERCISE 6-23

Study and calculate the value of the following integrals:

$$\int_0^b \frac{dx}{\sqrt{x}},\ \int_0^{\pi/2} \tan(x)\,dx,\ \int_0^\infty \frac{e^{-x}\sin(x)}{x}dx,\ \int_0^\infty \frac{x^{3/2}}{1+x^2}dx.$$

The first of the integrals presents a singularity at $x = 0$, so there may be problems in a neighborhood of 0. We have:

```
>> pretty(sym(limit(int(1/sqrt(x),x,a,b),a,0)))
```

```
    1/2
  2 b
```

```
>> pretty(simple(sym(int(1/sqrt(x),x,0,b))))
```

```
    1/2
  2 b
```

Thus the first integral is convergent and has the value $2\sqrt{b}$.

The second integral presents a unique singularity at $x = \pi/2$, and is divergent because:

```
>> pretty(sym(limit(int(tan(x),x,0,pi/2-b),b,0)))
```

inf

The third integral is convergent, since it can be calculated as:

```
>> pretty(simple(sym(int(exp(-x)*sin(x)/x,x,0,inf))))
```

1/4 pi

The fourth integral is divergent, because:

```
>> pretty(sym(limit(int(x^(3/2)/(1+x^2),x,1,b),b,inf)))
```

NaN

6.13 Parameter Dependent Integrals

Consider the function of the variable y: $\int_a^b f(x,y)dx = F(y)$ defined in the interval $c \le y \le d$, where the function $f(x,y)$ is continuous in the rectangle $[a, b] \times [c, d]$ with continuous partial derivative with respect to y in the rectangle, then for all y such that $c \le y \le d$ we have:

$$\frac{d}{dy}\left[\int_a^b f(x,y)dx\right] = \int_a^b \frac{d}{dy}f(x,y)dx$$

This result is very important, because it allows us to differentiate an integral by differentiating under the integral sign.

Integrals dependent on a parameter can also be improper, and in addition the limits of integration may also depend on a parameter.

If the limits of integration depend on a parameter, we have the following:

$$\frac{d}{dy}\left[\int_{a(y)}^{b(y)} f(x,y)dx\right] = \int_{a(y)}^{b(y)} \frac{df(x,y)}{dy}dx + b'(y) \cdot f[b(y),y] - a'(y) \cdot f[a(y),y]$$

provided $a(y)$ and $b(y)$ are defined on the interval $[c, d]$ and have continuous derivatives $a'(y)$ and $b'(y)$, and the curves $a(y)$ and $b(y)$ are contained in the rectangle $[a, b] \times [c, d]$.

Also, if the function $\int_a^b f(x,y)dx = F(y)$ is defined on the interval $[c, d]$ and $f(x,y)$ is continuous in the rectangle $[a, b] \times [c, d]$, then the following holds:

$$\int_c^d \int_a^b f(x,y)dxdy = \int_a^b \int_c^d f(x,y)dydx$$

i.e. integration under the integral sign is valid, and the order in which the integrals are evaluated can be reversed without affecting the result.

EXERCISE 6-24

Solve the following integrals using a parameter $a > 0$:

$$\int_0^\infty \frac{\tan^{-1}(ax)}{x(1+x^2)}\,dx, \int_0^\infty \frac{1-e^{-x^2}}{x^2}\,dx.$$

For the first integral, we will start by integrating the derivative of the integrand with respect to the parameter a, which will be easier to integrate. Once this integral is found we integrate with respect to a to find the original integral.

```
>> maple('assume(a>0)');
>> pretty(simple(sym((int(diff(atan(a*x)/(x*(1+x^2)),a),x,0,inf)))))
```

```
    pi
 --------
 2 a + 2
```

Now we integrate this function with respect to the variable a, to find the original integral:

```
>> pretty(simple(sym(int(pi/(2*a+2),a))))
```

```
1/2 log(2 a + 2) pi
```

To solve the second integral, we consider the following, using a as a parameter:

$$f(a) = \int_0^\infty \frac{1-e^{-ax^2}}{x^2}\,dx$$

As in the first integral, we differentiate the integrand with respect to the parameter a, find the integral, and then integrate with respect to a. The desired integral is then given by setting $a = 1$.

```
>> Ia = simple (sym (int (diff ((1-exp(-a*x^2)) / x ^ 2, a), x, 0, inf)))
```

```
Ia =
```

```
1/2/a ^(1/2) * pi ^(1/2)
```

```
>> s = simple(sym(int(Ia,a)))
```

```
s =
```

```
a ^(1/2) * pi ^(1/2)
```

Putting $a = 1$, we obtain the value $\sqrt{\pi}$ for the original integral.

6.14 The Riemann Integral

The definite integral of a function $f(x)$ gives the total area between the graph of the function and the x-axis contained between the two limits of integration, where areas under the x-axis are regarded as negative.

Riemann defined this integral as a certain limit. Given a partition of the domain of the function into intervals one can define two associated values, the *upper sum* and the *lower sum*. The *upper sum* is the sum of the areas of the rectangles with bases the intervals of the partition and heights given by the maximum of the function in the interval. The *lower sum* is similarly defined except the height of the rectangle is determined by the minimum of the function in the interval. Thus there are infinitely many upper sums and infinitely many lower sums. One can define the upper integral to be the infimum of the upper sums and the lower integral to be the supremum of the lower sums. If these two values are equal, then the function is Riemann integrable and the common value is its integral.

By dividing the domain into a large number of intervals with small widths one can approximate the integral. This method can be used when the integrand cannot be integrated algebraically.

If the function $y = f(x)$ we have to integrate is positive and continuous on the interval of integration $[a, b]$, the upper and lower sums can be calculated with the following MATLAB expressions:

> **suminf = (b-a)/n *symsum(abs(subs(f,a + k*(b-a)/n)),k,0,n-1)**

> **sumsup = (b-a)/n*symsum(abs(subs(f,a + k*(b-a)/n)),k,1,n)**

If the function we have to integrate is negative in certain subsets of its domain, we take the modulus of the function for the purpose of computing the integral and finding areas. One can apply this directly to the function without having to determine the subintervals on which it is negative.

In addition, MATLAB implements the command *rsums* whose syntax is as follows:

> **rsums (f)**   **approximates the integral of f using Riemann sums and produces a graphical representation of rectangles**

Using the *maple* command, loading the *student* library into the memory, the following commands are available:

> **leftsum(expr,variable=a..b)**

> > **approximates the integral of *expr* with respect to the variable ranging between *a* and *b* by Riemann sums, taking 4 rectangles of equal base whose heights are given by the value of the function *expr* at the left end points of each base interval. The result is given in the form of sum which can be evaluated using the command *value* (exact symbolic evaluation), or *evalf* (numerical approximation).**

> **leftsum(expr,variable=a..b, n)**

> > **same as the above except with *n* rectangles**

> **rightsum(expr,var=a..b)**

> > **same as leftsum except the heights of the 4 rectangles are determined by the right end points of each base interval**

> **rightsum(expr,var=a..b, n)**

> > **same as the above except with *n* rectangles**

> **middlesum(expr,var=a..b)**

> > **same as leftsum except the heights of the 4 rectangles are determined by the midpoints of each base interval**

> **middlesum(expr,var=a..b, n)**

> > **same as the above except with *n* rectangles**

EXERCISE 6-25

Approximate the value of the following integrals:

$$\int_0^1 \cos(\sin(x))\,dx, \ \int_2^5 \sin(x^2)\,dx, \ \int_2^7 \frac{dx}{\ln(x)}, \ \int_1^5 \frac{\sin(x)}{x}\,dx.$$

To approximate the integrals, we partition the range of integration into n intervals, find the middlesum, and then find the limit of these sums as n tends to infinity:

```
>> maple('with(student)')
>> pretty(sym(maple('evalf(limit(middlesum(cos(sin(x)),x=0..1,n),n=infinity))')))
```

0.8687400396

```
> evalf(limit(middlesum(sin(x)^2,x=2..5,n),n=infinity));
```

1.446804

```
> evalf(limit(middlesum(1/log(x),x=2..7,n),n=infinity));
```

3.711887986

```
> evalf(limit(middlesum(sin(x)/x,x=1..5,n),n=infinity));
```

0.6038481746

Alternative methods can be used. For example, to approximate the first integral, we can calculate the limit as the number of rectangles n tends to infinity of both the upper and lower sums. If these two limits match, then the function is integrable and the common value is the integral.

```
>> maple ('f: = x - > cos (sin (x))');
>> numeric(maple('limit((1-0)/n*sum(abs(f(0+(1-0)*k/n)),k=1..n),n=infinity)'))
```

ans =

0.8687

```
>> numeric(maple('limit((1-0)/n*sum(abs(f(0+(1-0)*k/n)),k=0..n-1),n=infinity)'))
```

ans =

0.8687

If we calculate the integral directly, we see that the values coincide:

```
>> numeric (int ('cos (sin (x))', 'x', 0, 1))
```

ans =

0.8687

We can produce a graphical representation of the rectangles as follows (see Figure 6-7):

```
>> syms x, f = cos (sin (x))
>> rsums (f)
```

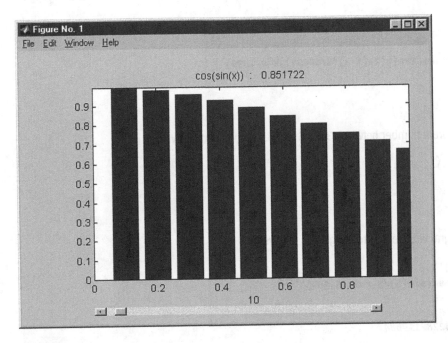

Figure 6-7.

We perform the same steps for the second integral:

```
>> maple ('g: = x - > sin (x) ^ 2');
>> numeric(maple('limit((5-2)/n*sum(g(2+(5-2)*k/n),k=0..n-1),n=infinity)'))
```

ans =
1.4468

```
>> numeric(maple('limit((5-2)/n*sum(g(2+(5-2)*k/n),k=1..n),n=infinity)'))
```

ans =
1.4468

Since the values coincide, this common value must be the integral. We confirm this:

```
>> numeric(int('sin(x)^2','x',2,5))
```

ans =
1.4468

To approximate the third integral we use 1,000 rectangles:

```
>> maple('h:=x->1/log(x)');
>> numeric('(7-2)/1000*sum(abs(h(2+(7-2)*k/1000)),k=1..1000)')
```

ans =
3.7096

```
>> numeric('(7-2)/1000*sum(abs(h(2+(7-2)*k/1000)),k=0..999)')
```

ans =
3.7142

The exact integral is therefore a number between 3.7096 and 3.7142, as shown by:

```
>> numeric(int('1/log(x)','x',2,7))
```

ans =
3.7119

To calculate the fourth integral we use 500 rectangles as follows:

```
>> maple('with(student)') ;
>> maple('evalf(middlesum(sin(x)/x,x=1..5,500))')
```

ans =
.6038471178876359136204 2282119684

This value matches that obtained by integrating directly using:

```
>> numeric(int('sin(x)/x','x',1,5))
```

ans =
0.6038

CHAPTER 7

■ ■ ■

Integration in Several Variables and Applications

In this chapter we will describe how to solve multivariate integrals with MATLAB, and give applications of double and triple integrals to calculate areas and volumes. We also give some other typical applications of multivariate integral calculus.

The relevant MATLAB functions have already been introduced in the previous chapter. They are the following:

> **syms x, int(f(x), x) or int('f(x)', 'x')**
>> **Computes the indefinite integral** $\int f(x)dx$

int (int ('f(x,y)', 'x'), 'y')
>> **Computes the double integral** $\int \int f(x,y)dxdy$

syms x and int (int (f(x,y), x), y)
>> **Computes the double integral** $\int \int f(x,y)dxdy$

int (int (int (... int ('f(x,y...z)', 'x'), 'y')...), 'z')
>> **Computes** $\int\int...\int f(x,y,...,z)dxdy...dz$.

syms x y z, int(int(int(...int(f(x,y...z), x), y)...), z)
>> **Computes** $\int\int...\int f(x,y,...,z)dxdy...dz$

syms x a b, int (f (x), x, a, b)
>> **Computes the definite integral** $\int_a^b f(x)dx$

int ('f (x)', 'x', 'a', 'b')
>> **Computes the definite integral** $\int_a^b f(x)dx$

int(int('f(x,y)', 'x', 'a', 'b'), 'y', 'c', 'd'))
>> **Computes the definite integral** $\int_a^b \int_c^d f(x,y)dxdy$

syms x y b c d, int (int (f(x,y), x, a, b), y, c, d)
>> **Computes the definite integral** $\int_a^b \int_c^d f(x,y)dxdy$

int(int(int(...int('f(x,y,...,z)', 'x', 'a', 'b'), 'y', 'c', 'd'),...), 'z', 'e', 'f')

Computes $\int_a^b \int_c^d ... \int_e^f f(x,y,...,z)\,dxdy...dz$

syms x y z a b c d e f, int (int (int (... int (f(x,y,...,z), x, a, b), y, c, d),...), z, e, f)

Computes $\int_a^b \int_c^d ... \int_e^f f(x,y,...,z)\,dxdy...dz$

In addition, with prior use of the command *maple*, the following commands can be used for integration:

int (f (x), x)

Computes the indefinite integral $\int f(x)dx$

int (f (x), x = a...b)

Computes the definite integral $\int_a^b f(x)dx$

int(f(x), x=a..b, continuous)

Computes the definite integral removing the check for continuity of the function in the interval (a, b)

int (int (f(x,y), x), y)

Computes the indefinite integral $\int \int f(x,y)dxdy$

int(int(int(...int(f(x,y,...,z), x), y),...), z)

Computes $\int \int ... \int f(x,y,...,z)\,dxdy...dz$

int (int (f(x,y), x = a..b, y = c...d))

Computes the definite integral $\int_a^b \int_c^d f(x,y)dxdy$

int (int (int (... int (f(x,y,...,z), x = a...b, y = c...d,..., z = e...f))))

Computes $\int_a^b \int_c^d ... \int_e^f f(x,y,...,z)\,dxdy...dz$

Commands for multivariate integration are also available in the *student* package, again requiring the prior use of the command *maple*. Their syntax is as follows:

Doubleint (expr, var1, var2, name)

Finds the inert double integral of the expression in the variables var1 and var2, where the domain of integration is specified by name

Doubleint (expr, var1=a1..b1, var2=a2..b2)

Finds the specified definite inert double integral

Tripleint (expr, var1, var2, var3, name)

Finds the specified indefinite inert triple integral

Tripleint (expr, var1=a1..b1, var2 = a2...b2, var3 = a3...b3)

Finds the specified inert definite triple integral

changevar (expr1=expr2,Fnc,var)

> Changes the variable in the expression *Fnc (Int, Limit, or Sum)*. The new variable is defined in terms of the old where *expr1* is an expression in the old variable (appearing in *Fnc*) and *expr2* is an expression in the new variable *var*. Used to change variables in integrals.

changevar ({eqn1,eqn2},Doubleint,[var1,var2])

> Change of variable in double integrals. The equations defining the new variables in terms of the old are in the form *expr1i = expr2i (i = 1, 2)*, where the *expr1i* are expressions in the old variables, and expr2i are expressions in the new variables *var1* and *var2*.

changevar ({eqn1,eqn2,eqn3},Tripleint,[var1,var2,var3])

> Change of variables for triple integrals

completesquare (expression)

> Completes the square with respect to all variables appearing in the specified polynomial expression

completesquare (expr, variable)

> Completes the square of the specified polynomial expression with respect to the given variable

integrand (expression)

> Extracts all integrands of an expression containing integrals *(Int, Doubleint, Tripleint)*

powsubs (expr1=expr2,expr)

> Replaces all occurrences of *expr1* in *expr* by *expr2* (*expr1* is a subexpression of *expr*)

powsubs ({eqn1,...,eqnn},expr) or subs([eqn1,...,eqnn],expr)

> Simultaneously performs the substitutions in expr described by the *n* equations *eqni* of the form *expr1i = expr2i, i = 1... n*

7.1 Areas and Double Integrals

If we consider an enclosure S, we can find its area through the use of double integrals. If the area S is determined by boundary curves whose equations are given in cartesian coordinates, its area A is given by the formula:

$$A = \iint_S dx\,dy$$

If, for example, S is determined by $a < x < b$ and $f(x) < y < g(x)$, the area will be:

$$A = \int_a^b dx \int_{f(x)}^{g(x)} dy$$

If S is determined by $h(a) < x < k(b)$ and $c < y < d$, the area will be:

$$A = \int_c^d dy \int_{h(a)}^{h(b)} dx$$

If the region S is determined by curves whose equations are given in polar coordinates with radius vector r and angle a, its area A is given by the formula:

$$A = \iint_S r\, da\, dr$$

If, for example, S is determined by $s < a < t$ and $f(a) < r < g(a)$ then

$$A = \int_s^t da \int_{f(a)}^{g(a)} r\, dr$$

EXERCISE 7-1

Calculate the area of the region above the *OX* axis bounded by the *OX* axis, the parabola $y^2 = 4x$ and the line $x + y = 3$.

First, we create a graphical representation of the problem, which is presented in Figure 7-1:

```
>> fplot ('[(4*x) ^(1/2), 3-x]', [0,4,0,4])
```

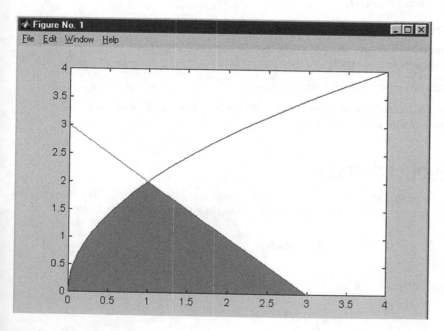

Figure 7-1.

We see that in the enclosed region y is limited between 0 and 2 $(0 < y < 2)$ and x is limited between the curves $x = (y\wedge 2)/4$ and $x = 3 - y$. We calculate the requested area as follows:

```
>> int(int('1','x','y^2/4','3-y'),'y',0,2)
```

ans =

10/3

EXERCISE 7-2

Calculate the area in the first quadrant bounded between the semicubical parabola $y^2 = x^3$ and the bisector of the first quadrant.

First, we graphically represent the problem (see Figure 7-2):

```
>> fplot ('[^(3/2) x, x]', [-4.5-1-4])
```

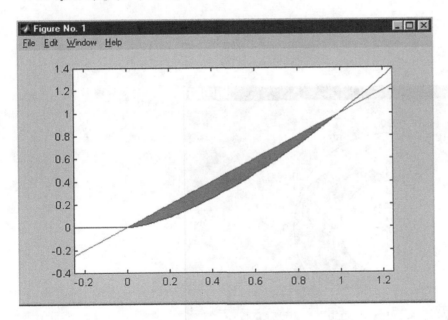

Figure 7-2.

Inspecting the graph we see that the enclosed area is defined for x ranging between 0 and 1 ($0 < x < 1$) and y ranging between the curves $y = x$ and $y = x \wedge (3/2)$. Therefore the area of the requested region can be calculated as:

```
>> int(int('1','y','x^(3/2)','x'),'x',0,1)
```

ans =

1/10

EXERCISE 7-3

Calculate the area outside the circle with polar equation $r = 2$, and inside the cardioid with polar equation $r = 2 (1 + cos (a))$.

First, we graphically represent the problem (see Figure 7-3):

```
>> a = 0:0. 1:2 * pi;
>> r = 2 * (1 + cos (a));
>> polar (a, r)
>> hold on;
>> r=2*ones(size(a));
>> polar (a, r)
```

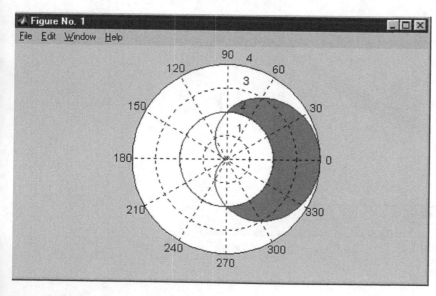

Figure 7-3.

Inspecting the graph, we see that, by symmetry, we can calculate half of the required area by varying a between 0 and $Pi/2$ ($0 < a < Pi/2$) and r between the curves $r = 2$ and $r = 2$ ($1 + cos$ (a)):

```
>> pretty(int(int('r','r',2,'2*(1+cos(a))'),'a',0,pi/2))
```

```
1/2 pi + 4
```

The required area is therefore $\pi + 8$ square units.

7.2 Surface Area by Double Integration

The surface area of a surface S defined by $z = f(x, y)$, where (x, y) ranges over a region R in the OXY plane, is given by:

$$S = \iint_R \sqrt{1 + \left(\frac{\partial z}{\partial x}\right)^2 + \left(\frac{\partial z}{\partial y}\right)^2}\, dx\, dy$$

The surface area of a surface S defined by $x = f(y, z)$, where (y, z) ranges over a region R in the OYZ plane, is given by:

$$S = \iint_R \sqrt{1 + \left(\frac{\partial x}{\partial y}\right)^2 + \left(\frac{\partial x}{\partial z}\right)^2}\, dy\, dz$$

The surface area of a surface S defined by $y = f(x, z)$, where (x, z) ranges over a region R in the OXZ plane, is given by:

$$S = \iint_R \sqrt{1 + \left(\frac{\partial y}{\partial x}\right)^2 + \left(\frac{\partial y}{\partial z}\right)^2}\, dx\, dz$$

EXERCISE 7-4

Calculate the area of the surface of the cone $x^2 + y^2 = z^2$, limited above the OXY plane and cut by the cylinder $x^2 + y^2 = b\,y$.

The projection of the surface onto the OXY plane is the disc bounded by the circle with equation $x^2 + y^2 = hy$ Then we can find the surface area via the first formula above as follows:

```
>> maple('z:=(x,y)->sqrt((x^2+y^2)/a)');
>> pretty(int(int('(1+diff(z(x,y),x)^2+diff(z(x,y),y)^2)^(1/2)','x','-(b*y-y^2)^(1/2)',
    '(b*y-y^2)^(1/2)'),'y',0,'b'))
               2            1/2
             b  pi (a + 1)
       1/4  -------------
                  1/2
                 a
```

EXERCISE 7-5

Calculate the area of the paraboloid $x^2 + y^2 = 2\,z$ limited below the plane $z = 2$.

```
>> maple('z:=(x,y)->(x^2+y^2)/2');
>> pretty(maple('(1+diff(z(x,y),x)^2+diff(z(x,y),y)^2)^(1/2)'))
```

$$(1 + x^2 + y^2)^{1/2}$$

This expression is suitable for a transformation to polar coordinates:

```
>> maple('m:=(x,y)->sqrt(1+x^2+y^2)');
>> pretty(simple('m(r*cos(a),r*sin(a))'))
```

$$(1 + r^2)^{1/2}$$

The requested integral is calculated as 4 times the integral delimited by the first quadrant of the circle $r = 2$:

```
>> pretty(simple(int(int('r*sqrt(1+r^2)','r',0,2),'a',0,pi/2)))
```

$$1/6\ (5\ 5^{1/2} - 1)\ pi$$

The result of the integral will be 4 times the previous value, i.e. $2\big(5\sqrt{5}-1\big)\pi/3$.

Figure 7-4 shows the graphical representation of the problem:

```
>> [x, y] = meshgrid(-3:.1:3);
>> z=(1/2)*(x.^2+y.^2);
>> mesh(x,y,z)
>> hold on;
>> z=2*ones(size(z));
>> mesh(x,y,z)
>> view(-10,10)
```

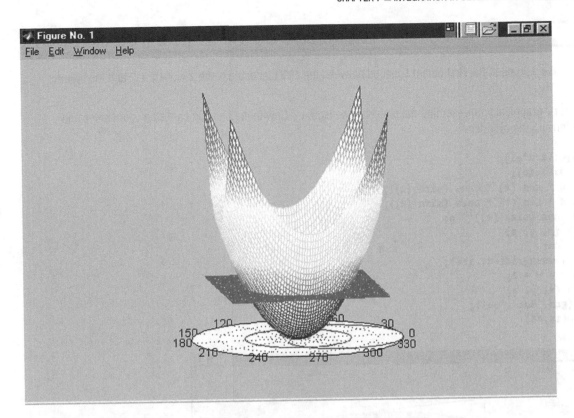

Figure 7-4.

7.3 Volume Calculation by Double Integrals

The volume V of a cylindroid limited in its upper part by the surface with equation $z = f(x, y)$, its lower part by the OXY plane and laterally by the straight cylindrical surface which cuts the OXY plane bordering a region R, is:

$$V = \iint_R f(x,y)\,dx\,dy = \iint_R z\,dx\,dy$$

The volume V of a cylindroid limited in its upper part by the surface with equation $x = f(y, z)$, its lower part by the OYZ plane and laterally by the straight cylindrical surface which cuts the OYZ plane bordering a region R, is:

$$V = \iint_R f(y,z)\,dy\,dz = \iint_R x\,dy\,dz$$

The volume V of a cylindroid limited in its upper part by the surface with equation $y = f(x, z)$, its lower part by the OXZ plane and laterally by the straight cylindrical surface which cuts the OXZ plane bordering a region R, is:

$$V = \iint_R f(x,z)\,dx\,dz = \iint_R y\,dx\,dz$$

EXERCISE 7-6

Calculate the volume in the first octant bounded between the *OXY* plane, the plane $z = x + y + 2$ and the cylinder $x^2 + y^2 = 16$.

We begin by graphically representing the problem (see Figure 7-5) with the plane in cartesian coordinates and parameterizing the cylinder:

```
>> t =(0:.1:2*pi);
>> u =(0:.1:10);
>> x = 4 * cos (t)'* ones (size (u));
>> y = 4 * sin (t)'* ones (size (u));
>> z = ones (size (t))'* u;
>> mesh (x, y, z)
>> hold on;
>> [x,y]=meshgrid(-4:.1:4);
>> z = x + y + 2;
>> mesh (x, y, z)
>> set(gca,'Box','on');
>> view(15,45)
```

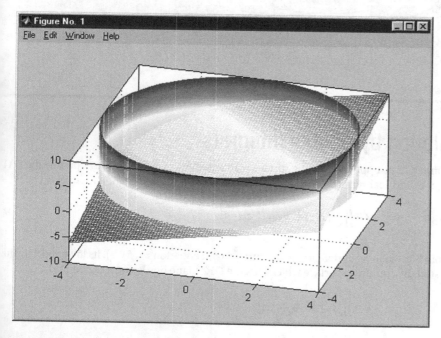

Figure 7-5.

The required volume is then given by the integral:

```
>> pretty(simple(int(int('x+y+2','y',0,'sqrt(16-x^2)'),'x',0,4)))
```

128/3 + 8 pi

EXERCISE 7-7

Calculate the volume bounded by the paraboloid $x^2 + 4y^2 = z$ and laterally by the cylinders with equations $y^2 = x$ and $x^2 = y$.

First, we graphically represent the problem (see Figure 7-6):

```
>> [x,y]=meshgrid(-1/2:.02:1/2,-1/4:.01:1/4);
>> z = x ^ 2 + 4 * y. ^ 2;
>> mesh(x,y,z)
>> hold on;
>> y=x.^2;
>> mesh(x,y,z)
>> hold on;
>> x=y.^2;
>> mesh(x,y,z)
>> set(gca,'Box','on')
>> view(-60,40)
```

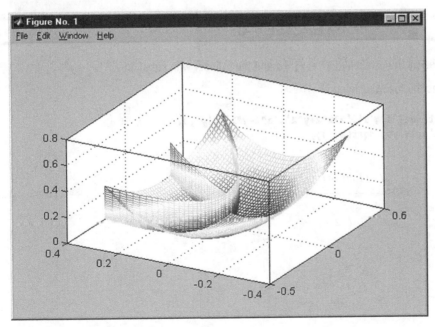

Figure 7-6.

The volume is calculated via the following integral:

```
>> pretty(int(int('x^2+4*y^2','y','x^2','sqrt(x)'),'x',0,1))
```

7.4 Volume Calculation and Triple Integrals

The volume of a three-dimensional region R whose boundary surface equations are expressed in cartesian coordinates is given by the triple integral:

$$\iiint_R dx\,dy\,dz$$

The volume of a three-dimensional region R whose boundary surface equations are expressed in cylindrical coordinates is given by the triple integral:

$$\iiint_R r\,dz\,dr\,da$$

The volume of a three-dimensional region R whose boundary surfaces equations are expressed in spherical coordinates is given by the triple integral:

$$\iiint_R r^2 \sin(b)\,dr\,db\,da$$

EXERCISE 7-8

Calculate the volume bounded by the paraboloid $x^2 + y^2 = z$ and the cylinder with equation $z = a^2 - y^2$.

The volume will be four times the following integral:

```
>> pretty(simple(int(int(int('1','z','a*x^2+y^2','a^2-y^2'),'y',0,
   'sqrt((a^2-a*x^2)/2)'),'x',0,'sqrt(a)')))
```

$$\frac{1}{8}\ \frac{a^4\ (\log(-a) - \log(a))}{(-2\ a)^{1/2}}$$

We can assume $a > 0$ and simplify the value of 4 times the previous integral as follows (note this gives the real part of the given expression):

```
>> pretty(simple(4*int(int(int('1','z','a*x^2+y^2','a^2-y^2'),'y',0,
   'sqrt((a^2-a*x^2)/2)'),'x',0,'sqrt(a)')))
```

$$\frac{1}{4} a^{7/2} \, 2^{1/2} \, pi$$

EXERCISE 7-9

Calculate the volume bounded by the cylinders $z = x^2$ and $4 - y^2 = z$.

First, we graphically represent the problem (see Figure 7-7):

```
>> [x, y] = meshgrid(-2:.1:2);
>> z = x ^ 2;
>> mesh(x,y,z)
>> hold on;
>> z = 4 - y. ^ 2;
>> mesh (x, y, z)
```

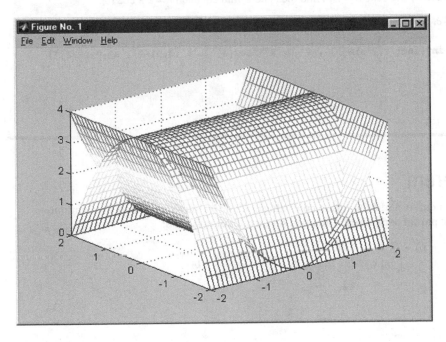

Figure 7-7.

17

The volume will be four times the following integral:

```
>> pretty(simple(int(int(int('1','z','x^2','4-y^2'),'y',0,'sqrt(4-x^2)'),'x',0,2)))
```

2 pi

The final result for the volme is therefore 8π.

EXERCISE 7-10

Calculate the volume enclosed by the cylinder $r = 4cos(a)$, the plane $z = 0$ and the sphere with equation $r^2 + z^2 = 16$.

The volume of the enclosure, given in cylindrical coordinates, is:

```
>> pretty(simple(int(int(int('r','z',0,'sqrt(16-r^2)'),'r',0,'4*cos(a)'),'a',0,pi)))
```

256/9 + 64/3 pi

EXERCISE 7-11

Calculate the volume enclosed by the cone $b = \pi/4$ and the sphere with equation $r = 2\ k\ cos\ (b)$.

The volume of the enclosure, given in spherical coordinates, will be four times the result of the following integral:

```
>> pretty(simple(int( int(int('r^2*sin(b)','r',0,'2*k*cos(b)'),'b',0,pi/4),'a',0,pi/2)))
```

```
       3
1/4  k  pi
```

The final result is therefore $k^3\pi$.

7.5 Green's Theorem

Let C be a simple closed planar curve, and R the region consisting of C and its interior. If f and g are continuous functions with continuous first partial derivatives in an open set D containing R, then:

$$\int_C m(x,y)\,dx + n(x,y)\,dy = \iint_R \left(\frac{\partial n}{\partial x} - \frac{\partial m}{\partial y}\right) dA$$

EXERCISE 7-12

Calculate the following integral using Green's theorem:

$$\int_C \left(x+e^{\sqrt{y}}\right)dx+(2y+\cos(x))dy$$

where C is the boundary of the region enclosed by the parabolas $y = x^2$, $x = y^2$.

The two parabolas intersect at the points (0,0) and (1,1). We graphically represent the problem (see Figure 7-8) and calculate the integral:

```
plot([x^2,sqrt(x)],x,0,1.2);
```

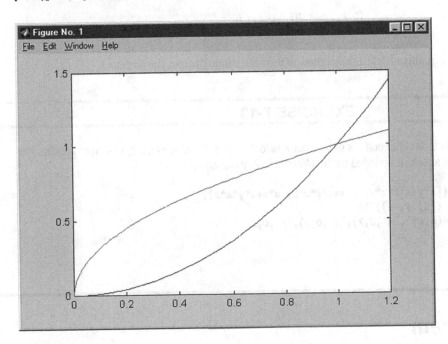

Figure 7-8.

```
>> maple ('m:=(x,y) - > x+exp (sqrt (y))');
>> maple ('n:=(x,y) - > 2 * y + cos (x)');
>> maple ('evalf (int (int (diff (n(x,y), x)-diff (m(x,y), y), y = x ^ 2.. sqrt (x)),
   x = 0.. 1))')
```

ans =

-.6764412004167925151253232665651204

The integral of the form can also be calculated as follows:

```
>> numeric(int(int('diff(n(x,y),x)-diff(m(x,y),y)','y','x^2','sqrt(x)'),'x',0,1))
```

ans =

-0.6764

7.6 The Divergence Theorem

Let Q be a domain with the property that each straight line passing through a point inside a domain cuts its border at exactly two points. In addition, suppose the boundary S of the domain Q is a closed oriented surface with exterior normal vector n. If f is a vector field that has continuous partial derivatives on Q, then:

$$\iint_S f \cdot n \, dS = \iiint_Q Div(f) \, dV$$

The left-hand side of this equality is called the outflow of the vector field f across the surface S.

EXERCISE 7-13

Use the divergence theorem to find the outflow of the vector field $f = (xy + x^2, yz + xy^2, z\,z, xz + xyz^2)$ across the surface of the cube in the first octant bounded by the planes $x = 2$, $y = 2$ and $z = 2$.

```
>> maple ('f: = vector([x*y+x^2*z*y, y*z+x*y^2*z, x*z+x*y*z^2])');
>> maple ('v: = vector ([x, y, z])');
>> int(int(int('diverge(f,v)','x',0,2),'y',0,2),'z',0,2)
```

ans =

72

7.7 Stokes' Theorem

Let S be an oriented surface of finite area defined by a function $f(x,y)$, having boundary C with unit normal n. Suppose is a continuous vector field defined on S such that the component functions of F have continuous partial derivatives at each non-boundary point of S. Then:

$$\int_C F \cdot dr = \iint_S (curl\,F) \cdot n \, ds$$

EXERCISE 7-14

Use Stokes' theorem to evaluate the line integral:

$$\int_C -y^3 dx + x^3 dy - z^3 dz$$

where C is the intersection of the cylinder $x^2 + y^2 = 1$ and the plane $x + y + z = 1$, and the orientation of C corresponds to counterclockwise rotation of the OXY plane.

The curve C bounds the surface S defined by $z = 1 - x - y = f(x,y)$ for (x, y) in the domain $D = \{(x,y) \mid x^2 + y^2 = 1\}$.

We put $F = -y^3 i + x^3 j - z^3 k$.

Now, we calculate the curl of F and integrate over the surface S:

```
>> maple ('F: = vector([-y^3,x^3,z^3])');
>> maple ('v: = vector ([x, y, z])');
>> pretty(sym(maple('curl(F,v)')))

          2     2
[0, 0, 3 x + 3 y]
```

Therefore, we have to calculate the integral $\int_D (3x^2 + 3y^2)\, dx\, dy$. Changing to polar coordinates, we obtain:

```
>> pretty(simple(int(int('3*r^3', 'a',0,2*pi),'r',0,1)))

3/2 pi
```

CHAPTER 8

■ ■ ■

Differential Equations

Although it implements only a relatively small number of commands related to this topic, MATLAB's treatment of differential equations is nevertheless very efficient. We shall see how we can use these commands to solve each type of differential equation algebraically. Numerical methods for the approximate solution of equations and systems of equations are also implemented.

The basic command used to solve differential equations is **dsolve**. This command finds symbolic solutions of ordinary differential equations and systems of ordinary differential equations. The equations are specified by symbolic expressions where the letter D is used to denote differentiation, or D2, D3, etc, to denote differentiation of order 2,3,..., etc. The letter preceded by D (or D2, etc) is the dependent variable (which is usually y), and any letter that is not preceded by D (or D2, etc) is a candidate for the independent variable. If the independent variable is not specified, it is taken to be x by default. If x is specified as the dependent variable, then the independent variable is t. That is, x is the independent variable by default, unless it is declared as the dependent variable, in which case the independent variable is understood to be t.

You can specify initial conditions using additional equations, which take the form $y(a) = b$ or $Dy(a) = b$,..., etc. If the initial conditions are not specified, the solutions of the differential equations will contain constants of integration C1, C2,..., etc. The most important MATLAB commands that solve differential equations are the following:

dsolve('equation', 'v')

> **Solves the given differential equation, where v is the independent variable (if 'v' is not specified, the independent variable is x by default). This returns only explicit solutions.**

dsolve('equation', 'condition_initial',..., 'v')

> **Solves the given differential equation subject to the specified initial condition**

dsolve('equation', 'cond1', 'cond2',..., 'condn', 'v')

> **Solves the given differential equation subject to the specified initial conditions**

dsolve('equation', 'cond1,cond2,...,condn', 'v')

> **Solves the given differential equation subject to the specified initial conditions**

dsolve('eq1', 'eq2',..., 'eqn', 'cond1', 'cond2',..., 'condn', 'v')

> **Solves the given differential system subject to the specified initial conditions (explicit)**

dsolve('eq1,eq2,...,eqn', 'cond1,cond2,...,condn' , 'v')

> **Solves the given differential system subject to the specified initial conditions**

There is another group of important MATLAB commands that solve differential equations, requiring the prior use of the command ***maple***. They are as follows:

dsolve (eqn, fnc (var))

> Symbolically solves the ordinary differential equation *eqn* for the function *fnc(var)*. The solution is usually returned in implicit form as an equation in *var*, *fnc (var)* and the implied constants $C\_1,..., C\_n$. *var* is an independent variable and *fnc* is the dependent variable. The result may also contain calls to the *DEsol* command.

dsolve (expr, fnc (var))

> Solves the differential equation *expr = 0*

dsolve({deqn,cond1,...,condn},fnc(var))

> Solves the differential equation *deqn* subject to the initial conditions *cond1,..., condn*

dsolve (deqn, fnc (var), explicit = true)

> Gives the solution in explicit form of the differential equation *deqn*, if possible

dsolve(deqn,fnc(var),method=laplace)

> Forces the use of the Laplace transform method in the solution of the differential equation

dsolve(deqn,fnc(var),type=series)

> Forces the use of the Taylor series method in the solution of the differential equation, with the degree of the polynomial solution determined by the global variable *Order*

dsolve(deqn,fnc(var),output=basis)

> The solution is given in terms of the specified basis

powseries[powsolve](deqn,cond1,...,condn)

> Solves the differential equation *deqn* subject to the initial conditions given in terms of power series

dsolve ({deqn1,..., deqnn}, {(var) fnc1... fncn (var)})

> Solves the specified system of differential equations for the independent variable *var* and the dependent variables *fnc1,..., fncn*

dsolve ({deqn1,..., deqnn, cond1,..., condm}, {(var) fnc1..)fncn (var)})

> Solves the specified system of differential equations for the independent variable *var* and the dependent variables *fnc1,..., fncn*, subject to the initial conditions *cond1,..., condm*

DEsol (deqn, fnc (var))

> Gives the solution of the differential equation *deqn* for the function *fnc(var)* in inert form

Examples are given below.

First, we solve differential equations of first order and first degree, both with and without initial values.

```
>> pretty(dsolve('Dy = a*y'))
```

exp(a t) C1

```
>> pretty(dsolve('Df = f + sin(t)'))
```

-1/2 cos (t) - 1/2 sin (t) + exp (t) C1

The previous two equations can also be solved in the following way:

```
>> pretty (sym (maple ('dsolve (diff (y (x), x) = a * y, y (x))')))
```

y (x) = exp(a x) _C1

```
>> pretty(sym(maple('dsolve(diff(f(t),t)=f+sin(t),f(t))')))
```

f(t) = - 1/2 cos(t) - 1/2 sin(t) + exp(t) _C1

```
>> pretty(dsolve('Dy = a*y', 'y(0) = b'))
```

exp(a t) b

```
>> pretty(dsolve('Df = f + sin(t)', 'f(pi/2) = 0'))
```

$$-1/2 \ cos \ (t) \ - \ 1/2 \ sin \ (t) \ + \ 1/2 \ - \ \frac{exp \ (t)}{exp(1/2 \ pi)}$$

Now, we solve an equation of second degree and first order:

```
>> y = dsolve ('(Dy) ^ 2 + y ^ 2 = 1', ' (0) = 0', 'y(s)')
```

y =

[sin (s)]
[-sin (s)]

We can also solve this in the following way:

```
>> pretty(maple('dsolve({diff(y(s),s)^2 + y(s)^2 = 1, y(0) = 0}, y(s))'))
```

y (s) = sin (s), y (s) = - sin (s)

Now we solve an equation of second order and first degree:

```
>> pretty (dsolve ('D2y = - a ^ 2 * y ', 'y (0) = 1, Dy (pi/a) = 0'))
```

cos (a t)

Next we solve a couple of systems, both with and without initial values:

```
>> pretty(dsolve('Dx = y', 'Dy = -x'))
```

x (t) = (t) C1 + C2 cos (t), y (t) = C1 cos (t) - C2 sin (t)

```
>> S=dsolve('Df = 3*f+4*g', 'Dg = -4*f+3*g');[S.f, S.g]
```

ans =

[exp(3*t)*cos(4*t)*C1+exp(3*t)*sin(4*t)*C2, -exp(3*t)*sin(4*t)*C1+ exp(3*t)*cos(4*t)*C2]

```
>> T= dsolve('Df = 3*f+4*g, Dg = -4*f+3*g', 'f(0)=0, g(0)=1') ;[T.f, T.g]
```

ans =

[exp(3*t)*sin(4*t), exp(3*t)*cos(4*t)]

This last system can also be solved in the following way:

```
>> pretty(maple('dsolve({diff(f(x),x)= 3*f(x)+4*g(x), diff(g(x),x)=- 4*f(x) + 3*g(x),
f(0)=0,g(0)=1}, {f(x),g(x)})'))
```

f (x) = exp (3 x) sin(4 x), g (x) = exp(3 x) cos(4 x)}

We now solve a differential equation by the Laplace transform method:

```
> dsolve ({diff (y (t), t$ 2) + 5 * diff (y (t), t) + 6 * y (t) = 0, y (y) (0) (0) = 0, D = 1},
(t), method = laplace);
```

(t) = - exp(-3 t) + exp(-2 t)

Next we solve a differential system in series form:

```
> dsolve({diff(y(x),x)=z(x)-y(x)-x,diff(z(x),x)=y(x),y(0)=0,z(0)=1},{y(x), z(x)}, type=series);
```

$$y(x) = x - x^2 + 1/2 \ x^3 - 5/24 \ x^4 + 1/15 \ x^5 + O(x^6),$$

$$z(x) = 1 + 1/2 \ x^2 - 1/3 \ x^3 + 1/8 \ x^4 - 1/24 \ x^5 + O(x^6)\}$$

8.1 Separation of Variables

differential equation is said to have separable variables if it can be written in the form $f(x) \ dx = g(y) \ dy$.

This type of equation can be solved immediately by putting $\int f(x) \ dx = \int g(y) \ dy + C$.

If MATLAB cannot directly solve a differential equation with the function *dsolve*, then we can try to express it the above form and solve the given integrals algebraically, which does not present particular difficulties for the rogram, given its versatility in symbolic computation.

EXERCISE 8-1

Solve the differential equation:

$$y\cos(x)\,dx - (1 + y^2)\,dy = 0, \quad y(0) = 1.$$

First of all we try to solve it directly. The equation can be written in the form:

$$y'(x) = \frac{\cos(x)y(x)}{1 + y(x)^2}.$$

```
>> dsolve('Dy = y * cos(x) /(1+y^2)')
```

ans =

$$exp(C33 + t*cos(x))*exp(-wrightOmega(2*C33 + 2*t*cos(x))/2)^0$$

Thus the differential equation appears not to be solvable with *dsolve*. However, in this case, the variables are separable, so we can solve the equation as follows:

```
>> pretty(solve('int(cos(x), x) = int((1+y^2) / y, y)'))
```

```
+-                        -+
|        /          2 \    |
|        |         y  |    |
|   asin| log(y) + -- |    |
|        \         2  /    |
|                          |
|        /          2 \  | |
|        |         y  |  | |
| pi - asin| log(y) + -- |  | |
|        \         2  /  | |
+-                        -+
```

Thus, after a little rearrangement, we see that the general solution is given by:

$$\sin(x) = \log(y) + 1/2\,y^2 + C.$$

We now find the value of the constant C via the initial condition, putting $x = 0$ and $y = 1$.

```
>> C = simple('solve(subs(x = 0, y = 1, sin(x) = log(y) + 1/2 * y ^ 2 + C), C)')
```

C =

-1/2

Thus the final solution is $\sin(x) = \log(y) + 1/2\,y^2 - \frac{1}{2}$.
In the same way you can solve any other differential equation with separable variables.
The above differential equation is also solvable directly by using:

```
>> pretty(maple('dsolve(diff(y(x), x) = y(x) * cos(x) /(1 + y(x) ^ 2), y(x))'))
```

$$log(y(x)) + 1/2\,y(x)^2 - sin(x) = \_C1$$

8.2 Homogeneous Differential Equations

Consider a general differential equation of first degree and first order of the form

$$M(x,y)\, dx = N(x,y)\, dy.$$

This equation is said to be homogeneous of degree n if the functions M and N satisfy:

$$M(tx, ty) = t^n\, M(x,y),$$

$$N(tx, ty) = t^n\, N(x,y).$$

For this type of equation, we can transform the initial differential equation (with variables x and y), via the change of variable $x = vy$, into another (separable) equation (with variables v and y). The new equation is solved by separation of variables and then the solution of the original equation is found by reversing the change of variable.

EXERCISE 8-2

Solve the differential equation:

$$(x^2 - y^2)\, dx + x\, y\, dy = 0.$$

First we check if the equation is homogeneous:

```
>> maple('m:=(x,y)->x^2-y^2');
>> maple('n:=(x,y)->x*y');
>> pretty(sym(maple('collect(m(t*x,t*y),t)')))
```

$$(x^2 - y^2)\, t^2$$

```
>> pretty(sym(maple('collect(n(t*x,t*y),t)')))
```

$$t^2\, y\, x$$

Thus the equation is homogeneous of degree 2. To solve it we apply the change of variable $x = vy$.

Before performing the change of variable, it is advisable to load the library *difforms*, using the command **maple('with(difforms)')**, which will allow you to work with differential forms. Once this library is loaded it is also convenient to use the command **maple('defform(v=0,x=0,y=0)')**, which allows you to declare all variables which will not be constants or parameters in the differentiation.

```
>> maple('with(difforms)');
>> maple('defform(v=0,x=0,y=0)');
```

Now we can make the change of variable $x = vy$, and group the terms in d(v) and d(y).

```
>> pretty(simple(sym(maple('subs(x=v*y,m(x,y)*d(x)+n(x,y)*d(y))'))))
```

$$(v^2\, y^2 - y^2)\, (y\, d(v) + v\, d(y)) + y^2\, v\, d(y)$$

```
>> pretty(sym(maple('collect(v^2*y^3*d(v)+v^3*y^2*d(y)-y^3*d(v),{d(v),d(y)}})')))
```

$$v^3 \ y^2 \ d(y) + (v^2 \ y^3 - y^3) \ d(v)$$

If we divide the previous expression by v^3y^3, and group the terms in $d(v)$ and $d(y)$, we already have an equation in separated variables.

```
>> pretty(sym(maple('collect(((v^2*y^3-y^3)*d(v)+v^3*y^2*d(y))/(v^3*y^3), {d(v),d(y)}})')))
```

$$\frac{(v^2 \ y^3 - y^3) \ d(v)}{v^3 \ y^3} + \frac{d(y)}{y}$$

The previous expression can be simplified.

```
>> pretty(maple('convert(collect(((v^2*y^3-y^3)*d(v)+v^3*y^2*d(y))/(v^3*y^3),
{d(v),d(y)}),parfrac,y)'))
```

$$\frac{(v^2 - 1) \ d(v)}{v^3} + \frac{d(y)}{y}$$

Now, we solve the equation:

```
>> pretty(simple(sym('int((v^2-1)/v^3,v)+int(1/y,y)')))
```

$$log(v) + \frac{1}{2 \ v^2} + log(y)$$

Finally we reverse the change of variable:

```
>> pretty(simple(sym('subs(v=x/y,log(v)+1/2/v^2+log(y))')))
```

$$log(x) + \frac{1}{2} \frac{y^2}{x^2}$$

Thus the general solution of the original differential equation is:

$$log(x) + \frac{1}{2} \frac{y^2}{x^2} = C.$$

Now we can represent the solutions of this differential equation graphically. To do this we graph the solutions with parameter C, which is equivalent to the following contour plot of the function defined by the left-hand side of the above general solution (see Figure 8-1):

```
>> [x,y]=meshgrid(0.1:0.05:1/2,-1:0.05:1);
>> z=y.^2./(2*x.^2)+log(x);
>> contour(z,65)
```

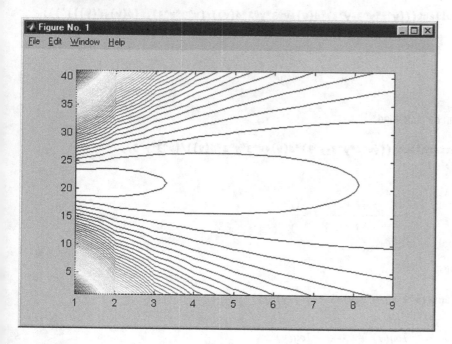

Figure 8-1.

3.3 Exact Differential Equations

he differential equation

$$M(x,y)\,dx + N(x,y)\,dy = 0$$

said to be exact if $\partial N/\partial x = \partial M/\partial y$. If the equation is exact, then there exists a function F such that its total differential F coincides with the left-hand side of the above equation, i.e.:

$$dF = M(x,y)\,dx + N(x,y)\,dy$$

herefore the family of solutions is given by $F(x,y) = C$.

The exercise below follows the usual steps of an algebraic solution to this type of equation.

EXERCISE 8-3

Solve the differential equation:

$$(-1 + y\, e^{xy} + y\cos(xy))\, dx + (1 + x\, e^{xy} + x\cos(xy))\, dy = 0.$$

First, we try to solve the equation with *dsolve*:

```
>> maple ('m:=(x,y) - > - 1 + y * exp(x*y) + y * cos(x*y)');
>> maple ('n:=(x,y) - > 1 + x * exp(x*y) + x * cos(x*y)');
>> dsolve ('m(x,y) + n(x,y) * Dy = 0')
```

ans =

[empty sym]

Thus the function *dsolve* does not give a solution to the proposed equation. We are going to try to solve the equation using the classical algebraic method.

First we check that the proposed differential equation is exact.

```
>> pretty(simple(diff('m(x,y)','y')))
```

(y exp(y x) - y sin(y x)) x + exp(y x) + cos(y x)

```
>> pretty(simple(diff('n(x,y)','x')))
```

(y exp(y x) - y sin(y x)) x + exp(y x) + cos(y x)

Since the equation is exact, we can find the solution in the following way:

```
>> solution1 = maple ('simplify (int (m(x,y), x) + g (y))')
```

solution1 =

*-x + exp(y*x) + sin(y*x) + g (y)*

Now we find the function *g(y)* via the following condition:

$$\text{diff(int(}m(x,y), x) + g(y), y) = n(x,y).$$

```
>> pretty(sym(maple('simplify(int(m(x,y),x)+g(y))')))
```

-x + exp(y x) + sin(y x) + g (y)

```
>> pretty (sym (maple ('simplify (diff (-x+exp(y*x) + sin(y*x) + g (y), y)'))))
```

$$exp(y\ x)\ x + x\ cos(y\ x) + \frac{d}{dy}\ g\ (y)$$

```
>> pretty (simple (sym ('solve (x * exp(y*x) + x * cos(y*x) + diff (g (y), y) = n(x,y),))))
((((diff (g (y), y))')))
```

ans = 1

Thus $g'(y) = 1$, so the final solution will be, omitting the addition of a constant:

```
>> pretty (simple (sym (maple ('subs (g (y) = int(1,y),-x+exp(y*x) + sin(y*x) + g (y))'))))
```

$-x + exp(y\ x) + sin(y\ x) + y$

To graphically represent the family of solutions, we draw the following contour plot of the above expression (Figure 8-2):

```
>> [x,y]=meshgrid(-2*pi/3:.2:2*pi/3);
>> z =-x+exp (y.*x) + free (y.*x) + y;
>> contour(z,100)
```

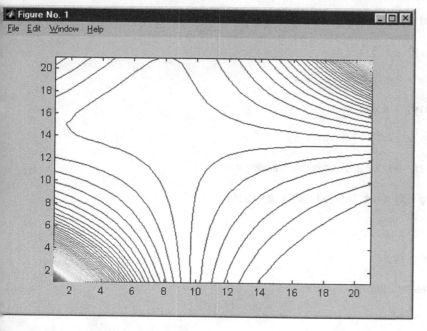

Figure 8-2.

In the following section we will see how any reducible differential equation can be transformed to an exact equation using an **integrating factor**.

8.4 Linear Differential Equations

A linear first order differential equation is an equation of the form:

$$dy/dx + P(x)y = Q(x)$$

where $P(x)$ and $Q(x)$ are given functions of x.

Differential equations of this type can be transformed into exact equations by multiplying both sides of the equation by the integrating factor:

$$e^{\int P(x)dx}$$

and the general solution is then given by the expression:

$$\left(e^{-\int P(x)dx} \right)\left(\int e^{\int P(x)dx} Q(x)dx \right).$$

MATLAB implements these solutions of linear differential equations, and offers them whenever the integral appearing in the integrating factor can be found.

EXERCISE 8-4

Solve the differential equation:

$$x \, dy/dx + 3 \, y = x \sin(x).$$

```
>> pretty (simple (dsolve ('x * Dy + 3 * y = x * sin (x)')))
```

```
1/3 x sin(x) + exp(-3 t/x) C1
```

Another more efficient solution of the differential equation that includes implicit solutions is as follows:

```
>> pretty(sym(maple('simplify(dsolve(x*diff(y(x),x)+3*y(x)=x*sin(x),y(x)))')))
```

```
          3            2
         x  cos(x) - 3 x  sin(x) + 6 sin(x) - 6 x cos(x) - _C1
y(x) = - ----------------------------------------------------
                                3
                               x
```

8.5 Ordinary High-Order Equations

An **ordinary linear differential equation of order** n has the following general form:

$$\sum_{k=0}^{n} a_k(x)y^{(k)}(x) = a_0(x)y(x) + a_1(x)y'(x) + a_2(x)y''(x) + \ldots + a_n(x)y^{(n)}(x)$$

$$= f(x).$$

If the function $f(x)$ is identically zero, the equation is called **homogeneous**. Otherwise, the equation is called **non-homogeneous**. If the functions $a_i(x)$ ($i = 1, \ldots, n$) are constant, the equation is said to have **constant coefficients**.

A concept of great importance in this context is that of a set of **linearly independent functions**. A set of functions $\{f_1(x), f_2(x), ..., f_n(x)\}$ is linearly independent if, for any x in their common domain of definition, the Wronskian determinant of the functions is non-zero. The **Wronskian determinant** of the given set of functions, at a point x of their common domain of definition, is defined as follows:

$$\begin{vmatrix} f_1(x) & f_2(x) & f_3(x) & \cdots & f_n(x) \\ f_1'(x) & f_2'(x) & f_3'(x) & \cdots & f_n'(x) \\ f_1''(x) & f_2''(x) & f_3''(x) & \cdots & f_n''(x) \\ \cdots & \cdots & \cdots & \cdots & \cdots \\ f_1^{(n-1)}(x) & f_2^{(n-1)}(x) & f_3^{(n-1)}(x) & \cdots & f_n^{(n-1)}(x) \end{vmatrix} = W(x)$$

The MATLAB command *maple('Wronskian')* allows you to calculate the Wronskian matrix of a set of functions. Its syntax is:

> **maple ('Wronskian(V,variable)')**
>
> > computes the Wronskian matrix corresponding to the vector of functions V with independent variable x.

A set $S = \{f_1(x), ..., f_n(x)\}$ of linearly independent non-trivial solutions of a homogeneous linear equation of order n

$$a_0(x)y(x) + a_1(x)y'(x) + a_2(x)y''(x) + ... + a_n(x)y^{(n)}(x) = 0$$

is called a set of **fundamental solutions of the equation**.

If the functions $a_i(x)$ $(i = 1, ..., n)$ are continuous in an open interval I, then the homogeneous equation has a set of fundamental solutions $S = \{f_i(x)\}$ in I.

In addition, the general solution of the homogeneous equation will then be given by the function:

$$f(x) = \sum_{i=0}^{n} c_i f_i(x)$$

where $\{c_i\}$ is a set of arbitrary constants.

The equation:

$$a_0 + a_1 m + a_2 m^2 + ... + a_n m^n = \sum_{i=0}^{n} a_i m^i = 0$$

is called the **characteristic equation** of the homogeneous differential equation with constant coefficients. The solutions of this characteristic equation determine the general solutions of the corresponding differential equation.

EXERCISE 8-5

Show that the set of functions

$$\{e^x, xe^x, x^2e^x\}$$

is linearly independent.

```
>> W=sym(maple('Wronskian(vector([exp(x),x*exp(x), x^2*exp(x)]),x)'))
```

```
W =
[exp(x),              x*exp(x),                         x^2*exp(x)]
[exp(x),    exp(x)+x*exp(x),          2*x*exp(x)+x^2*exp(x)]
[exp(x), 2*exp(x)+x*exp(x), 2*exp(x)+4*x*exp(x)+x^2*exp(x)]
```

```
>> pretty(determ(W))
```

```
      3
2 exp(x)
```

This gives us the value of the Wronskian, which is obviously always non-zero. Therefore the set of functions is linearly independent.

8.6 Higher-Order Linear Homogeneous Equations with Constant Coefficients

The homogeneous linear differential equation of order n

$$\sum_{k=0}^{n} a_k(x)y^{(k)}(x) = a_0(x)y(x) + a_1(x)y'(x) + a_2(x)y''(x) + \cdots + a_n(x)y^{(n)}(x)$$
$$= 0$$

is said to have **constant coefficients** if the functions $a_i(x)$ $(i = 1, ..., n)$ are all constant (i.e. they do not depend on the variable x).

The equation:

$$a_0 + a_1m + a_2m^2 + \cdots + a_nm^n = \sum_{i=0}^{n} a_im^i = 0$$

is called the **characteristic equation** of the above differential equation. The solutions $(m_1, m_2, ..., m_n)$ of this characteristic equation determine the general solution of the associated differential equation.

If the m_i $(i = 1, ..., n)$ are all different, the general solution of the homogeneous equation with constant coefficients is:

$$y(x) = c_1e^{m_1x} + c_2e^{m_2x} + \cdots + c_ne^{m_nx}$$

where $c_1, c_2, ..., c_n$ are arbitrary constants.

If some m_i is a root of multiplicity k of the characteristic equation, then it determines the following k terms of the solution:

$$c_ie^{m_ix} + c_{i+1}xe^{m_ix} + c_{i+2}x^2e^{m_ix} + \cdots + c_{i+k}x^ke^{m_ix} .$$

If the characteristic equation has a complex root $m_j = a + bi$, then its complex conjugate $m_{j+1} = a - bi$ is also a root. These two roots determine a pair of terms in the general solution of the homogeneous equation:

$$c_j e^{ax} \cos(bx) + c_{j+1} e^{ax} \sin(bx).$$

MATLAB directly applies this method to obtain the solutions of homogeneous linear equations with constant coefficients, using the command *dsolve* or *maple('dsolve')*.

EXERCISE 8-6

Solve the following equations:

$$3y'' + 2y' + 5y = 0$$

$$2y'' + 5y' + 5y = 0, \; y(0) = 0, \; y'(0) = \tfrac{1}{2}$$

```
>> pretty(dsolve('3*D2y+2*Dy-5*y=0'))
```

$$C1 \; exp(t) + C2 \; exp(-5/3 \; t)$$

```
>> pretty(dsolve('2*D2y+5*Dy+5*y=0','y(0)=0,Dy(0)=1/2'))
```

```
      1/2  1/2                        1/2  1/2
   2/15 3    5    exp(- 5/4 t) sin(1/4 3    5    t)
```

EXERCISE 8-7

Solve the differential equation

$$9y'''' - 6y''' + 46y'' - 6y' + 37y = 0.$$

```
>> pretty (simple (dsolve('9*D4y-6*D3y+46*D2y-6*Dy+37*y=0')))
```

```
                                          / t \                      / t \
   C46 cos(t) + C47 sin(t) + C44 cos(2 t) exp| - | + C45 sin(2 t) exp| - |
                                          \ 3 /                      \ 3 /
```

Looking at the solution, it is evident that the characteristic equation has two pairs of complex conjugate solutions.

```
>> solve('9*x^4-6*x^3+46*x^2-6*x+37=0')
```

ans =

```
[        i]
[       -i]
[1/3 + 2 * i]
[1/3-2 * i]
```

You can also solve the equation as follows:

```
>> pretty (sym (maple ('dsolve (9 * diff (y (x), x$ 4) - 6 * diff (y (x), x$ 3) + 46 * diff
(y (x), x$ 2)-6 * diff (y (x), x) + 37 * y (x) = 0 y (x))')))
```

y (x) =

_C1 exp(1/3 x) sin(2 x) + _C2 exp(1/3 x) cos(2 x) + _C3 sin (x) + _C4 cos (x)

8.7 Non-Homogeneous Equations with Constant Coefficients. Variation of Parameters

Consider the non-homogeneous linear equation with constant coefficients:

$$\sum_{k=0}^{n} a_k(x) y^{(k)}(x) = a_0(x)y(x) + a_1(x)y'(x) + a_2(x)y''(x) + \cdots + a_n(x)y^{(n)}(x)$$

$$= f(x).$$

Suppose $\{y_1(x), y_2(x),\ldots, y_n(x)\}$ is a linearly independent set of solutions of the corresponding homogeneous equation:

$$a_0(x)y(x) + a_1(x)y'(x) + a_2(x)y''(x) + \cdots + a_n(x)y^{(n)}(x) = 0.$$

A **particular solution of the non-homogeneous equation** is given by:

$$y_p(x) = \sum_{i=1}^{n} u_i(x)y_i(x)$$

where the functions $u_i(x)$ are obtained as follows:

$$u_i(x) = \int \frac{f(x)W_i[y_1(x), y_2(x),\ldots,y_n(x)]}{W[y_1(x), y_2(x),\ldots,y_n(x)]} dx \quad (i=1,\ldots,n).$$

Here $W_i[y_1(x), y_2(x), \ldots, y_n(x)]$ is the determinant of the matrix obtained by replacing the i-th column of the Wronskian matrix $W[y_1(x), y_2(x), \ldots, y_n(x)]$ by the transpose of the vector $(0,0,\ldots, 0, 1)$.

The solution of the non-homogeneous equation is then given by combining the general solution of the homogeneous equation with the particular solution of the non-homogeneous equation. If the roots m_i of the characteristic equation of the homogeneous equation are all different, the general solution of the non-homogeneous equation is:

$$y(x) = c_1 e^{m_1 x} + c_2 e^{m_2 x} + \cdots + c_n e^{m_n x} + y_p(x).$$

If some of the roots are repeated, we refer to the general form of the solution of a homogeneous equation discussed earlier.

EXERCISE 8-8

Solve the following differential equations:

$$y'' + 4y' + 13y = x\cos^2(3x),$$

$$y'' - 2y' + y = e^x \ln(x).$$

We will follow the algebraic method of variation of parameters to solve the first equation. We first consider the characteristic equation of the homogeneous equation to obtain a set of linearly independent solutions.

```
>> solve('m^2+4*m+13=0')
```

ans =

```
[- 2 + 3 * i]
[- 2 - 3 * i]
```

```
>> maple ('f: = x - > x * cos(3*x) ^ 2');
>> maple ('y1: = x - > exp(-2*x) * cos(3*x)');
>> maple ('y2: = x - > exp(-2*x) * sin(3*x)');
>> maple ('W: = x - > Wronskian ([y1 (x), y2 (x)], x)');
>> pretty(simple(sym(maple('det(W(x))'))))
```

3 exp(-4 x)

We see that the Wronskian is non-zero, indicating that the functions are linearly independent. Now we calculate the functions $W_i(x)$, $i = 1, 2$.

```
>> maple ('W1: x-= > array ([[0, y2 (x)], [1, diff ((y2) (x), x)]])');
>> pretty(simple(sym(maple('det(W1(x))'))))
```

-exp(-2 x) sin (3 x)

```
>> maple ('W2: x-= > array ([[y1 (x), 0], [diff ((y1) (x), x), 1]])');
>> pretty(simple(sym(maple('det(W2(x))'))))
```

exp(-2 x) cos(3 x)

Now we calculate the particular solution of the non-homogeneous equation.

```
>> maple('u1:=x->factor(simplify(int(f(x)*det(W1(x))/det(W(x)),x)))');
>> maple ('u1 (x)')
```

ans =

1/14652300*exp(2*x)*(129285*cos(9*x)*x-6084*cos(9*x)-28730*sin(9*x)*x-
13013*sin(9*x)+281775*cos(3*x)*x-86700*cos(3*x)-187850*sin(3*x)*x-36125*sin(3*x))

```
>> maple('u2:=x->factor(simplify(int(f(x)*det(W2(x))/det(W(x)),x)))');
>> maple ('u2 (x)')
```

ans =

*1/14652300 * exp(2*x) * (563550 * cos(3*x) * x+108375 * cos(3*x) + 845325 * sin(3*x) * x-260100 * sin(3*x) + 28730 * cos(9*x) * x+13013 * cos(9*x) + 129285 * sin(9*x) * x-6084 * sin(9*x))*

```
>> maple ('yp: = x - > factor (simplify (y1 (x) * (x) u1 + y2 (x) * u2 (x)))');
>> maple('yp(x)')
```

ans =

-23/1105 * x * cos(3*x) ^ 2 + 13436/1221025 * cos(3*x) ^ 2 + 24/1105 * cos(3*x) * sin(3*x) * x + 3852/1221025 * cos(3*x) * sin(3*x) + 54/1105 * x-21168/1221025

Then we can write the general solution of the non-homogeneous equation:

```
>> maple (' y: = x - > simplify (c1 * y1 (x) + c2 * y2 (x) + yp (x))');
>> maple ('combine (y (x), trig)')
```

ans =

C1 * exp(-2*x) * cos(3*x) + c2 * exp(-2*x) * sin(3*x)-23/2210 * x * cos(6*x) + 1/26 * x + 6718/1221025 * cos(6*x)-2/169 + 12/1105 * x * sin(6*x) + 1926/1221025 * sin(6*x)

Now we graphically represent a set of solutions, for certain values of c1 and c2 (see Figure 8-3)

```
>> ezplot(simple(sym(maple('subs(c1=-5,c2=4,y(x))'))),[-1,1])
>> hold on
>> ezplot(simple(sym(maple('subs(c1=-5,c2=-4,y(x))'))),[-1,1])
>> ezplot(simple(sym(maple('subs(c1=-5,c2=-2,y(x))'))),[-1,1])
>> ezplot(simple(sym(maple('subs(c1=-5,c2=2,y(x))'))),[-1,1])
>> ezplot(simple(sym(maple('subs(c1=-5,c2=1,y(x))'))),[-1,1])
>> ezplot(simple(sym(maple('subs(c1=-5,c2=-1,y(x))'))),[-1,1])
>> ezplot(simple(sym(maple('subs(c1=5,c2=-1,y(x))'))),[-1,1])
>> ezplot(simple(sym(maple('subs(c1=5,c2=1,y(x))'))),[-1,1])
>> ezplot(simple(sym(maple('subs(c1=5,c2=2,y(x))'))),[-1,1])
>> ezplot(simple(sym(maple('subs(c1=5,c2=-2,y(x))'))),[-1,1])
>> ezplot(simple(sym(maple('subs(c1=5,c2=4,y(x))'))),[-1,1])
>> ezplot(simple(sym(maple('subs(c1=5,c2=-4,y(x))'))),[-1,1])
```

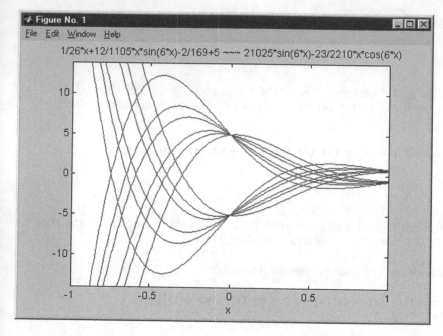

Figure 8-3.

There is a MATLAB command that allows you to solve differential equations by the method of variation of parameters directly. Its syntax is as follows:

maple ('DEtools [varparam]([expr1,...,exprn], exprrhs, varind)')

> Finds the general solution by the method of variation of parameters of an ordinary differential equation in the independent variable *varind*, where *exprrhs* is the right-hand side of the original equation (non-homogeneous part) and the *expri (i = 1... n)* are the solutions of the corresponding homogeneous equation of order *n*. The command value can help to obtain the final solution.

For the second differential equation we directly apply *dsolve*, obtaining the solution. First, we find the general solution of the homogeneous equation:

```
>> maple ('solhomog: = dsolve (diff (y (x), x$ 2) - 2 * diff (y (x), x) + y (x) = 0 y (x))')
```

ans =

*solhomog: = y(x) = _C1 * exp (x) + _C2 * exp (x) * x*

As the differential equation is of order 2 we must take two solutions (for two pairs of any values of C1 and C2). The simplest solutions that can be taken are those which form a basis for the set of solutions (*exp (x)* and *x exp (x)*), which can be found directly as follows:

```
>> maple('solhomog:=dsolve(diff(y(x),x$2)-2*diff(y(x),x)+y(x)=0,y(x),output=basis)')
```

ans =

*solhomog := [exp(x), exp(x)*x]*

As the inhomogeneous part of the right-hand side of the equation is $e^x \ln(x)$, and the independent variable is x, we can already apply the command *varparam* as follows:

```
>> pretty(sym(maple('DEtools[varparam](solhomog,exp(x)*ln(x),x)')))
```

$$\_C[1]\ exp(x) + \_C[2]\ exp(x)\ x + (-\ 1/2\ x^2\ log(x) + 1/4\ x^2)\ exp(x)$$

$$+ (x\ log(x) - x)\ exp(x)\ x$$

The second differential equation is solved directly as follows:

```
>> pretty(simple(dsolve('D2y-2*Dy+y=exp(t)*log(t)')))
```

$$1/4\ exp(t)\ (2\ t^2\ log(t) - 3\ t^2 + 4\ C1 + 4\ C2\ t)$$

8.8 Non-Homogeneous Linear Equations with Variable Coefficients. Cauchy-Euler Equations

A non-homogeneous linear equation with variable coefficients of the form

$$\sum_{k=0}^{n} a_k x^k y^{(k)}(x) = a_0 y(x) + a_1 xy'(x) + a_2 x^2 y''(x) + \ldots + a_n x^n y^{(n)}(x)$$
$$= f(x)$$

is called a **Cauchy–Euler equation**.

This equation can be reduced to a homogeneous linear equation with constant coefficients by replacing $x = e^t$.

This leads us to solve the equation:

$$a_0 + a_1 k + a_2 k(k-1) + \cdots + a_n k(k-1)\cdots(k-n+1) = 0$$

The roots k_i of multiplicity α_i correspond to the solutions:

$$x^{k_i},\ x^{k_i} \ln x,\ x^{k_i} \ln^2 x, \ldots, x^{k_i} \ln^{\alpha_i-1} x$$

The complex roots $p \pm qi$ of multiplicity α correspond to the solutions:

$$x^p \cos(q \ln x), x^p \ln x \cos(q \ln x), \ldots, x^p (\ln x)^{\alpha-1} \cos(q \ln x).$$

$$x^p \sin(q \ln x), x^p \ln x \sin(q \ln x), \ldots, x^p (\ln x)^{\alpha-1} \sin(q \ln x).$$

MATLAB solves this type of equation directly with the command *dsolve* or *maple('dsolve')*.

EXERCISE 8-9

Solve the following differential equation:

$$x^3 y''' + 16x^2 y'' + 79xy' + 125y = 0.$$

```
>> pretty(simple(dsolve('x^3*D3y+16*x^2*D2y+79*x*Dy+125*y=0')))
```

$$
\frac{C1 + C2 \; sin(3 \; log(x)) \; x + C3 \; cos(3 \; log(x)) \; x}{x^5}
$$

8.9 The Laplace Transform

Suppose $f(t)$ is a function defined in the interval $(0, \infty)$. The **Laplace transform** of $f(t)$ is the function $F(s)$ defined by:

$$F(s) = L\{f(t)\}(s) = \int_0^\infty e^{-st} f(t)\,dt.$$

We say that $f(t)$ is the inverse Laplace transform of $F(s)$, so that

$$L^{-1}\{F(s)\}(t) = f(t).$$

MATLAB provides the commands *maple('laplace')* and *maple('invlaplace')* to calculate the Laplace transform and inverse Laplace transform of an expression with respect to a variable. The syntax is as follows:

maple ('laplace (expression, t, s)')

> **Calculates the Laplace transform of a given expression with respect to t. The transformed variable is s.**

maple ('invlaplace (expression, s, t)')

> **Computes the inverse Laplace transform of the given expression with respect to s. The inverse variable is t.**

Here are some examples:

```
> pretty(sym(maple('laplace(t^(3/2)-exp(t)+sinh(a*t), t, s)')))
```

$$
3/4 \; \frac{pi^{1/2}}{s^{5/2}} - \frac{1}{s-1} + \frac{a}{s^2-a^2}
$$

```
> pretty(sym(maple('invlaplace(s^2/(s^2+a^2)^(3/2), s, t)')))
```

$$t \; BesselJ(1, a\,t) \; a + BesselJ(0, a\,t)$$

The Laplace transform and its inverse are used to solve certain differential equations. The method is to calculate the Laplace transform of each term of the equation to obtain a new differential equation, which we then solve. Finally, we find the solution of the original equation by applying the inverse Laplace transform to the solutions just found.

MATLAB provides the 'laplace' option in the maple('dsolve') command, which forces the program to solve the differential equation using the Laplace transform method. The syntax is as follows:

```
maple ('dsolve (equation, func (var), 'laplace'))
```

EXERCISE 8-10

Solve the differential equation

$$y'' + 2y' + 4y = x - e^{-x}, \; y(0) = 1, \; y'(0) = 1$$

using the Laplace transform method.

First, we calculate the Laplace transform of each side of the differential equation, and we apply the initial conditions.

```
>> maple('L:=s->laplace(diff(y(x),x$2)+2*diff(y(x),x)+4*y(x),x,s)');
>> pretty(simple(sym(maple('subs(y(0)=1,(D(y))(0)=1,L(s))'))))
```

$$laplace(y(x), \; x, \; s) \; s^2 \; - \; s \; - \; 3 \; + \; 2 \; laplace(y(x), \; x, \; s) \; s \; + \; 4 \; laplace(y(x), \; x, \; s)$$

```
>> maple('L1:=s->laplace(x-exp(-x),x,s)');
>> pretty(simple(sym('L1(s)')))
```

$$\frac{1}{s^2} - \frac{1}{s+1}$$

We then solve the Laplace transformed differential equation:

```
>> pretty(simple(sym(maple('solve(L(s)=L1(s),laplace(y(x),x,s))'))))
```

$$\frac{s^4 \; y(0) + (3 \; y(0) + D(y)(0)) \; s^3 + (2 \; y(0) + D(y)(0) - 1) \; s^2 + s + 1}{s^2 \; (s^3 + 3 \; s^2 + 6 \; s + 4)}$$

Now we substitute the given initial conditions into the solution.

```
>> maple('TL:=s->solve(L(s)=L1(s),laplace(y(x),x,s))');
>> pretty(simple(sym('subs(y(0)=1,(D(y))(0)=1,TL(s))')))
```

$$\frac{s^4 + 4 \; s^3 + 2 \; s^2 + s + 1}{s^2 \; (s + 1) \; (s^2 + 2 \; s + 4)}$$

This gives the solution of the Laplace transformed equation. To calculate the solution of the original equation we calculate the inverse Laplace transform of the solution obtained in the previous step.

```
>> maple('TL0:=s->simplify(subs(y(0)=1,(D(y))(0)=1,TL(s)))');
>> solution=simple(sym(maple('invlaplace(TL0(s),s,x)')));
>> pretty(solution)
```

$$1/4 \; x \; - \; 1/8 \; - \; \frac{1}{3 \; exp(x)} \; + \; 5/8 \; \frac{sin(3^{1/2} \; x) \; 3^{1/2}}{exp(x)} \; + \; \frac{35}{24} \; \frac{cos(3^{1/2} \; x)}{exp(x)}$$

This gives the solution of the original differential equation.

We could also have solved it directly via:

```
>> pretty(simple(sym(maple('dsolve({diff(y(x),x$2)+2*diff(y(x),x)+4*y(x)= x-exp(-x),
y(0)=1,D(y)(0)=1},y(x),laplace)'))))
```

$$y(x) \; = \; 1/4 \; x \; - \; 1/8 \; - \; \frac{1}{3 \; exp(x)} \; + \; 5/8 \; \frac{sin(3^{1/2} \; x) \; 3^{1/2}}{exp(x)} \; + \; \frac{35}{24} \; \frac{cos(3^{1/2} \; x)}{exp(x)}$$

8.10 Systems of Linear Homogeneous Equations with Constant Coefficients

A system of differential equations, written as $X'(t) = AX(t)$, has a general solution of the form:

$$X(t) = \sum_{i=1}^{n} c_i V_i e^{\lambda_i t}$$

where the eigenvalues $\{\lambda_k\}$ ($\kappa = 1, 2, \dots n$) corresponding to the eigenvectors $\{V_k\}$ of the matrix A of the system are all assumed to be different.

If an eigenvalue λ_k is a complex number $a_k + b_k i$, then it generates the following component of the overall solution:

$$C_{k_1} W_{k_1} e^{\lambda_k t} + C_{k_2} W_{k_2} e^{\lambda_k t}$$

where:

$$W_{k_1} = \frac{1}{2}\left(V_k + \overline{V}_k\right)\cos(b_k t) + \frac{i}{2}\left(V_k - \overline{V}_k\right)\sin(b_k t),$$

$$W_{k_2} = \frac{i}{2}\left(V_k - \overline{V}_k\right)\cos(b_k t) - \frac{1}{2}\left(V_k + \overline{V}_k\right)\sin(b_k t).$$

Here V_k is the eigenvector corresponding to the eigenvalue λ_k and $\overline{V}_k$ is its conjugate.

If there is an eigenvalue λ_i of multiplicity $m > 1$, then it will generate a portion of the general solution of the form:

$$c_i e^{\lambda_i t} V_i + c_{i+1} t e^{\lambda_i t} V_{i+1} + c_{i+2} t^2 e^{\lambda_i t} V_{i+2} + \dots + c_{i+k} t^k e^{\lambda_i t} V_k$$

MATLAB can solve this type of system directly, simply by using the command *dsolve* or *maple('dsolve')* with the familiar syntax.

EXERCISE 8-11

Solve the following system of equations:

$$x' = -5x + 3y,$$

$$y' = -2x + 10y.$$

```
>> S = dsolve('Dx=-5*x+3*y,Dy=-2*x-10*y','t');
>> pretty(sym([S.x,S.y]))
```

[-2 C1 exp(-8 t) + 3 C1 exp(-7 t) + 3 C2 exp(-7 t) - 3 C2 exp(-8 t) ,

-2 C1 exp(-7 t) + 2 C1 exp(-8 t) + 3 C2 exp(-8 t) - 2 C2 exp(-7 t)]

You can also use the following syntax:

```
>> pretty (sym (maple ('dsolve ({diff (x (t), t) =-5 * x (t) + 3 * y (t), diff (y (t), t) =
-2 * x (t) - 10 * y (t)}, {x (t), y (t)})')))
```

{x(t) = -2 _C1 exp(-8 t) + 3 _C1 exp(-7 t) + 3 _C2 exp(-7 t) - 3 _C2 exp(-8 t)

y(t) = -2 _C1 exp(-7 t) + 2 _C1 exp(-8 t) + 3 _C2 exp(-8 t) - 2 _C2 exp(-7 t)}

8.11 Systems of Linear Non-Homogeneous Equations with Constant Coefficients

Now let us consider systems of non-homogeneous differential equations with constant coefficients of the form $X' = AX + F(t)$.

The general solution of the homogeneous system $X' = AX$ takes the form $X = \Phi(t)C$. A particular solution of the non-homogeneous system is:

$$X_p = \Phi(t)\int \Phi^{-1}(t)F(t)dt.$$

The general solution of the non-homogeneous system will be $X = \Phi(t)C + X_p$, which is, using the previous expression:

$$X = \Phi(t)C + \Phi(t)\int \Phi^{-1}(t)F(t)dt.$$

This method is a generalization to systems of equations of the method of variation of parameters for simple equations.

MATLAB can solve such systems of equations directly with the command *dsolve* or *maple('dsolve')*, provided the integrals that appear in the solution can be evaluated.

EXERCISE 8-12

Solve the following system of equations:

$$x' - y' = e^{-t}$$
$$y' + 5x + 2y = sin(3+t)$$

with initial conditions $x(0) = x0$ and $y(0) = y0$.

```
>> S=dsolve('Dx-Dy=exp(-t),Dy+5*x+2*y=sin(3+t)','x(0)=xo,y(0)=yo','t');
>> pretty(simple(sym([S.x,S.y])))
```

```
  [5/7 xo exp(-7 t) + 2/7 xo - 2/7 yo + 2/7 yo exp(-7 t) - 1/6 exp(-t)
   - 5/42 exp(-7 t) + 2/7 - 7/50 exp(-7 t) sin(3) + 1/50 exp(-7 t) cos(3)
   + 7/50 sin(3 + t) - 1/50 cos(3 + t) ,


   - 5/7 xo + 5/7 xo exp(-7 t) + 2/7 yo exp(-7 t) + 5/7 yo + 5/6 exp(-t) - 5/42 exp(-7 t)
   - 5/7- 7/50 exp(-7 t) sin(3) + 1/50 exp(-7 t) cos(3) + 7/50 sin(3 + t)- 1/50 cos(3 + t)]
```

8.12 Higher Order Equations and Approximation Methods

When the known algebraic methods for solving differential equations and systems of differential equations offer no solution, we usually resort to methods of approximation. The approximation methods can involve both symbolic and numerical work. The symbolic approach yields approximate algebraic solutions, and its most representative technique is the Taylor series method. The numerical approach yields a solution in the form of a finite set of solution points, to which a curve can be fitted by various algebraic methods (interpolation, regression,...). This curve will be an approximate solution of the differential equation. Among the most common numerical methods is the Runge–Kutta method.

Approximation methods are most commonly employed to find the solution of equations and systems of differential equations of order and degree greater than one, where the exact solution cannot be obtained by other methods.

8.13 The Taylor Series Method

This method provides approximate polynomial solutions of general differential equations, and is based on the Taylor series expansion of functions. MATLAB offers the option *'series'* for the command *maple('dsolve')*, which allows you to solve equations by this method. Its syntax is as follows:

```
maple ('dsolve (equation, func (var), 'series'))
```

There is also the command *maple('powsolve')*, which gives a power series solution of linear differential equations, and whose syntax is as follows:

```
maple ('powseries [powsolve](equation, cond1,...,condn) ')
```

Using the command *maple('convert(polynom)')* you can convert a complicated solution to a polynomial in powers of the variable.

EXERCISE 8-13

Solve the following two equations by the Taylor series method:

$$4x^2 y'' + 4xy' + \left(x^2 - 1\right)y = 0,$$

$yy'' + (y')^2 + 1 = 0$ *with the initial conditions* $y(0) = 1$ *and* $y'(0) = 1$.

```
>> pretty(simple(sym(maple('dsolve(4*x^2*diff(y(x),x$2)+4*x*diff(y(x),x)+
   +(x^2-1)*y(x)=0,y(x),series)'))))
```

$$y(x) = (\_C1\ x\ (1 - 1/24\ x^2 + 1/1920\ x^4 + O(x^6)) + \_C2\ \log(x)\ (O(x^6))$$

$$+ \_C2\ (1 - 1/8\ x^2 + 1/384\ x^4 + O(x^6)))\ /\ x^{1/2}$$

```
>> pretty(simple(sym(maple('convert(",polynom)'))))
```

$$y(x) = \_C1\ x^{1/2}\ (1 - 1/24\ x^2 + 1/1920\ x^4) + \frac{\_C2\ (1 - 1/8\ x^2 + 1/384\ x^4)}{x^{1/2}}$$

```
>> pretty(simple(sym(maple('dsolve({y(x)*diff(y(x),x$2)+diff(y(x),x)^2+1=0,
   y(0)=1,D(y)(0)=1},y(x),series)'))))
```

$$y(x) = 1 + x - x^2 + x^3 - 3/2\ x^4 + 5/2\ x^5 + O(x^6)$$

EXERCISE 8-14

Solve the following two systems of equations using the Taylor series method:

$$x'' + y' - 4x + 12 = 0$$

$$y'' - 10x' - y + 7 = 0$$

$$x(0) = y(0) = x'(0) = y'(0) = 1$$

and

$$x'' + 2x' + 2y' + 3z' + x = 1$$
$$y' + z' - x = 0$$
$$x' + z = 0.$$

```
>> pretty(simple(sym(maple('dsolve({diff(x(t),t$2)+diff(y(t),t)-4*x+12=0,
diff(y(t),t$2)-10*diff(x(t),t)-y(t)+7=0,x(0)=1,y(0)=1,D(x)(0)=1,D(y)(0)=1},
{x(t),y(t)},series)'))))
```

$$\{y(t) = 1 + t + 2\ t^2 - 89/6\ t^3 + 1/6\ t^4 + \frac{147}{40}\ t^5 + O(t^6),$$

$$x(t) = 1 + t - 9/2\ t^2 + \frac{53}{24}\ t^4 - 1/30\ t^5 + O(t^6)\}$$

```
>> pretty(simple(sym(maple('dsolve({diff(x(t),t$2)+2*diff(x(t),t)+2*diff(y(t),t)+ +3*diff
(z(t),t)+x(t)=1,diff(y(t),t)+diff(z(t),t)-x(t)=0,diff(x(t),t)+z(t)=0}, {x(t),y(t),z(t)},
series)'))))
```

$$\{x(t) = x(0) + D(x)(0)\ t + (- D(x)(0) - 1/2\ x(0) + 1/2)\ t^2$$

$$+ (1/2\ D(x)(0) + 1/3\ x(0) - 1/3)\ t^3 + (- 1/6\ D(x)(0) - 1/8\ x(0) + 1/8)\ t^4$$

$$+ (1/24\ D(x)(0) + 1/30\ x(0) - 1/30)\ t^5 + O(t^6),$$

$$z(t) = z(0) + x(0)\ t + 1/2\ D(x)(0)\ t^2 + (- 1/3\ D(x)(0) - 1/6\ x(0) + 1/6)\ t^3$$

$$+ (1/8\ D(x)(0) + 1/12\ x(0) - 1/12)\ t^4$$

$$+ (- 1/30\ D(x)(0) - 1/40\ x(0) + 1/40)\ t^5 + O(t^6),$$

$$y(t) = y(0) + x(0)\ t + 1/2\ D(x)(0)\ t^2 + (- 1/3\ D(x)(0) - 1/6\ x(0) + 1/6)\ t^3$$

$$+ (1/8\ D(x)(0) + 1/12\ x(0) - 1/12)\ t^4$$

$$+ (- 1/30\ D(x)(0) - 1/40\ x(0) + 1/40)\ t^5 + O(t^6)\quad\}$$

8.14 The Runge–Kutta Method

The Runge–Kutta method gives a set of data points to which you can fit a curve, approximating the solution of a differential equation. Maple provides the option *numeric* for the command *maple('solve')* which enables the calculation of approximate numerical solutions of differential equations. Its syntax is:

```
maple ('dsolve (equation, func (var), 'numeric'))
```

EXERCISE 8-15

Solve the following equation using the Runge–Kutta method:

$3(y'')^2 = y'''y'$ with the initial conditions $y'(0) = y''(0) = 1$.

```
>> maple ('f: = dsolve ({3 * diff (y (x), x$ 2) ^ 2 = diff (y (x), x$ 3) * diff (y (x), x),
y (0) = 1/2, D (y) (0) = 1, (D@@2) (y) (0) = 1}, y (x), numeric)');
```

Now, in order to graph the solution, we calculate various points of the solution function f generated above (see Figure 8-4).

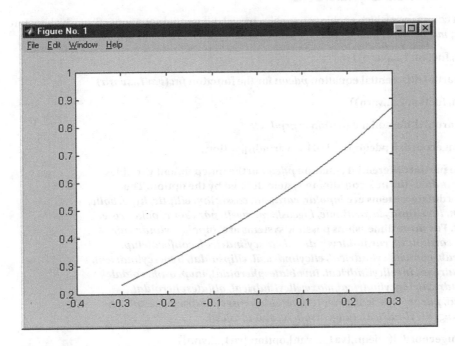

Figure 8-4.

```
>> [maple('f(-0.3)'),maple('f(-0.2)'),maple('f(-0.1)'),maple('f(0)'), maple('f(0.1)'),
maple('f(0.2)'),maple('f(0.3)')]
```

ans −

$\{x = -.3, y(x) = .2350889359260396\}\{y(x) = .3167840433732281, x = -.2\}$ $\{y(x) = .4045548849869109, x = -.1\}\{y(x) = .5000000000000000, x = 0\}$ $\{x = .1, y(x) = .6055728090006967\}\{y(x) = .7254033307597474, x = .2\}$ $\{y(x) = .8675444679682489, x = .3000000000000000\}$

```
>> y = [.2350889359260396,.3167840433732281,.4045548849869109,.5,.6055728090006967,.725403330
7597474,.8675444679682489];
```

```
>> plot ((-0.3:.1:0.3), y)
```

We find the degree 2 polynomial which is the best fit to the set of solution points. The equation of this parabola will be an approximate solution of the differential equation.

```
>> pretty(vpa(poly2sym(polyfit((-0.3:.1:0.3),y,2))))
```

$$.5747427827483573 \; x^2 + 1.041293962469090 \; x + .4991457846921903$$

This yields a degree 2 polynomial approximation to the solution $y(x)$ of the equation.

8.15 Partial Differential Equations

MATLAB implements several commands which enable you to solve partial differential equations, all of which require the prior use of the command *maple*. We have:

pdesolve (pdeqn, fnc(var1,...,varn))

> Solves the partial differential equation *pdeqn* for the function *fnc(var1,..,varn)*

pdesolve (exprpd, fnc(var1,...,varn))

> Solves the partial differential equation *exprpd = 0*

DEtools[PDEchangecoords](pdeqn,[varind1,...,varindn],option)

> Converts the partial differential equation *pdeqn* in the independent variables *varind1, varindn* to the new coordinate system defined by the option. The possible coordinate systems are *bipolar, cardioid, cassinian, elliptic, hyperbolic, invcassinian, invelliptic, logarithmic, logcosh, maxwell, parabolic, polar, rose,* and *tangent.* For three dimensions possible systems are *bipolarcylindrical, bispherical, cardioidal, cardioidcylindrical, casscylindrical, confocalellip, confocalparab, conical, cylindrical, ellcylindrical, ellipsoidal, hypercylindrical, invcasscylindrical, invellcylindrical, invoblatespheroidal, invprospheroidal, logcoshcylindrical, logcylindrical, maxwellcylindrical, oblatespheroidal, paraboloidal, paracylindrical, prolatespheroidal, rosecylindrical, sixsphere, spherical, tangentcylindrical, tangentsphere,* and *toroidal.*

DEtools [PDEchangecoords](pdeqn,[va1,...,van],option,[vn1,...,vnn])

> Performs the change of coordinates specifying the new independent variables

DEtools[PDEchangecoords]({pdeqn1,...,pdeqnm},[varind1,...,varindn],option)

> Performs the change of coordinates in the specified system of partial differential equations

Here are some examples:

```
pretty(sym(maple('pdesolve( diff(f(x,y),x,x)+5*diff(f(x,y),x,y)=3, f(x,y) )')))
```

$$f(x, y) = 3/2 \; x^2 + \_F1(y) + \_F2(y - 5 \; x)$$

```
>> pretty(sym(maple('pdesolve( 3*diff(g(x,y),x)+7*diff(g(x,y),x,y)=x*y, g(x,y) ) ')))
```

$$g(x, y) = 1/6 \ x^2 \ y - 7/18 \ x^2 + \_F1(y) + exp(- \ 3/7 \ y) \ \_F2(x)$$

```
>> pretty(sym(maple('pdesolve( diff(h(x,y),x,x)-diff(h(x,y),y,y)=0, h(x,y)) ')))
```

$$h(x, y) = \_F1(y + x) + \_F2(y - x)$$

```
>> pretty(sym(maple('pdesolve(y*diff(U(x,y),x)+x*diff(U(x,y),y)=0, U(x,y) ) ')))
```

$$U(x, y) = \_F1(-x^2 + y^2)$$

8.16 Finite Difference Equations

MATLAB enables commands that allow you to solve finite difference equations and recurrence equations in general, the prior use of the command **maple** is always required. We have:

rsolve (reqn, fnc (var))

> Solves the recurrence equation *reqn* for the function *fnc(var)*. You can use the command *asympt* to find asymptotic solutions.

rsolve (expr, fnc (var))

> Solves the recurrence equation *expr = 0*

rsolve ({reqn1,..., reqnm}, {fnc1 (var1),..., fncm (varm)})

> Solves the set of recurrence equations given by the specified functions

rsolve ({reqn1,..., reqnn}, {fnc1,..., fncm}, 'genfnc' (var))

> (for linear recurrences with constant coefficients and systems of linear recurrences with constant coefficients) returns the generating functions *fnc1,..., fncn* of the sequences defined by *reqn1,...,reqnn.*

rsolve({reqn1,...,reqnn},{fnc1,...,fncm},'makeproc')

> (for any single recurrence that can be uniquely solved for the highest indexed function) returns a procedure body for evaluating the function defined by *reqn1,...,reqnn.*

REsol (reqn, fnc (var), {cond1,..., condm})

> Represents the solution of the inert recurrence equation *reqn* for the function *fnc (var)* subject to the specified initial conditions *cond1,..., condn*

(with (LREtools))

> Loads into the memory a library of commands for work with linear recurrence equations

constcoeffsol (reqn, fnc (var), {cond1,..., condm})

> Returns the solution of the recurrence equation with constant coefficients *reqn* according to *fnc(var)* and with initial conditions *{cond1,..., condn}*

constcoeffsol(reqn,fnc(var),{cond1,...,condm},output=basis)

> Returns a basis for the solutions of *reqn*

hypergeomsols(reqn,fnc(var),{cond1,...,condm})

> Returns hypergeometric solutions of *reqn*. Also supports the option *output = basis*. With the option *output = onesol* gives a simple solution.

polysols (reqn, fnc (var), {cond1,..., condm})

> Returns polynomial solutions of *reqn*. Supports the additional options *output = basis* and *output = onesol*.

ratpolysols (reqn, fnc (var), {cond1,..., condm})

> Returns rational polynomial solutions of *reqn* with the given initial conditions

REcreate(reqn,fnc(var),{cond1,...,condn})

> Creates a recurrence equation for *reqn*

REcreate ({reqn1,..., reqnn}, {(var) fnc1,..., fncn (var)}, {cond1,..., condm})

> Creates *n* recurrence equations

REcontent (reqn, fnc (var), {cond1,..., condm})

> Returns the content of the recurrence equation *reqn*

REprimpart(reqn,fnc(var),{cond1,...,condm})

> Returns the primitive part of the recurrence equation

REreduceorder (reqn, fnc (var), {cond1,..., condm}, expr)

> Reduction of order for the recurrent equation *reqn* where *expr* is a partial solution

REreduceorder (reqn, fnc (var), {cond1,..., condm}, [expr1,..., exprn])

> Specifies *n* partial solutions

REtoDE (reqn, fnc (var), {cond1,..., condm})

> Converts a recurrence equation *reqn* to a differential equation

REtodelta (reqn, fnc (var), {cond1,..., condm})

> Converts the recurrence equation *reqn* to a difference equation

REtoproc(reqn,fnc(var),{cond1,...,condm})

> Converts the recurrence equation *reqn* into a procedure

shift(expr, var, int)

> Coincides with *subs(var=var+int,expr)*

shift(expr, var)

> Takes *int = 1* in the above by default

> **Delta (expr, var, n)**
>
>> Executes the difference of order *n* for the expression *expr* with respect to the variable *var*
>
> **Delta (expr, var, n)**
>
>> Executes the difference of order 1. We have that shift(expr,var,1)-expr = delta (expr, var)

Here are some examples:

```
>> pretty(sym(maple('LREtools[REtodelta](u(n+2)-2*u(n+1)+u(n),u(n),{})')))
```

$$LREtools[Delta][n]^2$$

```
>> maple('rec:= a(n+2)-(2*n+1)*a(n+1)/n+n*a(n)/(n-1)=n*(n+1): ')
>> maple('re:= LREtools[REcreate](rec, a(n), { })')
```

ans =

re := RESol({a(n+2)*n^2-a(n+2)*n-2*a(n+1)*n^2+a(n+1)*n+a(n+1)+n^2*a(n) = n^4-n^2},{a(n)},{a(3) = a(3), a(2) = a(2), a(1) = 0},INFO)

```
>> pretty(sym(maple('LREtools[polysols](re, output=basis) ')))
```

$$1/9\ n^4 - 5/18\ n^3 - 1/9\ n^2 + \_C[1]\ n + 5/18 - \_C[1]$$

```
>> pretty(sym(maple('LREtools[REtoDE]((18+12*n)*t(n)+(-20-7*n)*t(n+1)+ (4+n)*t(n+2),t(n), {t(0) = 0,
t(1) = 2}, y(z)) ')))
```

$$DESol(\{(-18\ z^2 + 13\ z - 2)\ y + (-12\ z^3 + 7\ z^2 - z)\ D(y) + 6\ z\}, \{y\},$$

$$\{y(0) = 0,\ D(y)(0) = 2\})$$

```
>> maple('rec:= a(n+4) = -a(n+3)+3*a(n+2)+5*a(n+1)+2*a(n): ')
>> pretty(sym(maple('constcoeffsol(rec, a(n), { })')))
```

$$-2\ (-\ 1/18\ a(1) - 1/54\ a(0) - 1/54\ a(3) - 1/18\ a(2))\ 2^n$$

$$+ \left(14/9\ a(1) + \frac{68}{27}\ a(0) - \frac{13}{27}\ a(3) - 4/9\ a(2)\right)\ (-1)^n$$

$$+ (-\ 8/3\ a(1) - 20/9\ a(0) + 7/9\ a(3) + 1/3\ a(2))\ (-1)^n\ (n + 1)$$

$$+ 1/2\ (a(1) + 2/3\ a(0) - 1/3\ a(3))\ (-1)^n\ (n + 1)\ (n + 2)$$

EXERCISE 8-16

Find the solutions to the following recurrence equations:

$$y_{m+1} = my_m + (m+1)! \quad y_1 = 2,$$
$$y_{2n} = 4y_n + 5 \quad y_1 = a,$$
$$y_{n+2} - 3y_{n+1} + 2y_n = 4^n \quad y_0 = y_1 = 1$$

```
>> pretty(sym(maple('rsolve({y(m+1)=m*y(m)+(m+1)!,y(1)=2},y)')))
```

$$1/2 \; GAMMA(m) \; (m^2 + m + 2)$$

```
>> pretty(sym(maple('rsolve({y(2*n)=4*y(n)+5,y(1)=a},y) ')))
```

$$a \; n^2 + n^2 \; (-20/3 \; (1/4)^{\frac{log(n)}{log(2)} + 1} + 5/3)$$

```
>> pretty(sym(maple('rsolve({y(n+2)-3*y(n+1)+2*y(n)=4^n,y(0)=1,y(1)=1},y) ')))
```

$$4/3 - 1/2 \; 2^n + 1/6 \; 4^n$$

EXERCISE 8-17

Find the general term of the sequences of real numbers defined by the following recurrence laws:

$$x_n - nx_m {}^* x_n {}^* x_{n+1} = x_{n+1} \quad x_0 = 1,$$
$$y_{n+2} - 2y_{n+1} + 5y_n = cos(3n) \quad y_0 = y_1 = 1$$

```
>> pretty(sym(maple('rsolve({x(n)-n*x(n)*x(n+1)=x(n+1),x(0)=1},x) ')))
```

$$\frac{2}{n^2 - n + 2}$$

```
>> pretty(sym(maple('simplify(evalf(rsolve({x(n+2)-2*x(n+1)+5*x(n)=
=cos(3*n),    x(0)=1,x(1)=1},x))) ')))
```

$.4373424525 \; exp((.8047189562 - 1.107148718 \; I) \; n)$

$\qquad + .4373424525 \; exp((.8047189562 + 1.107148718 \; I) \; n)$

$$- .9160727930 \cos(n - 3.)^{3} + .4362567143 \cos(n - 5.)^{3}$$

$$+ .1725076052 \cos(n - 2.)^{3} - .1986350636 \cos(n - 4.)^{3}$$

$$- .06265675740 \; I \; exp((.8047189562 + 1.107148718 \; I) \; n)$$

$$+ .06265675750 \; I \; exp((.8047189562 - 1.107148718 \; I) \; n)$$

$$+ .7931668115 \cos(n - 3.) + .07520876265 \cos(n - 2.)$$

Get the eBook for only $10!

Now you can take the weightless companion with you anywhere, anytime. Your purchase of this book entitles you to 3 electronic versions for only $10.

This Apress title will prove so indispensible that you'll want to carry it with you everywhere, which is why we are offering the eBook in 3 formats for only $10 if you have already purchased the print book.

Convenient and fully searchable, the PDF version enables you to easily find and copy code—or perform examples by quickly toggling between instructions and applications. The MOBI format is ideal for your Kindle, while the ePUB can be utilized on a variety of mobile devices.

Go to www.apress.com/promo/tendollars to purchase your companion eBook.